URBAN LEGENDS
OF ROCK & ROLL
(You Never Can Tell)

Dale Sherman

Photo Credits
Rock Classics - jablake@wwdc.com
Cover: Led Zeppelin (2), Marilyn Manson, Eric Clapton, Stevie Nicks.
Pages: 13, 38, 96, 154, and color pages 1, 2, 4, 5, 6, 7, 8.
Hot Wacks - www.log.on.ca/hotwacks
Pages - 14, 29, 30, 106.

We acknowledge the financial support of the Government of Canada through
the Book Publishing Industry Development Program for our publishing activities.
Published by Collector's Guide Publishing Inc., Box 62034,
Burlington, Ontario, Canada, L7R 4K2
URBAN LEGENDS OF ROCK & ROLL / Dale Sherman
ISBN 1-896522-78-5
©2002 Collector's Guide Publishing Inc.

URBAN LEGENDS

OF ROCK & ROLL
(You Never Can Tell)

Dale Sherman

Table of Contents

Introduction

It was September 1969. Frank Zappa had just heard that one of his label's talents, Alice Cooper, had killed chickens on stage during a performance at the Toronto Rock 'n' Roll Revival by ripping off their heads and drinking their blood. Zappa contacted Alice to verify the story.

"Did you really do that?" Zappa asked.

"No," replied Alice.

"Well," Zappa responded, "whatever you do, don't tell anybody you didn't do it!"

Every day, we read or hear about stories from friends and acquaintances that are bizarre, disgusting, humorous, and/or ironic. The stories may be about celebrities or about people we have no background for. The stories may have a moral to them, a lesson to be learned, or just a punch line to make us laugh. Many times the stories sound preposterous, yet for some odd reason are just likely enough that we never can quite pinpoint if the story is true or not. Some are even so outrageous that you immediately shake your head in astonishment that anyone would even believe such a thing; and yet, in the back of your mind you cannot help but wonder if maybe it's all true. In time, you find yourself repeating the story to others, sometimes adapting the story a little in order to make it sound better than when you first heard it.

We all know the kind of stories being talked about here. There's the women who washes her dog and then puts it in the microwave to dry off, only to have it pop like a balloon when she turns the microwave on. Another is the man who picks up a teenage girl hitchhiking along the side of the road, only to find out after dropping her off that the girl had been dead for years. Don't forget the woman's beehive hairdo that's infested with spiders, or a certain bubble-gum that has spider eggs in it. Of course, there's the commercial stories, like that the leading fast-food company puts worms in its hamburger meat to make it juicier, and the soap company that has a secret pact with Satan.

All of these stories have a couple of things in common. First off, they're not true. None of the stories has even a shred of truth to them. No woman has ever put her dog into the microwave to dry it off; nor has a woman died from her spider-infested hairdo. Nobody puts spider eggs in bubble-gum and no fast-food place is going to risk upsetting customers by putting ground worms into their burgers.

But there's something else about these stories that bring them together in one place – they've all been told to us "by a friend, who heard it from a friend." No doubt, that friend heard it from a "friend of a friend' as well. They never had a solid basis for backing up the stories, as they are always a case of someone supposedly reading about the case somewhere or "having a cousin, who has a friend, who has a nephew twice removed that had such-and-such happen to them."

As made famous by researcher Jan Harold Brunvand, such stories have become known as "urban legends." They are myths created and told by people around the country and even around the world that provoke humor, tell tales of danger, or try to elicit outrage or sympathy. More importantly, they are not true, or are true stories that have been stretched so far out of shape that they no longer represent what really happened in relation to the event being discussed. These urban legends travel from person to person, in the office, at school, and (thanks to the internet) through chat rooms and emails at an alarming speed. On top of that, the stories remain for years and get recycled – sometimes with new individuals involved, sometimes with a different twist, but usually with the same resolution to the story at the end.

It doesn't stop with stories detailing events that happened to anonymous individuals either ("this happened to a guy in another state . . ."). In fact, many urban legends have been created over the years dealing with famous individuals: from sports figures to political leaders to movie stars and even rock stars. Such "celebrity" urban legends have a slightly different life than that of the normal urban legends in that there is a recognizable face for people to hang these stories on. There are also enough elements of truth or background about the performers involved that the stories seem to stick to them and cannot be shaken off. Look no further than Mariah Carey's supposed quote about "starving children" for proof of that.

After some thought and research, most urban legends can be recognized as being false. When it comes to rock and roll urban legends, finding the truth is a little harder. As seen from the snippet at the beginning of this introduction pertaining to Alice Cooper and the infamous "chicken incident" (see the entry for "Cooper, Alice" for more details), sometimes the lie is deemed better than the truth. It is seen as publicity for the artist because it keeps the performer's name fresh in people's minds. After all, who wouldn't want to talk to their friends about "that crazy guy who takes out a chicken and kills it on stage every night!" It's a great, albeit twisted, way to promote a performer.

So, as the old saying goes, when the legend is better than the truth, print the legend. In doing just that, over the years there has grown a lot of misinformation about rock performers who have made it into the history books based on the fact that no one wants to "spoil the fun." After all, rock music is supposed to be rebellious, even shocking. It is also a music that draws young people who have a lot of imagination and who want to be outside of the norm. When the story went around that Ozzy Osbourne was killing puppies on stage during his shows, parents and people in authority were outraged – all the better for enticing teenagers to sneak out and see Ozzy perform in concert. Further, if Ozzy actually didn't kill puppies on stage during the show, what would keep a kid from telling schoolmates who didn't attend that Ozzy did perform such an act? To the kid, he would be considered cool for sneaking out and seeing such a thing; and who really gets hurt in the process? Even Ozzy's reputation rises a notch due to the fact that even more kids would want to see him after such a rumor was circulated.

Therefore, it's not easy to separate the facts from fiction when dealing with rock and roll urban legends. Still, with this book we will attempt to look at some of the more prevalent urban legends from over the years and decipher how they were created and why. In some cases, we will discover that the bizarre rock and roll stories are actually true. Sometimes we'll find that a story long thought to be true has no truth to it whatsoever.

We will also see urban legends that were taken up by the artists themselves and even improved upon in order to gain maximum exposure.

The book is designed in an encyclopedia format, with the artists' (or bands') names in alphabetical order. For some artists, an urban legend told about them may be so similar to another artist's story (for instance, the "gross-out contest" legend), that the entry for the story will simply refer the reader to another artist's entry for further detail. There were also a few legends that have been told so many times of such a wide variety of artists that the stories have earned their own separated entries in the book. These entries are:

- Backmasking and Subliminal Messages – the consistent cautionary tales of messages hidden in rock music that are supposed to turn listeners into mindless zombies.
- Satanic Rock – the still ongoing belief of religious fanatics that rock music will turn children into Satan-worshipers. Somewhat similar to "Subliminal Messages," but with far more "blatant" examples and directed towards a certain segment of the population.
- Death (and the Conspiracy of Life) – the many urban legends dealing with made-up flamboyant deaths of certain rock stars, along with the continuing belief that certain performers never died and are merely hiding out for one reason or another.
- The Stomach-Pump Story – an urban legend that has been rehashed so many times over the years about so many different artists (both male and female) that there was no choice but to give it a separate entry in the book.

The reasons that urban legends are created are many and will be discussed along with an examination of the legends in the entries contained in the book. To get a jump-start on the proceedings, however, here is a small list of common reasons for the creation of urban legends (along with a few examples):

Collective Amnesia – This is the only logical explanation for why some of these supposedly true stories never get documented anywhere. This usually involves stories of horrible accidents, murders, animal abuse, and just plain sick behavior occurring before a large audience. For some reason, although large audiences witnessed what in many cases are obviously criminal acts, there is never any evidence that at least one person went to the police or even the press about the incident when it occurred. Of course, the logical reason for that is because they never occurred. A good example of this type of Urban Legend would be the "Gross-out Contest" (see the entry for Alice Cooper for more details) or stories of puppies, kittens, baby chicks and other cute, fuzzy animals being stomped, kicked or otherwise brutalized on stage. As one would imagine, these actions would lead to arrests and public complaint, or at the very least, public protest by animal activists. Still, there is no evidence of any public outcry, leaving the reviewer with "collective amnesia" being the only logical reason nothing was ever reported.

Conspiracy Theories – In some cases, however, stories do not have the full characteristics of an urban legend. Any documentation or witnesses needed to prove the basics of the story are said to have been lost, destroyed, or covered up as part of some type of conspiracy. Government conspiracies have increasingly become the norm over the past three decades, leading to paranoid stories about situations that have no basis for any other conclusion than normal ones (such as accidental deaths). In some cases, these conspiracy theories have hit the public so hard that they have taken on a life of their own, for which they will be examined in some depth in this book. In other cases, the stories of conspiracy are so preposterous or so little-known that they have not been covered in this book. For example, the urban legend that Mama Cass Elliott died from choking to death on a ham sandwich is covered; the conspiracy theory that she was made to choke on it by a group of CIA agents wanting to keep her quiet about a known drug king, is not. The conspiracy theory in this case is so over-the-top, so ludicrous, that is can be easily seen by most people as not true.

He Said / She Said – Stories that have no real basis in proof except for the word of one or two people who supposedly saw or participated in the event. Usually one person will say that something occurred for such-and-such a reason, while another person will counter the claim with their own version of the story. All fine and good, but neither will provide proof that their story is the accurate one and there will be no other witnesses beyond what they say occurred. In some cases, the story is so oriented in personality clashes that all one can observe is what the two opposing individuals have to say. The Byrds story about why David Crosby is replaced by a horse on the cover of their album, THE NOTORIOUS BYRD BROTHERS, would be a good example of this type of tale. David Crosby insisted that it was done intentionally, while Roger McGuinn stated it was just a coincidence. Neither can be faulted for his logic, nor can he be praised for his evidence.

Opinion – Stories that are based specifically on the opinion of the speaker. For example, someone who cannot stand listening to a particular artist will make up a story about them in order to "prove" to others that the artist is terrible. The "Stomach Pump" story (see that entry for more details) is a good example of the type of slur, created to make a particular artist look horrible in the eyes of others. Sometimes such a story can work both ways, good and bad. For example, the "KISS stands for Knights In Satan's Service" rumor may have scared off some people from the band, but there were probably a few kids who thought the rumor was cool and started listening to the band just for that reason alone.

Stretching the Truth – In some cases, what has been commonly believed to be an Urban Legend is actually true. Still, sometimes a piece of the story will be turned around and stretched in order to make it sound better. Some artists over the years were and/or still are known for doing this, feeling that keeping the legends alive is better for their careers. "Weird Al" Yankovic's gentle nudging of the "27" legend in his work is a rather innocent variation of this type of legend.

Too Good To Die – An urban legend that may have any of the above elements, with the major additional value of being so memorable that people can't forget it. In most such cases, a majority of people know the legend is false, and proof will be readily available to those who at first believe it to be true. No matter, people will still make comments referring to the rumor because it has become part of our way of thinking as a society. "Elvis is Alive" is a perfect example of this type of urban legend.

Because urban legends are created every day for both new artists and old, a book of this type can only hope to cover the tip of the iceberg. No doubt, as time goes by, more legends will be created around several of the popular artists contain herein, while new artists will have brand new ones (or even variations of the old ones) created in their "honor" by the fans and those who resent or are confused by them. As is readily apparent, researching urban legends is a never-ending study, and some readers may be interested in knowing how they can research newer stories themselves. To help those readers, a section at the end of this book deals with research techniques designed to clarify stories, both truthful and fictional. In doing so, some of the future urban legends of rock and roll can be seen for what they are before they start any kind of panic amongst fans.

I should make mention of some of the people that have helped with the book, including Barbara and David P. Mikkelson of http://www.snopes.com, who allowed me to reference some of their columns from their excellent web site of urban legends. I have also benefited from the work of previous researchers in the field of urban legends, such as Jan Harold Brunvand, William Poundstone, Hal Morgan, Kerry Tucker, and the team over at Cecil Adams' web site, The Straight Dope. On a more personal note, I wish to thank Mats Sexton, Mark Landwehr, and the folks over at the Electric Bayou web site, along with that of all the fans out there who have worked diligently on FAQ(s) (a.k.a. "frequently asked questions") about their favorite musicians. Their work, along with that of biographers and music-researchers has helped formulate many parts of this book (as the sources listed can verify). Lastly, I wish to thank the following people who have been there every step of the way during the writing of this book: Mike DeGeorge for his help and suggestions; Brian Schnau, Larry Blake, Carlyn Nugent, and the people over at the dawghouse for their suggestions and encouragement; my family and co-workers for their support; and, as always, my wife Jill for putting up with all of this.

For those readers who have additional stories to add to the list, please feel free to contact that author at the following email address: mailto:justabob@iglou.com. You can also contact the author at the following postal address:

Dale Sherman
P O Box 406795
Louisville, KY 40204
USA

Who knows? With the number of legends created daily, it may only be a matter of time before The Urban Legends of Rock 'N' Roll, Part II is out on the bookshelves.

10CC

> *The band's name came (no pun intended) from the measure given to the average amount of semen ejaculated at climax. According to legend, the average amount was 9cc, and since the band was "above average," they would be 10cc.*

Such an urban legend begs the question, "someone actually would measure such a thing?" This urban legend had been around for years and was even referred to by Dave Marsh in his overall excellent resource book, The Book of Rock Lists (later revised as The New Book of Rock Lists). The name actual refers to a dream that promoter Jonathan King had about a successful band named 10cc. With the band (featuring Eric Steward, Graham Gouldman, Kevin Godley and Lol Crème) soon to release their first single in August 1972, King thought it to be an omen and thus the band changed their name from Hotlegs to 10cc.

Yes, admittedly the true story is nowhere near as exciting as the legend.

Source: Marsh, Dave. THE NEW BOOK OF ROCK LISTS, Fireside Books, New York. 1994 Page 262.
Dolgins, Adam. ROCK NAMES: FROM ABBA TO ZZ TOP. Citadel Press, New Jersey. 1998. Pages 254-255.

311

> *The name "311" stands for 3 times the eleventh letter of the alphabet, which is K. In other words, "KKK." The band uses the name 311 as a sly way to state their allegiance to the Ku Klux Klan.*

The band's name actually comes from the Omaha, Nebraska's police code for indecent exposure. The band's original guitarist, P-Nut, had gone skinny-dipping in a public pool and was arrested by the police. 311 was the code used on the ticket P-Nut received and the band thought it sounded like a funny name for their band. After the novelty wore off, they decided to keep the name not only because people knew it, but also because it was nonsensical enough that they knew the name of the band would not fixate them into a certain style of music (as some band names can).

No one is quite sure how the whole "311 stands for the KKK" urban legend started, but the rumor went so far as to force some schools to change their dress codes so that students could not wear T-shirts promoting 311. After finding out about the situation, the band made an official announcement against the rumor, stating that the band's lyrics clearly show they are not pro-KKK at all. The statement also ended with a comment that the name stood for "five friends from Omaha making music" (or 3 + 1 + 1 = 5). This is a completely different origin of the name than that given originally, yet it should be taken as a "new" definition and not some type of revision in the band's history.

Source: Mikkelson, Barbara and David P. "311 NOT OKKK?" Urban Legend Reference Pages. January 30, 2000.
http://www.snopes.com/music/artists/311.htm

ABBA

ABBA recorded an album, never released, called Opus 10.

The rumor goes that the group had gotten together in 1981 to record a full-length album. A Swedish newspaper article at the time stated that the album would be the tenth one released by the group, and subsequently referred to the album as their tenth opus, or rather as "Opus 10." In making a flip reference to the album, the writer created a legend. For years, ABBA fans had heard about an unreleased album called Opus 10 (or, in some version of this story, "Opus 10" is an unreleased track).

In later years, bootleggers have taken an early instrumental version of the song "Anthem" from the musical Chess (created by the two men in the group) and issued it as "Opus 10," but this is far from the truth, as one can tell.

As ABBA authority Carl Magnus Palm stated on the abbafiles.com web site, "ABBA never used working titles for their albums." Thus, the newspaper writer's reference is even further shown to be merely a joke and nothing more. The band did attempt recording some new material in 1982, but fell back on releasing a "best of" double album, with two new tracks instead.

Source: Palm, Carl Magnus. OPUS 10, Abbafiles, http://www.abbafiles.com

AC/DC

The band's name is an acronym for "Anti-Christ / Devil's Children" ("Anti-Christ / Devil Crusade.")

The name actually came about through the sister of the brothers in the group. Margaret Young thought of the name when she saw it on the back of a vacuum cleaner. Because the symbol designated electricity and power, it was deemed a good name for a hard-rocking band. No one in the band knew at the time that the term was slang for bisexuality in other parts of the world, and they ran into problems at first convincing clubs that they were a "straight" act.

As to the "Anti-Christ / Devil's Children" ("Anti-Christ / Devil Crusade" and "After Christ, the Devil will Come" being a couple of the many alternatives given in variations of the legend), that came about during the latter part of the 1970s when fanatical Christian groups were determined to prove that every popular rock band on the radio was satanic. In the case of AC/DC, thanks to songs like *Highway to Hell* and *Back in Black*, the connotation was not that hard to achieve, although the acronym that was arrived at was certainly a stretch, even for the religious fanatics.

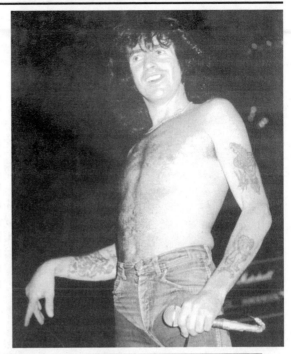

Bon Scott of AC/DC

Source: Putterman, Mark. SHOCK TO THE SYSTEM. Omnibus Press, England. 1999.

The B-52's

> 1. The line "Tin roof rusted" in the song Love Shack is a Southern term for pregnancy.
> 2. The cover for the WHAMMY! album shows cocaine falling down on the band.

1: Mishearing lyrics of popular songs is something everyone has done at one time or another. In some cases, it is certainly understandable (see *Louie Louie* in the entry for Kingsmen), and of course one of the main complaints people have about rock music is that no one can understand what is being said. It had even become a popular conversation starter, with people comparing notes on songs they could not understand. There have even been books written about what people thought the lyrics to popular songs were.

The B-52's' song *Love Shack* has a moment like this. However, there is an additional twist to the story leading to the creation of an urban legend, as once the lyric is understood, it is still not quite understood.

Love Shack was a major hit from this group of out Athens, Georgia, coming from their 1989 album COSMIC THING. As is typical for B-52's' material, the melody and lyrics seems to have an almost sub-conscious link to the "pleasure" portion of the brain, making it hard for listeners not to smile, if not get up and dance. In fact, the song is exactly that, an anthem to getting together and "getting down." Of course, with a title like *Love Shack*, the urgent need to "get down" and "banging on the door" (or floor) would suggest something other than dancing, and that's where the urban legend comes into play.

Cindy Wilson

In the last quarter of the song, the music stops as band member Fred Schneider appears to be shouting, "You're what?," (he is actually saying "Your what?," which would lead to a question about something owned instead of something wrong), whereupon band member Cindy Wilson replies with "tin roof . . . rusted!" The song then starts up again.

What was amusing, or rather frustrating, for many listeners at the time, was the fact that they were unable to figure out what Wilson had said. This was mainly due to the somewhat nonsensical nature of the line. However, the urban legend arose mainly due to this, because once people did figure out the line, they felt it had to mean something important in the song. Certainly, it had to mean something for the song to break down and for Schneider to say, "You're what?" with such urgency.

Thus, all of this led to the birth of an urban legend. Since the song could be naturally construed to be about sex, it was assumed that "tin roof rusted" was a slang term meaning the girl was pregnant. Since no one had ever heard the term before, people then assumed it was southern slang or even strictly one from Athens, Georgia that the band members had heard when living there.

Another major variation of the legend stated that the term didn't mean she was pregnant, but rather having her menstrual cycle (which at least dealt with the visual image of a red-tinted, rusted roof more logically than the "pregnant" version of the legend). There was even a third variation of the legend as well – this one stating that the term meant the person was crazy (again, not that farfetched, as a roof is on the top and rust would be a defect).

Nevertheless, none of these variations is what the band had in mind when composing the song. Mats Sexton – creator of the official "unofficial" web site for the band (http://www.b52s.com) and author of the book THE B-52'S UNIVERSE (Plan-B Books, 2002) – pointed out to the author the obvious reference is that a building with a tin roof would tend to rust, and that in Georgia buildings often have tin roofs. Mats went on to tell the band's side of the creation of the lyric:

"The way the band writes music is by jamming in the studio. Rarely are songs 'written' in the traditional sense of pen and paper first. While in the studio and jamming on ideas (everyone singing, Keith [Strickland] playing music) Cindy had sung 'Tin Roof . . .' at that moment Keith, for whatever reason, stopped the music. Cindy finished her thought and sang . . . 'Rusted.' The band thought it was so funny, so they worked it into the song. It was just a spontaneous thing during the jam session and has no hidden meaning."

In other words, what seemed like a funny, somewhat nonsensical lyric turned out to be exactly that. Ironically, before Wilson added the line, the band was about to drop work on the song as it was deemed too slow and not coming together. It would go on to become one of their biggest hits.

2: The cover of the 1983 album, WHAMMY! shows the band with a dog standing in front of a black backdrop. There is white powder on the floor and it appears that more white powder is about to fall on them. This powder suspended above them in the photo was thought by some to be cocaine. It is actually flour. Photographer William Wegman decided to drop the flour on the band during the photo shoot and happened to catch it in mid-flight. As Mats Sexton pointed out, "again, no hidden meaning (and a miracle that he captured the flour in mid-motion)."

Source: Mats Sexton, B-Hive – The B-52's Fan Club, http://www.b52s.com

Backmasking and Subliminal Messages

> *Backmasking – the production art of taking a spoken message, reversing it and then hiding it in a musical track – has been done many times over the years by many different musicians. It and other subliminal messages are used in order to try to brainwash the listeners into doing what the artist wants them to do.*

Magician-Comedian Penn Jillette once put this urban legend into a clear perspective: "[The evil of backmasking] is, of course, hysterical grandstanding. If subliminal messages really worked, Ozzy Osbourne would be Prime Minister of England."

The genesis of the whole "subliminal message" movement goes back to a much publicized event in 1956 when subliminal messages were first attempted. The event involved an advertising expert named James Vicary and his company called the Subliminal Projection Company. At a movie theater in Fort Lee, New Jersey, a device was used during the screening of the movie PICNIC for six weeks. The device would flash messages on the screen every five seconds for 1/3,000th of a second that tried to entice the audience members to "Eat Popcorn" and "Drink Coke." According to the studies made by Vicary's company, cola sales increased 18 percent, while popcorn sales went up 58 percent.

It was a fascinating idea for advertisers and marketers, but it immediately worried people who believed Vicary had perfected a way for people to be coerced into doing things against their will via the subliminal messages. By the early 1970s the FCC had ruled that subliminal messages could not be used due to the possibility that such messages would unethical.

At the same time that this type of "flashed" subliminal message was being restrained, another type of subliminal message was being reviewed by a researcher named Wilson Bryan Key. Key began to advocate that hidden messages (usually sexual in nature) could be found in advertising that would entice prospective customers to buy the product. This led to the infamous study of Ritz cracker ads that had the word "sex" hidden in them, or that a naked man could be seen in the drawing of a camel on the Camel cigarette package. Not only were the images there, Key insisted, but they were there purposefully – to make customers buy the product for subconscious reasons manifested by the subliminal messages.

This is where music comes into play. In the 1960s, experiments were being done thanks to rapid progress in the development of recording equipment (especially in the later part of the 1960s). The Beatles, Phil Spector, and the Beach Boys were just some of the popular artists who began experimenting with what they could do with recordings and equipment, trying to find new sounds to use that would bring something to the music that hadn't been heard before. For the Beatles in particular, this meant trying things backwards, forwards, sideways, cut up and thrown in the air then retaped together – anything. None of it was taken seriously, but the listeners could tell that something was going on and tried to figure out what was being done. This led to listeners trying to play things backwards (which on many record players was easier said than done), and turning up the sound to pick things out. In some cases, the fans were right in thinking that something was there (such as King Lear being heard in the background of *I Am the Walrus*); in other cases, they were completely wrong (Lennon's "Cranberry sauce" sounding like "I buried Paul" and thereby helping to start an Urban Legend in that direction).

It wasn't long before other musicians started trying similar tricks in their tracks, and one of the easiest things to do was to record a message, play it backwards, and then put it into the music. In many cases, this was done not on a subliminal level, but rather audibly in plain sight (plain sound?). Pink Floyd was notorious for doing this somewhere on their albums, most specifically on the track *Empty Spaces* from THE WALL. At about the 1:13 mark, a voice can be heard saying something that when reversed clearly becomes, "Congratulations, you have just discovered the secret message. Please send your answer to old pink, care of the funny farm, Chalfont . . ."

Many of the clear backward messages on albums are along this humorous line, specially made to entice people into trying to figure out what the message is and then poking fun at these people for wasting their time doing so. Here are a few examples:

Electric Light Orchestra, *Fire on High* from FACE THE MUSIC: about 25 seconds into the song a message occurs that says, "The music is reversible, but time – turn back! Turn back! Turn back!"

- Weird Al Yankovic, *Nature Trail to Hell* on IN 3-D: "Satan eats Cheez Whiz." Al followed this up a few years later on the song *I Remember Larry* from the album BAD HAIR DAY: "Wow, you must have an awful lot of free time on your hands."
- Petra, *Judas Kiss* on MORE POWER TO YOU: Just before the song starts a backward message appears that says: "What are you looking for the Devil for, when you ought to be looking for the Lord?"

And so on. While these were simply in fun, it took on a sinister edge from the standpoint of the religious leaders who believed Rock music in all its forms were instruments of satanic corruption. These individuals were convinced by the studies of Vicary and Key that such messages probably were being put on albums by "satanic" musicians in order to corrupt unknowing kids into evil. By the mid-1980s, a massive amount of money and time was spent trying to find backward messages (by then commonly referred to as "backmasking" due to the messages being hidden "under" the music so they would be even harder to find) and other subliminal messages in many songs of popular (and even some never-to-be-known) artists. For these people, finding anything that sounded like a message was good as gold for them and a pile of "messages" were put together that would sound like gibberish to everyone else but those "trained" to find them.

Such messages would be the backbone of the religious right's fight against Rock music in the 1980s and into the 1990s. It was also the focus of landmark cases dealing with supposed backmasking and subliminal messages from Ozzy Osbourne and Judas Priest (see entries under these names for more details). Whenever such a case came up, both Key's and Vicary's work were cited as proof that such messages really worked, making people do things that they may not have done without the subconscious message coming through.

The problem with that, however, is that the research by both Vicary and Key has various flaws in it. Key's research was built on his necessity to prove his theory and so he did it without using a "control group" to see if advertising without the "subliminal messages" he had found produced the same, greater, or lesser effect. Because of this, there can be no solid proof that the messages really motivated people to do anything at all. Nor did Key prove that such messages were put there deliberately by the companies that produced the products and/or advertising. In many cases, the companies would deny doing so, but this only spurred on the people who believed that Key was right and that these companies were lying.

As for Vicary, he admitted in 1962 to ADVERTISING AGE that he had fabricated the research done by the machine he had created to flash subliminal messages. He merely wanted to increase customers for his marketing firm and never expected that the results he reported would cause such widespread and long-lasting panic. In fact, as Vicary said in the interview for the magazine, "we hadn't done any research . . . and what we had shouldn't have been used promotionally."

In other words, the research done at that time did not prove at all that popcorn and coke sales went up when subliminal messages were shown. To compound this, subsequent experiments have not shown subliminal messages to influence behavior. It seems that a sham is what it has actually turned out to be. Still, the press and the public tend to believe the old stories without even bothering to find out the facts behind them; and with these faulty "facts" many urban legends are born.

Sources: Poundstone, William. BIGGER SECRETS. Houghton Mifflin, Boston. 1998. Pages 227-231.

Pratkanis, Anthony. THE CARGO-CULT SCIENCE OF SUBLIMINAL PERSUASION, Skeptical Inquirer. Spring 1992.

The Beatles

1. *John created most of the characters for the movie, YELLOW SUBMARINE.*
2. *The infamous "butcher cover" for the YESTERDAY AND TODAY album was done in protest by the Beatles over the "butchering" of their music by Capitol Records.*
3. *Most of the Beatles work with Bob Dylan on an album called the MASKED MARAUDERS.*
4. *The Beatles reunite in the 1970s as the band Klaatu.*
5. *The reunion on SATURDAY NIGHT LIVE that didn't happen due to a slow taxi driver*
6. *Paul is dead, and has been since 1966.*
7. *John Lennon had a homosexual affair with Brian Epstein during the early 1960s.*
8. *Paul McCartney and John Lennon booted Pete Best from the band due to his ability to attract women, as they wanted to be the "cute" ones in the band.*
9. *John Lennon had gotten Mama Cass Elliott pregnant in 1974, but she died before she could give birth.*
10. *The Beatles were so into drugs that many of their songs ended up being advertising for drugs (Lucy in the Sky with Diamonds, Little Help From My Friends, Yellow Submarine, etc.).*
11. *Sexy Sadie was written by John Lennon about the Maharishi after the Maharishi supposedly attacked Mia Farrow during their communion stay.*

1:   In several interviews before his death Lennon had stated that the production crew of the animated movie YELLOW SUBMARINE stole several ideas from him without due credit. In particular, he pointed out the vacuum-cleaner monster and even the Blue Meanies as being creations he made for the animators when visiting them in the studio. As Lennon himself stated in David Sheff's important Lennon book THE PLAYBOY INTERVIEWS WITH JOHN LENNON AND YOKO ONO, he wrote the song *Hey Bulldog* specifically about the people behind the movie, as they were "gross animals apart from the guy who drew the paintings for the movie. They lifted all the ideas for the movie out of our heads and didn't give us any credit."

According to Robert Hieronimus' book, INSIDE THE YELLOW SUBMARINE, such accusations by Lennon were rubbish. The key animator, Alan Ball, stated that Lennon's accusation was very unlikely, going on to say that both the vacuum-cleaner monster and the Meanies were original concepts drawn by illustrator Heinz Edelmann before the film was even started.

Sources: Hieronimus, Robert R. INSIDE THE YELLOW SUBMARINE. Krause
Publications, Iola, WI. 2002, page 51.
Sheff, David. The Playboy Interviews With John Lennon and Yoko Ono.
Playboy Press, New York. 1981, page 172.

2:   In June 1966, a new Beatles album was released in the US, YESTERDAY AND TODAY.
Promotional copies of the album, a collection of tracks from, amongst others, the UK
versions of RUBBER SOUL and REVOLVER, were sent out to disc jockeys and other
important people in the business in hopes of another smash hit for Capitol Records.
Imagining another group of happy pop tunes from the foursome, people were shocked
when they looked at the cover and saw the four "mop-tops" wearing butchers'
smocks, with raw meat and decapitated baby dolls around them and on them. The
four look delirious, almost mad as a baby doll's head is held up for inspection. It was
startling and gruesome, especially for the time.

The outcry was immediate. Capitol withdrew the album immediately and a new
cover was created that showed the Beatles around a steamer trunk.

When Capitol realized that they couldn't release the 750,000 copies already
produced with the cover that caused such outrage, they had to come up with a cheap
solution. Instead of destroying the cover, a new album sized sheet showing the revised
cover was glued over the "butcher" cover and then released to record stores. This
lead to the collectabillity of not only the album in its original cover, but also the copies
that had the revised cover glued over the original. Over time, the "butcher cover"
album became one of the most sought-after record albums of all time, while also one
of the most widely believed urban legends in rock music.

To understand how this legend grew around the "butcher cover," one has to
understand how Capitol Records was releasing the Beatles' music in the US during
the 1960s. First, one must remember that distribution in foreign countries, even ones
so closely related in business as the US and the UK, did not lead to the same products
being released at the same time (or even released at all). Although the Beatles had
become a phenomenon in the UK, in 1962 the record labels in the US were unsure
about the band. When it was finally realized how successful the Beatles really were,
the US wing of EMI (the Beatles' label) found itself lagging behind what had already
been released in overseas.

This, as it turned out for those in charge at Capitol, was not necessarily a bad thing.
They found themselves with enough material that they could easily drop five "cover"
songs (songs originally recorded and made popular by other artists, and thought at
the time to be too "old fashioned" for release) and add some more recent non-album
singles to fill up the playing time and produce a sure-selling album from the mix.
When the first album, MEET THE BEATLES, was a smash, Capitol simply took the five
songs deleted from the first album, added some A & B-sides from singles, along with
a couple of tracks recorded but unreleased at the time, and produced the second US
Beatles album called, cleverly enough, THE BEATLES' SECOND ALBUM.

This was just the beginning; with the success of the second reworked package of
material Capitol saw that they were sitting on a gold mine. In shortening the length

of subsequent albums, adding tracks left off of earlier albums or non-album-related singles – not to mention adding movie orchestration tracks (such as in the case of the soundtrack albums for HARD DAY'S NIGHT and HELP!) – Capitol found they could release nearly twice the amount of new product as their British counterpart. With Beatlemania sweeping the country, Capitol could string the public along quite nicely and make a bundle off the material still in the vaults. The people at Capitol were quite happy about it.

However, the speculation was that the Beatles were not at all happy with the seemingly random reworking of their albums. This would certainly seem logical, as it was evident that the band was becoming more engrossed with the production of their albums as they became increasingly disenchanted with touring. They began to view their completed albums to be the whole purpose of their work as a group, and to see the US label tear up the logic of their completed work in order to make a few additional dollars . . ., one would have to think that the band members were less than thrilled.

Which brings us to YESTERDAY AND TODAY.

On June 15, 1966, a new Beatles album was released in the US, YESTERDAY AND TODAY. The album was no different from the others before it, put together with bits and pieces from the HELP! soundtrack album, the RUBBER SOUL and REVOLVER albums, and both sides of a previous single. As it stood, the usage of three tracks from the REVOLVER album was were the legend would be born. REVOLVER had yet to be released and was to be another step in the evolution of album recording for the band after the remarkable RUBBER SOUL in 1965. Now, because the US label needed filler for their next hodge-podge bag of tunes, three songs had been taken from REVOLVER just weeks before it was released in the US.

With that in mind, it was no wonder that fans soon began to suspect that the redrawn "butcher cover" was a statement by the band over what was happening with their music in the US. As it turned out, it wasn't at all. As it stood, the Beatles had little concern with what was happening in the US with the album until after it was released (with the cutting of three tracks from Revolver being one of the key elements of that change). Before then, the Beatles were largely unaware of how their albums were treated in the US, besides knowing that they were selling.

Furthermore, the "butcher cover" photo (as it has become known) was photographed back on March 1966 – a month before the three tracks from REVOLVER used on YESTERDAY AND TODAY were even recorded, and nearly three months before the release of the album. On top of that, the photo had already begun appearing in association to the band before YESTERDAY AND TODAY was released (including a print ad for the *Paperback Writer* single, the cover of DISC magazine and the promotional films made for *Paperback Writer* and *Rain*). Therefore, the cover was not a one-off association with the "butchering" of the albums by the US record label.

Nor was there any intention to use it as a cover at all. The photographer, Robert Whitaker, had originally shot the photo as part of a larger project he was working on dealing with the band's resentment to always being the happy, lovable "mop-tops" in their promotional photos. Whitaker, a close associate of the band (and, ironically enough, the photographer of the photo used in the substitution of the "butcher" cover) had worked with the band on a series of photos that was to represent the Beatles as "just as real and human as everyone else." As Whitaker told GOLDMINE magazine in 1991, the "butcher" cover was entitled A SOMNAMBULANT ADVENTURE, and was to demonstrate a shocking contrast to the "happy" image the band had at the time. This photo, along with three others, were to be used together to form a larger overview of the band. Instead, it was used by Capitol erroneously as another "fun, madcap" photo of the Beatles in action.

In retrospect, the band's image created the opportunity for such an error to be made without question by the people at Capitol Records. On the other side of the coin, the fans insistence that the band would strike back at their label in their own iconoclastic way created the opportunity for an urban legend to be born. In the end, neither turned out to be the correct assumption.

Sources: York, Robert. WHO BUTCHERED THE BEATLES?
http://www.eskimo.com/~bpentium/whobutch.html
Tamarkin, Jeff. "Photographer Bob Whitaker Talks about the 'Butcher Cover' and His Experiences with the Beatles," Goldmine. 1991 Vol., 17, Issue 295.

3: See the entry for Bob Dylan for more details.

4: See the entry for Klaatu for more details.

5: People forget, but there was a time when everyone watched SATURDAY NIGHT LIVE. Starting back in the mid-1970s, the show was an escape for high school and college-aged viewers who wanted a comedy show of their own, and featured many actors and writers that would go on to bigger things in the 1980s. The show continues to be a starting place for many young comedic writers today.

The show had evolved over time, but one essential element was the impression of intimacy that it had in the early years. There was also a sense of cheapness about SNL, as if it was a group of people pooling their money together to make the show run.

This led directly to an early classic moment on the show. At a time when there had been several stories of the Beatles being offered multi-millions to regroup and tour, the people on SNL decided to parody the whole thing. This was done on an April 1976 episode by having the producer and co-creator of the series, Lorne Michaels, go before the cameras and offer $3,000 to the Beatles to reunite on the program (the joke was extended a few weeks later, when Michaels reappeared to announce that the ante had been bumped up to a "massive" $3,200). The joke was obvious and was even referred to in later broadcast (commonly when a former Beatle appeared on the show, as when a latter episode that season featured George Harrison and offered viewers a teaser where Michaels was explaining to Harrison that the $3,200 was for all four Beatles, not just one).

It was a great gag, yet it also produced its own urban legend. According to the legend, John Lennon and Paul McCartney were watching SATURDAY NIGHT LIVE that particular night at Lennon's place in Manhattan. As a joke, the two decided to go to the NBC network studios nearby. Unfortunately, the driver of the taxi they took got hopelessly lost and did not arrive at the studios until the show was long over. Thus, the possible reunion of the Beatles, or even the reunion of McCartney and Lennon together on the same stage – even as an extension of a joke on SNL – never came to be.

The oddest thing about this legend is that there really is a certain amount of truth to the story. Lennon and McCartney were in New York that night, and were at Lennon's apartment in the Dakota building. On top of that, they were actually watching SATURDAY NIGHT LIVE at the time and saw the offer made by Michaels on the show. As it turned out, McCartney at the time was making it a habit to come over to Lennon's place every so often to play guitar together and generally have a friendly chat. There was no taxi driver getting lost, however, as there was no taxi in the first place. As John Lennon himself explained in THE PLAYBOY INTERVIEWS WITH JOHN LENNON AND YOKO ONO: "We were watching it and almost went down to the studio, just as a gag. We nearly got into a cab, but we were actually too tired."

Rather an anti-climatic ending to the story; perhaps even more so than the urban legend based around it.

Ironically enough, as Doug Hill and Jeff Weingrad mentioned in their book about SNL, SATURDAY NIGHT, Michaels had a concern that Lennon and McCartney would take him up on the offer and then not be allowed past NBC security if they arrived in time for the show. Although he prepared the pages at the studio to keep an eye out for Lennon and McCartney, his hopes never materialized.

We can hardly blame him for wishing, however.

Sources: Hill, Doug and Weingrad, Jeff. SATURDAY NIGHT. Vintage Books, New York. 1987, Pages 134-135.
Sheff, David. The Playboy Interviews with John Lennon and Yoko Ono. Playboy Press, New York, NY. 1981, page 69.

6: One of the most famous and long-lasting rock music urban legends ever is that commonly referred to simply as "Paul is dead." At least two books have been written about the subject, numerous references to the legend appear in various biographies about the Beatles and McCartney, and it has a universal "household" status amongst the public. People may have never heard about Klaatu being the Beatles, or even the "butcher cover," but everyone has heard about "that guy in the Beatles that was supposedly dead."

The essential elements of the legend are as follows: The Beatles are working on their next album in November 1966. Paul leaves the studio one day only to become involved in a horrible car accident due to not noticing that a traffic light had changed. The car is destroyed and McCartney's body is so horribly disfigured as to be unrecognizable.

Brian Epstein and the rest of the Beatles decide to hush up the whole incident so as not to destroy the large following they had already built up around themselves. To do this, a replacement for McCartney had to be found and a secret contest was held to find someone that looked like McCartney.

The winner was a young Scotsman named William Campbell. Campbell already looked a bit like McCartney, but he was given extensive plastic surgery to make him appear as close to McCartney as possible. The surgery was almost a complete success, although a small scar was left on his upper lip from the surgery.

After going through all these elaborate activities in order to keep the world from knowing that McCartney has been replaced, the other Beatles began to feel guilty about lying to their fans and to the world. In order to counteract this, the Beatles decided that a series of gentle, almost undetectable clues on their albums and in other subsequent appearances would be a good way to let fans in on the situation. It was not until 1969 that the clues came to the public's attention.

Although some sources say the story started in September of that year, an announcement about the rumor on a radio show on October 12, 1969 is usually pointed to as the major breakout point of the story. Less than two weeks after the release of the album ABBEY ROAD, a radio disc jockey named Russ Gibb supposedly received an anonymous phone call from someone claiming that McCartney was dead. The caller further went on to state that the evidence could be found if one played *Strawberry Fields Forever* backwards. At the end of the song, one would supposedly hear John saying, "I buried Paul" (it was actually John saying "cranberry sauce"). Gibb did this and announced the findings on the Detroit, Michigan radio station WKNR-FM. From there, the story blossomed into a full-fledged side phenomenon about the Beatles. Soon, everyone was looking at the album covers, playing songs backwards, looking at pictures of Paul "before" and "after" – anything and everything in order to find clues that would relate to the death of Paul and his replacement.

That was just the start. With just a little bit of imagination, all kinds of things seemed to interpretable as further clues in the legend:

- Paul being barefoot on the cover of ABBEY ROAD, along with the progression of the band members on the cover that made John, George and Ringo each a member of a funeral procession. Not to mention a Volkswagen in the background that had a license plate reading "28 IF," supposedly meaning Paul's age at the time if he had lived.
- Clues that were frontward in songs, such as "he blew his mind out in a car" in *A Day in the Life* meaning that Paul was decapitated in an automobile accident at a traffic light; or the Walrus of *I am the Walrus* being a symbol of death.
- Paul wearing a black carnation while the others wore red during the dance-sequence for *Your Mother Should Know* in the film MAGICAL MYSTERY TOUR.

And onward up to the present day, with hundreds and hundreds of clues having been accumulated.

Today, many people find the rumor to be strictly a morbid yet fascinating game. There is little doubt that everyone accepts the fact that McCartney did not die in 1966, and even if he had, that Campbell character has played the part so well that it hardly seems important anymore to seriously consider him to be anyone but Paul McCartney. The question remains, however, why would anyone at the time take the story so seriously that they would bother trying to find clues?

We have to remember, that at the time of the story in 1969, the band was starting to break up. Rumors of a break-up kept circulating and, as many biographies since have made clear, the band members were starting to distance themselves from each other publicly. With the release of ABBEY ROAD, Paul had taken a sabbatical away from the band, the public, and the press. Meanwhile, the rest of the Beatles were still in the public eye. Therefore, when the rumors started that Paul was dead, Paul was not immediately available to counteract the rumors. Nor was it thought to make much of a difference if the people working for the band had bothered trying on their own. As Ringo Starr stated in THE BEATLES ANTHOLOGY, "There was no way to prove he was alive. We said, 'Well, how can we prove this rumor isn't true? Let's take a photo!' But, of course, they would say, 'That's just his stand-in in the photo.'"

While the band and their people in the offices snickered a bit at the story and saw it as great publicity for the new album, everyone soon grew tired of the story. George Martin stated in the book THE BEATLES – AN ORAL HISTORY that he had started getting phone calls "at three o'clock in the morning, asking you if Paul is really dead!" Meanwhile, Paul was having people react to him strangely in person, as if they were unsure if the story were true and he really was some type of double. Peter Blake, the designer of the SGT. PEPPER album cover stated that Paul also got a brief kick out of the story as well: "We talked about the rumors and he said, 'You know, I'm not Paul McCartney ... Look I've got a scar. I'm a stand-in.' And, just for a moment, I wasn't sure.'"

Still, Paul finally went public about his supposed death after a reporter from LIFE magazine tracked him down in November of that year. As suspected by all involved, that did little to stop the stories. After that, the band had other problems to deal with, and the urban legend of Paul's supposed death in 1966 became little more than an oddly humorous story in their shared history and nothing more. After the death of John Lennon in 1980 (and Harrison's death in 2001), the humor level of the legend has become even more remote.

In a final analysis, the possibility that such a story could have even the slightest possibility of being true was put to rest by John Lennon years ago. As he stated, "Paul McCartney couldn't die without the world knowing it. The same as he couldn't get married without the world knowing it. It's impossible – he can't go on holiday without the world knowing it. It's just insanity – but it's a great plug for ABBEY ROAD."

Sources: Beatles. THE BEATLES ANTHOLOGY. Chronicle Books, San Francisco. 2000 Page 342.
Brown, Peter and Gaines, Steven. THE LOVE YOU MAKE. McGraw Hill, New York. 1983, pages 372-373.
Morgan, Hal and Tucker, Kerry. RUMOR!. Penguin Books, New York. 1984, pages 82-87.
Norman, Philip. SHOUT! THE BEATLES IN THEIR GENERATION. Warner Books, New York. 1981, pages 482-483.

Sources: Pritchard, David and Lysaght, Alan. THE BEATLES – AN ORAL HISTORY.
Hyperion, New York. 1998, pages 293-294.

7: Did John Lennon and Brian Epstein have a brief affair in the early 1960s? Hard to say for sure, although the breakthrough book to put forth such a story was THE LOVE YOU MAKE by Peter Brown and Steven Gaines. Brown was a personal acquaintance of Brian Epstein and worked formally for the band, while the book was written in conjunction with several interviews done with many former associates of the band. With that type of history, it would seem assured that the true story about the band would be told.

Their book was not the first to suggest that Brian, a closeted homosexual, had interest in John on a more sexual level, but it was one of the first to openly suggest that they actually did have sex together. At least one could guess at that by the way the story is told in the book.

The story goes that Brian went on a vacation to Barcelona and had asked John along on the trip. According to Brown and Gaines, John went along on the trip knowing full well that Brian may try to make an advance on him, and eventually the two did have sex; yet, Brown and Gaines use innuendo in such a way that they never flat out say such a thing occurred. Thus, in trying to clear the air about a rumored sexual liaison between the two, the authors clouded up the issue even more.

The Beatles themselves discussed the vacation Lennon and Epstein took in their BEATLES ANTHOLOGY book. From Paul, nothing is flat-out stated either way, but he saw the move by Lennon not one of sexual curiosity, but rather an opportunity for Lennon to get on the good side of their manager. As Paul stated in the book, "he wanted Brian to know whom he should listen to. That was the relationship."

In an excerpt from an interview with Lennon used in THE BEATLES ANTHOLOGY, he was livid when the stories began to surface that he and Epstein had an affair while in Spain, leading to a famous punch-up with Bob Wooler after the man had insinuated the rumor to Lennon. As Lennon reported in the interview, while the relationship between he and Epstein was "pretty intense," it was never a sexual relationship.

Sources: Beatles. THE BEATLES ANTHOLOGY. Chronicle Books, San Francisco.
2000 Page 98.
Brown, Peter and Gaines, Steven. THE LOVE YOU MAKE. McGraw Hill,
New York. 1983, pages 93-94.

8: Pete Best was in the Beatles as their drummer until August 16, 1962 and there was little doubt that he was certainly the best looking guy in the group. With rugged, working man features, along with a way of inciting women to clamor towards him, he was obviously a favorite. Because of this, many viewed at the time and still to this day that Pete was sacked for no other reason than jealousy from Paul and John, who wanted a chance at getting the girls after the show as much as Pete had.

Of course, in retrospect, this thinking doesn't make a whole lot of sense. As evident in many biographies about the band, the members of the group pretty much had their hands full of girls, left and right, and if Best had a chance to get a few himself, it hardly would be the type of thing that would account for his leaving the band. Mainly such thinking came from those who were fans of Best (including his own family), who wanted to prove that Best was the "better man" by showing that he was fired because of his looks and for no other reason.

The evidence supports other reasons, however. Pete had been hired into the band at a time when they needed a drummer; they knew he had his own drum kit and knew he could keep a steady beat. The problems came when Pete demonstrated that he was not the same type of person that the others in the band were. While the others were partying after the shows, Pete stayed to himself; while the others kept popping pills to keep going, Best avoid them; in the end Pete didn't share the same life as the others. As Paul McCartney pointed out in THE BEATLES ANTHOLOGY: "It was a personality thing. We knew that he wasn't that good a player. He was slightly different from the rest of us; not quite as 'studenty'."

More importantly, due to illness, Pete was known for missing shows over time, leading to the band having to "borrow" drummers left and right in order to fulfill gigs already set up for them. That led to tension between Best and the others as well. It also led to Best not developing at the same pace as the others, because he couldn't be there with them. Because of the substitutions, the others also got to know the drumming style of Richard "Ringo" Starkey, as Ringo substituted for Best at several shows over time.

When the time came that the band got a chance to play for a record producer, George Martin (who would remain the band's producer for nearly their entire existence as a band), they were willing to do what it took to keep an "in" into the recording industry. So when Martin suggested that the best thing for the band would be if Best was replaced with another drummer for the recordings, it was the final blow to his position in the band. Soon after, Best was out and Ringo was in.

At the time, the dropping of Best was considered sacrilege by some of the fans (especially the girls that came mainly to see Best). The matter soon dropped after Ringo had been in the band for a time and Best had moved on to other bands as well. In the end, the success of the band made Ringo a famous name, along with George, John, and Paul, while Best stayed in Liverpool and built his own life there.

Source: The Beatles. THE BEATLES ANTHOLOGY. Chronicle Books, San Francisco. 2000. Page 70-71.

9: See the entry for Mama Cass Elliott for more details.

10: For years the Beatles have had to live with the assumption that many of their songs were written specifically to promote drugs. It doesn't seem to matter whether it was true or not, but both pro- and anti-drug segments of the population just knew they had to be singing about drugs.

Here's a few of the songs that were supposed to be about drugs:

- *Lucy in the Sky with Diamonds* – the obvious one of the songs as the initials of the song spell out LSD. With the psychedelic lyrics that describes everything from a girl with "kaleidoscope eyes" to "newspaper taxies" it was apparent that something not real was happening within the song and the rumor about the LSD initials led to the obvious conclusion. This story had always been denied by members of the band and backed up with the same genesis for the song from everyone involved: that John's young son, Julian, showed him a picture he had drawn of a classmate named Lucy, flying through a sky full of diamonds. John liked the title of the artwork so much that he used it for the title of the song.
- *Hey Jude* – Thanks to the lyrics, "Remember to let her under your skin, then you'll begin to make it better," some concluded that the song was about shooting heroin ("under the skin ... make it better"). As McCartney would state in several interviews over the years, the song was actually written for John's son, Julian (or Jules for short). McCartney was using the song as a way to tell Julian (and himself, as he later realized) to accept the changes in John Lennon's life after he had left Julian's mother and started living with Yoko Ono. "Remember to let her under your skin," merely deals with acceptance, not with heroin.
- *With A Little Help From My Friends* – thanks to the title lyric and the line, "I get high with a little help from my friends," it was considered a song saluting pill-popping. In the context of the song, however, it is obvious that the song refers to the happiness found in having friends. The reference to getting "high" merely means this, not that the friends are some type of pill. It is a misreading of the lyrics and simply that.
- *Yellow Submarine* – supposedly about a pills, once again. This one is a bit of a grasping at straws, as it is clearly a children's song with nonsensical lyrics. However, soon after the song was released, some drug pushers began using the name to describe a type of pill they had, so one can understand where the connotation came from.

There are others, no doubt, but these are some of the best remembered of the rumored "drug songs" done by the band. The thing was, the band did write about drug experiences in their songs, but usually in such a way that it told a story instead of being a huge, obnoxious banner promoting drugs. *She Said, She Said*, is a good example of this, being a song that Lennon wrote about a horrible drug experience he had. The band members rarely discussed the topic in interviews and usually kept to themselves (unlike some other bands and singers that publicly endorsed heroin and LSD, amongst other things). As pointed out in THE BEATLES ANTHOLOGY, the band also avoided anything harsher than marijuana in the studio because they were there to work, not "goof off."

When word would reach the band members that a song was taken out of context and turned into a "drug song," they usually just shook their heads. They were probably quite used to it, as there are other songs in the Beatles' repertoire that have been misread and misunderstood.

Source: The Beatles. THE BEATLES ANTHOLOGY. Chronicle Books, San Francisco. 2000.

11: Lennon had said in interviews that the song *Sexy Sadie* was a poke at the Maharishi after their experience staying with him in 1968. The rumor was that George and John had left after it was discovered that the Maharishi had either made a pass at or literally attacked actress Mia Farrow. From reports later on it was questioned if such an attack or pass really did occur, but it was too late to stop the media from suggesting that the Beatles (actually Paul and Ringo had already left after a brief stay by that point) had become disillusioned with the Maharishi.

John picked up on this point when he mentioned in interviews later that he had been disillusioned by the Maharishi, and ever the one to prick holes in the ideals of others, saw this as a perfect opportunity to give it to the Maharishi in song.

As both Lennon and Harrison reported, a line in the song originally went, "Maharishi, what have you done? You've made a fool of everyone." Harrison disagreed with the lyric, especially in light of the fact that there was no proof anything had occurred between the Maharishi and Farrow in the first place, just a vicious rumor. Lennon eventually agreed and changed the lyric to "Sexy Sadie" if not for Harrison's reason then for the sake of avoiding a slander suit at some point.

Source: The Beatles. THE BEATLES ANTHOLOGY. Chronicle Books, San Francisco. 2000.

Captain Beefheart

Captain Beefheart took part in a "gross-out" contest with Frank Zappa back in the early 1970s.

See the entry for Alice Cooper for more details.

Pat Benatar

Hit Me with Your Best Shot *is a song about sado-masochism.*

The rumor that *Hit Me with Your Best Shot* was a song about sado-masochism (sexual fulfillment via giving or receiving mental or physical punishment) has been around since the song became a hit back in the late 1970s for singer Pat Benatar. It is also a case of people reading far too much and/or not reading enough into the song just by the title and chorus itself.

As is evident from listening to the song, it is not about sado-masochism at all. Instead, the song is about bravado, with a girl setting her sights on a guy known for "loving 'em and leaving 'em," knowing full well that she can do the same to him just as easily. As Benatar and her husband and lead-guitarist Neil Giraldo pointed out to GOLDMINE magazine in 1999, the whole song was tongue-in-cheek (no pun intended). Due to the nature of the song and the urban legend based around it, Benatar looks back on the song as "ridiculous and so beat to death." As Benatar said in the interview: "They'd think it was serious. They just didn't get the sarcasm. That's the problem; I can't do it the serious way, and they don't get it the other way."

Benatar also ran into a similar problem with the song *Hell is for Children* – a song against child abuse that for some reason people have interpreted as being pro child abuse. It also became a "joke" at Benatar's expense by critics, pointing out the "irony" that such an anti-abuse song would be on the same album as *Hit Me with Your Best Shot.* However, any person of normal intelligence who read the lyrics would see that the joke was not only lame but also lacking in any basis of fact.

Source: Sharp, Ken. "Pat Benatar & Neil Giraldo: Fire Away." Goldmine. Issue 496, July 30, 1999. Page 40.

Blondie

> *In the early 1970s, Deborah Harry was kidnapped by serial killer Ted Bundy.*

Debbie Harry was the lead singer of the popular late 1970s / early 1980s band Blondie, and a successful actress and artist in her own right. Back in the early 1970s, however, she was struggling to make it in New York, just like most others in the city.

Ted Bundy was an infamous serial killer and sex offender whose known murders occurred in the mid-1970s. He was executed for his murders on January 24, 1989 in Florida.

Bundy's execution was very high-profile, which may have led to Harry remembering an incident that occurred to her in the early 1970s and why she felt it worth discussing to reporters in late 1989 and early 1990 (at a time when she was promoting her album, DEF, DUMB AND BLONDE). The story Harry told was that in the early 1970s during the

summer (she never gives a specific date), she was in the lower east side of Greenwich Village waiting for a cab when a man in a white car pulled up and offered her a lift. Getting into the car, she noticed that, even though it was a hot day, all the windows were rolled partially rolled-up. When she went to roll down the window, she noticed that there was no crank to roll down the window or door handle to open the door on her side of the car.

Knowing something was wrong, Harry reached through the car window and stretched her arm down to the car handle on the outside. When the driver noticed this, he tried to stop her as they turned a corner. Harry opened the door as they turned the corner and she fell out on to the street. The driver then pulled away and back into traffic, never to be seen by Harry again.

With Bundy's execution, Harry remembered the incident from her past and concluded that it must have been Bundy who attempted to kidnap her that day. However, Bundy's known killing spree did not begin until 1974 from all accounts and took place mainly in Utah and Colorado, far west of New York. Harry states in her interviews that the incident occurred before she was even in a band, which would have made it sometime before Bundy starting killing, as she began working in bands by 1973. He was also prone to killing women not by picking them up, but by entering their homes; nor is there any evidence that he was ever in the New York area in the early 1970s; nor did it appear that he ever visited New York during his lifetime.

In other words, while it is very possible that Harry was picked up by someone who had terrible plans for her and that she made a miraculous escape from a criminal, it does not appear that it was Ted Bundy.

Sources: Aparicio, Nester. "Encounter With a Killer?" St. Petersburg Times. November 8, 1989. Page A3.
Mikkelson, Barbara and David P. "'Call Me!' Disbelieving, Blondie," Urban Legends Reference Pages. February 3, 2000.

David Bowie

> *Mick Jagger was caught having sex with David Bowie by Bowie's wife.*

See the entry for Rolling Stones for more details.

Kate Bush

> *Kate posed nude for the International version of PENTHOUSE magazine in September 1978.*

Probably one of the most recurring of urban legends for Kate Bush, this story can usually be put to rest once someone actually sees the photos of Kate Simmons, the women posing in that issue of PENTHOUSE from September 1978.

Of course, even the slightest of similarities between Bush and Simmons certainly can lead to some confusion by a less-than-astute reader (viewer?), and there were just enough similarities to do exactly that. Both have or had brown hair, brown eyes and the same first name. Simmons is also listed in the accompanying article (yes, there are such things in men's magazines) as working on her first album, and 1978 also saw the release of Kate Bush's first album. It is also evident that at least two photos were posed and lit in such a fashion that it appears the photographer was intentionally trying to make Simmons look like Bush. From there the rumor snowballed until some people (although typically not fans of Kate Bush) thought the story to be true. One photo from the pictorial even turned up as the cover to a Kate Bush bootleg album (DREAMTIME).

The subject was eventually brought up to Bush in an interview for MUSICIAN magazine in 1990 whereupon Bush clearly put the matter to rest, stating that she had never posed nude for any photos in her career. However, anyone that looks at the photos instead of just listening to the innuendo would clearly see that the two women really look nothing alike.

Sources: "Kate," Penthouse (International Edition), September 1978. Pages 91-102.
    Diliberto, John. "Kate Bush's Theater of the Senses," Musician, February, 1990.

The Byrds

> 1. *Glen Campbell played lead guitar on* EIGHT MILES HIGH.
> 2. *David Crosby was replaced by a horse on the cover of the album Byrds album he contributed to,* THE NOTORIOUS BYRD BROTHERS.

1: There is this assumption that session players were used a lot by starting bands in the early to mid-1960s. This was usually due to the record executives' believing that the performers they were hiring may be "good," but "good" wasn't enough for making hit records. New bands, upon being told that sessions players would do the music "at first" (sometimes it never got past a "first") may put up a fuss, but they were usually reluctant to say no. In fact, Roger McGuinn was the only member of the Byrds to perform on their first single, *Mr. Tambourine Man*. The other session players there, however, did not include an up and coming Glen Campbell.

Campbell was working as a studio musician in the mid-1960s, working for such artists as Johnny Cash and even the Mamas and the Papas. He even replaced Brian Wilson in the Beach Boys for several months at the beginning of 1965. In 1966 he did work with Gene Clark as a studio musician following Clark's departure from the Byrds on the album, GENE CLARK AND THE GOSDIN BROTHERS, for Columbia Records. This was the only work Campbell did in relation to any of the Byrds members, but it was probably enough to convince some fans to fancy that he had worked with the Byrds in some capacity instead of just one former member.

After *Mr. Tambourine Man*, the Byrds would never resort to hired studio musicians again.

Source: Adams, Cecil. THE STRAIGHT DOPE. Ballantine Book, Toronto. 1984.
         Page 319.

2: In 1967, the Byrds were becoming a huge sensation in the U.S., but tension within the group was beginning to make it fall apart. The band, made up of Roger McGuinn, Chris Hillman, Michael Clarke and David Crosby, was beginning work on their next album, which would become THE NOTORIOUS BYRD BROTHERS, when things came to a head. Michael Clarke, the drummer, was vocal in stating that he was less than happy with his status in the band (so vocal that the argument between the band members was caught on tape and eventually appeared as a cut on the CD version of the album released years later). Soon after, Clarke left the band and was replaced by a series of studio musicians.

The problems in the band didn't stop there, however. Crosby, had been increasing his control of the band in both the studio and on stage, leaving McGuinn and Hillman less than satisfied with their own take on things. There had also been a recent incident at the famous Monterey Pop Festival where Crosby had derailed their performance with a rambling rant about "the government cover-up" of the Kennedy Assassination that had embarrassed the rest of the band. Crosby also created friction by playing with Buffalo Springfield during the festival without telling the others that he planned to do so, further distancing himself from the rest of the Byrds.

Crosby's problems with Hillman and McGuinn came to a head when he refused to record a song written by Gerry Goffin and Carole King because it was beneath his talents and would knock one of his own songs off the album. An argument followed that lead to McGuinn throwing Crosby out of the studio and later informing Crosby at his home that he was no longer a member of the band.

The album was completed with a number of session players (including original guitarist Gene Clark for a three-week period) and the return of Michael Clarke to the band for an additional track. The album was then released with a cover that seemed to speak volumes about Crosby's status in the band. The cover shows what appears to be a stable with four windows. In each of the first three windows, left to right, stood a member of the band: Chris Hillman, Roger McGuinn, and Michael Clarke. In the fourth appeared a horse. Crosby was nowhere to be found, even though he was a long-time member of the band and played on half the album.

Crosby immediately took offense, figuring it was McGuinn that came up with the concept of making it appear that Crosby had been replaced by a horse (or was so insignificant that even a horse was better to see on the cover than Crosby). McGuinn denied the story, saying that the horse belonged to Clarke and had come to the window on his own just as publicity photos were being taken and the photo just turned out looking so good that they decided to use it.

In this case, the legend becomes one of "He said / She said," since it will never be determined for sure if McGuinn and the others were really trying to make a statement about Crosby's importance in the band or if it was just a coincidence. On one hand, you can plainly see that Clarke is holding the horse's rein so that the horse can't leave the window (leading us to suggest that it wasn't just a coincidence in the making); on the other hand, as McGuinn said himself, "If we had intended to do that, we would have turned the horse around."

Sources: Rogan, Johnny. THE BYRDS: TIMELESS FLIGHT REVISITED. Rogan House, London. 1998.
Mikkelson, Barbara and David. "Equinimity," Urban Legends Reference Pages. May 30, 1999.
http://www.snopes.com/music/hidden/horse.htm

Mariah Carey

> *During a 1996 on-line interview, Mariah Carey said, "When I watch TV and see those poor starving kids all over the world, I can't help but cry. I mean, I'd love to be skinny like that, but not with all those flies and death and stuff."*

This legend is a perfect example of the power of the Internet. As the old saying goes, "people believe what they read." Unfortunately, what was created as a parody for an on-line web site soon took on a life of its own and has continued to plague the artist it was supposed to be from even though she never said any such thing.

The story began with the web site http://www.cupcake.com. A writer, going by the name Cindy Zee, created an article that was a supposedly an interview with singer Mariah Carey. Viewing it, a reader would have instantly known that the interview was a parody, and a crude variation of the punch line of a "dumb blonde" joke, but that didn't stop the British magazine VOX from reprinting it as an actual quote from Carey. From there, the story spread – through countless magazines, newspapers, Internet newsgroups, and emails. It became an infamous quote that everyone had heard about in shock and dismay. Many believed it to be true. Many more wanted to believe it was true, even if they couldn't believe that she would actually say such a thing.

Why? Because Mariah Carey had become a phenomenon, with hit singles and albums thanks not only to her singing voice, but also to her position – she was a wife of the president of her record label. Because of her position, many thought she had achieved her success not on the strength of her character and ability, but based on who she was married to. The next step for those who believed this was to put Carey down in any way possible, and the quote was a delicious delight to people wanting to knock her down a peg or two. It made Carey appear to be bubble-headed and vain. It matched the expected stereotype.

At first, Carey and her record label tried to ignore the quote, hopeful that fans and the public would realize that it didn't come from her. They also worried that any denial made would only publicize the "quote" even more. After it refused to die, it was decided to go public with a press conference in Britain, where she addressed the issue with the following statement:

> "What was said was horrible and if anyone ever thought I would remotely say or think about anything like that, please understand I would not. Cupcake treated it as though it was a real interview with real quotes. It's not like they were saying things that I could laugh off. The internet is a great thing but it's also a dangerous thing. I know people love it, but people in this position can get really screwed over."

In the end, Mariah's response to the press never had the life that the parody quote did, and people still believe she said the "starving children" quote to this day. As a final irony, the Cupcake site does not exists today, giving the joke the longest lasting contribution of the site to the ages.

It should be mentioned that another parody quote supposedly said by Carey has been past around from friend to friend since 1999. The quote was rumored to have come from USA TODAY or the CNN web site and reportedly was Carey's response after being told about the death of Jordan's King Hussein in February 1999.

> "I'm inconsolable at the present time. I was a very good friend of Jordan, he was probably the greatest basketball player this country has every seen. We will never see his like again."

The joke, of course, being that Carey had somehow confused King Hussein of Jordan with basketball player, Michael Jordan. As evident, the parody is not as good as the earlier one from 1996.

Sources: Mikkelson, Barbara and David P. "Carey on Starving," Urban Legends Reference Pages, http://www.snopes.com/quotes/carey.htm, October 26, 1966.
"Mariah Carey's Cupcake Quote Falls Flat," Wall of Sound, http://mcarticles.hypermart.net/96/96_wof.htm, August 29, 1996.
Roeper, Richard. URBAN LEGENDS. Career Press, New Jersey. 2001, Pages 229-231.

The Cars

> The Cars got their name in connection with a contest where audience members at one of their shows got a chance to beat up on an old car with a sledge hammer.

During the early days of the band, they did participate in a concert in the southern U.S. where a radio station ran such a promotion – allowing people to take a swing at an old car with a sledge hammer for the price of a ticket. However, the band was already called the Cars before being associated with that particular concert. As guitarist Elliot Easton told Jere Chandler on his site, Rewind, the name was chosen because a car was so much a part of growing up as a teenager and a part of the "rock and roll experience."

Source: Chandler, Jere. "Elliot Easton of the Cars," Rewind.
http://members.aol.com/jerec7/cars.html

Cher

> 1. Sonny and Cher were actually a lesbian couple – Sonny was actually a woman. If not that, then they are actually brother and sister.
> 2. Cher, in a bid for a younger, slimmer figure, has had ribs surgically removed.

1: The rumor that Sonny Bono was actually a woman came about around the time the pair were having their first run of success in the late 1960s. The story lost a lot of steam once it became apparent that Sonny really was a man, especially after their television success and Bono's later career as a politician (not to mention the several children Bono had fathered over the years). As to the idea that Sonny and Cher were related, this rumor had even less steam than the "Sonny is a woman" one.

Source: Morgan, Hal and Tucker, Kerry. RUMOR!. Penguin Books, New York. 1984, page 72.

2: The rumor that Cher had ribs removed in order to have a slimmer figure goes back to previous rumors about all the cosmetic surgery that she has supposedly had over the years. While Cher has had some plastic surgery done – the best known being the

surgeries to her nose and breasts – there has never been any substantiation of other surgeries done. As reported by Barbara and David P. Mikkelson for their Urban Legends Reference Pages web site, the story about Cher having extensive surgery done, including having two ribs removed, was first reported in a magazine called PARIS MATCH in 1988. Although Cher sued the magazine over the allegations, these allegations were just what those who never cared for Cher were just dying to hear. The frustration of people who were upset over Cher's youthful appearance and ability to stay thin as she grew older was now happily alleviated by the "knowledge" that Cher must have used artificial means to keep her shape and beauty.

Cher would try at various times to prove the rumors false, even going so far as to hire a physician in 1990 to examine her and report to the public about the work done on her body (he found only that which she had always said had been done). None of it has stopped the rumors from continuing, and, unfortunately, they will probably remain in circulation for decades to come.

The legend that Cher had ribs removed has been a rumor that others have had to face in recent years, in particular Marilyn Manson (although for reasons other than wanting to look thin – see the entry for Marilyn Manson for more details). This kind of surgery has never been performed for cosmetic reasons (if performed at all) because of its risky nature – and surely the amount of scar tissue that would occur from such a surgery would make the whole thing pointless anyhow. With Cher in 1988 wearing outfits that readily showed off her midriff, it is publicly clear that no such surgery was ever done.

Source: Mikkelson, Barbara and David P. "Getting Waisted," Urban Legends Reference Pages. June 22, 2000.
http://www.snopes.com/horrors/vanities/ribs.htm

Chicago

> *Lead guitarist Terry Kath committed suicide by playing Russian Roulette.*

Fans of this popular rock band that mixed guitars, keyboards and brass instruments into a successful number of hit singles were shocked when the news came over the radio on

January 24, 1978. The story told at the time was that Kath had accidentally shot himself in the head while playing with a gun at a party the night before.

As it stood, the news carried that day in the newspapers and on the radio was pretty much the entire story. The strange part is how this story has gathered bits of urban legend to it over the years, even though the truth of the incident has always been available and never covered up in any way. There is the assumption that, because he died at his own hands, Kath was suicidal.

Many would contest that assumption. Although Kath found himself drifting a bit from the band as their style was shifting away from his own, there was no way to deny that Chicago was a major success and still growing. Kath also had a family he deeply loved to care for. In essence, there was fame, fortune, and love in his life. Nor have family or friends over the years suggested that he was despondent in any way.

What can be seen, however, is that Kath liked to party and had partied too much on the night of the shooting. He was also an avid gun-enthusiast, who usually carried a pistol. This unfortunate combination led to his death. After a party at the home of a road crew member by the name of Don Johnson, Kath began playing with the pistol he had, making Johnson nervous in the process. When Johnson asked him to put the gun away, Kath assured him it was not loaded. To prove his point, Kath put the gun to his head and pulled the trigger. He died instantly.

The suicide rumor started when it became clear that he had put the gun to his head and pulled the trigger. Once the words "Russian Roulette" started being used (because his actions were similar to those who would play such an insane, death-defying game), the rumor continued to grow. By doing so, the tragic nature of his death became even more tragic as some fans gained an image of Kath that from all reports is not even remotely true.

Eric Clapton

> *1. While being interviewed on the Tonight Show back in 1969, Eric Clapton stated that Phil Keaggy was the best guitarist he had ever heard.*
> *2. A man heckling the lead guitarist of Grand Funk Railroad and challenged to come on stage and do a better job of playing guitar. The heckler? Eric Clapton, who proceeds to blow the entire, embarrassed band off the stage.*

1: See the entry for Keaggy under Jimi Hendrix for more details.

2: The story of Eric Clapton heckling a band from the audience has been told many times in different ways – sometimes with an unknown band being up on stage instead of Grand Funk Railroad; sometimes with the band being the Guess Who – nearly always with Clapton as the heckler, however.

The usual version of the story goes like this: Grand Funk Railroad is playing a concert to an enthusiastic crowd in a hall. Everyone is really into the show with the exception

of one man in the crowd who keeps heckling the band (typically the lead guitarist). After the heckling continues for some time, someone in the band tells the heckler to come on stage and play "if you think you're so much better." At that point, the heckler bounces on stage and is revealed to be Eric Clapton. Clapton proceeds to outplay the band to the wild applause of the audience. The band slowly moves off stage, dejected and embarrassed while Clapton finishes the show.

Now the problems with the story:

In some versions of the story, Clapton is still an unknown guitarist at the time. This of course would be impossible if the story is being told about Grand Funk Railroad at their peak (and the story is often told as being a band that is playing a large, sold-out show). Grand Funk Railroad was in the early 1970s, long after Clapton had made a name for himself as one of the "Guitar Gods" of the 1960s. In other versions of the story, everyone is enjoying the concert with the exception of one lone heckler. This also seems impossible at a show in even a large theater unless the heckler was sitting in the first or second row. If so, there would be a good chance that the band would have deduced who was sitting there (as well as most of the audience if Clapton had come in before the performance) and avoiding looking foolish by demanding that the heckler come on stage and play "if he's so great." Sometimes this problem is solved by saying that the band is playing a small dive. This neglects the fact that the band performing is supposed to be a major successful band, such as Grand Funk Railroad was at the time in the early 1970s. If it were a successful band, why would they be playing a "small dive?" Also, why would Clapton be going to a "small dive" to see the band?

Of course, that leads to one of the most common questions about this story: why would Clapton even be at such a concert? Moreso, if he truly hated the band playing so much, why would he bother with staying around long enough to heckle them to the point where action is taken? It also seems highly unlikely that an audience or the management of the hall, dive, etc. would allow a heckler to continue abusing the band that the audience are "enthusiastically enjoying."

As to the ending of the story, the purpose is to show the band leaving the stage in embarrassment when they are taken to task by a superior musician. As pointed out by Barbara and David P. Mikkelson on the Snopes.com Urban Legend web site, this is the reason Grand Funk Railroad is usually named as the band Clapton destroys on stage and is perfectly logical from the standpoint of popular opinion at the time. Many critics and the more stuffy rock fans viewed Grand Funk Railroad as a terrible band that succeeded for no reasons that could be clearly comprehended. Clapton, on the other hand, was considered a "god" amongst rock musicians and would be a good first choice for the role of the heckler in the story. The problem is, why would the band suddenly be embarrassed to be playing with Clapton on stage? Even if the guitarist left in anger, would the drummer leave when he had a clear chance to play with a "god" of rock musicians? Would anyone else leave? Hard to fathom that occurring. On the flip side, if the band was really that angry about the heckler, would it matter who jumped up on stage? A heckler is a heckler, and most performers have a very little tolerance for such people, no matter who they are.

A final dagger to the heart of this story is the publicity surrounding this event – there isn't any! As common with many Urban Legends of this sort, a "collective amnesia" must have occurred to the band, Clapton, and the audience, because no one has ever stated that they saw this event occur, nor is there documented proof that it ever occurred.

What this story does recall is a similar story often told about Keith Moon and his tryout for the Who back in the early 1960s. The story goes that the band was in desperate need of a drummer, with their original drummer quitting and his replacement being a high-priced temporary. After hearing the Who play part of a set, Moon challenges them to let him play a few songs, since he was bound to be better than who they had on stage with them. Taking him at his word, the other members of the Who allow him to play during the next set and he blows everyone away with his ability behind the drums. This story demonstrates a clear similarity to the heckler story told about Clapton and may even been the basis of where the story came from.

As for the Keith Moon story . . . well, perhaps that one needs a closer look as well (see the entry for The Who for more details).

Sources: Mikkelson, Barbara and David P. "Slow Band," Urban Legends Reference
        Pages. January 20, 2000.
        http://www.snopes.com/music/artists/clapton2.htm
        Roeper, Richard. URBAN LEGENDS. New Pages, New Jersey. 2001. Pages
        165-167.

Joe Cocker

Jarvis Cocker of the band Pulp is Joe Cocker's son or nephew.

Not true. See the entry for Pulp for more details.

Phil Collins

> *The popular song* In the Air Tonight *was written by Phil Collins about a murder he witnessed that he was unable to stop in time.*

One of the more popular urban legends in Rock and Roll, is the one surrounding the popular Phil Collins song *In the Air Tonight*. Collins, the drummer of the band Genesis, had a hit on his hands with the song, but he also had created a monster of an urban legend when fans started trying to figure out exactly what the song meant. The legend even became a part of someone else's song when Eminem referred to it in his song, *Stan*. Typically, the urban legend goes like this:

Collins, on vacation at an ocean resort, is standing on shore when he spots a man drowning far off in the distance. Unable to get to the man, Collins notices that there is another man in a boat, close enough to save the drowning man. His relief soon turns to shock as he sees the man in the boat glide on past the drowning victim without a glance, allowing the first man to drown before any other help is possible.

Feeling bitter about the experience, Collins writes a song about it called *In the Air Tonight*, while simultaneously tracking down the man in the boat. Once the man is found, Collins sends the man two front row tickets to one of his concerts. The man arrives and is enjoying the show as Collins introduces his new song and begins performing it. As the song starts, a spotlight is directed at the man in the audience, who begins to become uncomfortable with the attention. Collins then jumps off the stage and confronts the man in song. The man, realizing that he had been found out, flees in terror and commits suicide in the lobby of the hall as Collins and the audience cheers his death and rock the night away.

Well, that's at least one variation of the urban legend. There are other versions, but many of the elements are the same:

Collins witnesses a drowning (of a stranger, of his wife, or that he himself is drowning) and is unable to help.
Someone passes by the drowning victim and refuses to help.
Collins writes the song (sometimes immediately, sometimes years later).
Collins sings the song as a confrontation with the guilty party (sometimes with the man at the concert; sometimes in "spirit").
The man (if he is at the concert), realizes the song is about him and either confesses, leaves, or commits suicide (and in some versions, does so right on the spot, in front of the audience).

There is also a variation of the urban legend that claims Collins wrote the song after his wife was raped and Collins tracked down the rapist. All the other elements of the story remain the same, however.

The problem with the story is that it is so obviously staged. A song no one has heard before is instantly recognized not only by the man, but by the audience as well, as being a song directed at the man for ignoring a drowning victim. How that would be possible is anyone's guess, but the story assumes that the listener knows the song so well that he will skip over this obvious error. It is also odd that the audience would cheer the suicide of an audience member, especially when there is no way the audience would know why the man did such a thing and why – according to this version of the legend – Collins would be cheering the man's death.

Also, most versions of the legend make it out to be that Collins spots the man in the audience at one of his concerts. The coincidental element that Collins would write a song about a man who just happens to appear at one of his concerts the night he decides to debut the song, on top of the fact that it would be virtually impossible for Collins to have spotted the man in the crowd and for Collins to jump into said crowd and have a spotlight on the man and confront him face-to-face is a bit too astonishing to be believed. One would also think such an incident would have been reported in the papers and be featured as part of Collins' biography. Of course, it isn't because it never happened.

In truth, Collins had written the song at the time of his divorce from his first wife, with the lyrics being his angry feelings directed at his soon-to-be ex-wife. It had nothing to do with witnessing a drowning or a rape; nor did he ever confront someone about such an incident, and certainly not in front of a concert audience. Collins himself finally made mention to this urban legend in his appearance on the VH1 television concert series, VH1 Storytellers, on April 14, 1997:

> "The way I write lyrics is: I open my mouth and I see what comes out. And I was going through an unpleasant divorce. And I guess I was very angry, I was very bitter, I was very upset. And I think you can probably tell that from the song. But all these stories . . . it's like Chinese whispers. Whenever I come to America, then I hear a new bit. There's this person, who reckons that I saw someone drowning and I witnessed the thing, and then I invited the guy to come to the concert and sat him down at the front row and sang the song. All I did was write the song, really. But anything you hear – let it be said, right here, right now – anything you hear about this song is not true."

Even so, the legend lives on.

Sources: Mikkelson, Barbara and David P. "In the Air Tonight," Urban Legends Reference Pages. http://www.snopes.com/music/songs/someair.htm September 12, 2000.
VH-1 Storytellers. April 14, 1997.
Zimmerman, Eric. Phil Collins World. http://www.PhilCollinsWorld.de. March 10, 2002.

Alice Cooper

1. Alice took part in a "gross-out" contest with Frank Zappa back in the early 1970s.

> 2. *Alice stomped on baby chicks with his platform shoes, killed puppy dogs, and beheaded real babies during his concerts.*
> 3. *Alice Cooper got his name when the name appeared to Alice and the other band members while playing with an Ouija board. Alice later found out that the name belong to a witch who was burned at the stake in the 17th Century.*
> 4. *Alice played Eddie Haskell on LEAVE IT TO BEAVER.*
> 5. *The large balloons thrown out into the audience at this end of his shows were full of maggots. When the balloons popped, the audience was covered in maggots.*
> 6. *Alice Cooper was the son of a Mormon Bishop, who quit the church when he was on a mission in England.*
> 7. *An old woman died while sitting next to Alice Cooper on a plane.*

1: The Gross-out Contest is one of the more sickening urban legends dealing with rock music. It also happens to be one of the more endearing and recurring ones from the years as well. Not only has this story been told about Cooper, Zappa and other artists like Captain Beefheart repeatedly, but also variations have been told about such other "crazed" artists as Ozzy Osbourne, Marilyn Manson, Faith No More, and many others. No doubt, it will continue for years to come, with new artists to replace the old standbys.

The story? The story about Alice and Frank goes something like this: Alice and Frank are touring together in the early 1970s. Both are known for being eccentric rock performers that do outlandish things on-stage, and the topic came up before a concert. Of course, the rumor was as well, that both would do disgusting things during a concert and were not just simply "eccentric." As the story goes, the two were discussing their status as being "gross-out kings," when one challenged the other to a contest. The objective was to keep committing sickening acts until one of them could not go any further.

Some variations of this story put this "gross-out" contest as happening backstage, while others have it occurring in front of the audience. Either way, the contest began with some type of disturbing act – typically Zappa and/or Alice taking a puppy and stomping it to death (sometimes it is a baby chick or kitten that is killed). All the variations of the story then continue with increasingly grotesque acts until finally one of them (usually Alice) pulls down his pants and defecates in front of the people watching. In retaliation, the other (typically Zappa) pulls out a fork, digs into the stool, and begins eating it, thereby becoming the winner of the contest.

This kind of story was typical for a couple of artists who were considered crazy and perhaps even dangerous to Middle America. Parents were warned to keep their kids away from their shows, and the kids noticed it, and turned it into their own "cool" story in a typical juvenile fashion. The whole story just reeks (no pun intended) of kids trying to come up with the worst possible thing they could think of for someone to do in such a contest. It is also built upon the assumption that Alice and Frank toured together, and while Alice was on Zappa's Bizarre label for a brief time at the start of his career, they rarely performed at the same show early on, and certainly never toured together as the story would suggest. To deal with this factor, later variations of the story have it that one was visiting backstage instead of actually on tour with the other artist.

We must point out that there have been known cases of artists trying variations of this story in concert, but typically these artists have been known more as cult-status performers rather than popular musicians (Jayne County eating dog food from a toilet bowl on stage is one example of a restaging of the story.) Of course, the idea that such a thing would happen in front of a paying audience in a mainstream concert hall yet not to be reported in many sources seems highly unlikely. Both Alice and Zappa also found the story too incredible to believe. Zappa discussed the legend in a Playboy interview:

> "There never was a gross-out contest. That was a rumor. Somebody's imagination ran wild. Chemically-bonded imagination. The rumor was that I went so far as to eat shit on stage. There were people who were terribly disappointed that I never ate shit on stage. But no, there never was anything resembling a gross-out contest."

Sources: Zappa, Frank. THE REAL FRANK ZAPPA BOOK. Poseidon Press, New
York. 1989.
Sheff, David. "Frank Zappa," Playboy. April 1993.

2: Marilyn Manson today has many stories told about him killing animals on stage, but all of these stories go back to the days of the early 1970s when Alice Cooper was paraded around as the mass-murderer of small, defenseless animals. Sometimes the story would be that Alice would let loose a small group of baby chicks on stage and then stomped them to death with his high-heel platform shoes (probably one of the more common stories revised for other artists over the years, including Manson). At times the story was puppies instead of baby chicks, and that Alice would either stomp on them or carve them up with a sword on stage and throw pieces out to audience members. Other times, like a similar story told of Ozzy Osbourne when he became a solo artist, the story went that Alice would throw an animal, typically a puppy, out to the audience, and refused to continue with the show until audience members had killed the puppy and thrown the carcass back on stage. Some people would even go so far as to suggest that Alice didn't even bother with animals but rather got hold of real human babies and carved them up on stage.

The baby rumor no doubt started when someone saw that Alice used to cut up a baby doll on stage (with a hatchet, a sword, or even just tearing it apart by hand). As to the animals, there is some history based around this rumor, all leading back to an event that did happen to Alice in 1969. It occurred in front of a movie camera filming the band's performance at the 1969 Toronto Rock 'N' Roll Revival.

Alice Cooper, which at the time was the name of the entire band as well as the lead singer, was a relatively unknown band on Frank Zappa's Bizarre record label. The band had been doing some extensive touring and had developed a very visual act that involved everything including the kitchen sink being thrown around on stage. Anything to grab the audience's attention – fire extinguishers being set off; feather pillows being torn apart and feathers flying out into the crowd; food sometimes being thrown out into (and come hurtling from) the audience, etc.

At the Toronto show, the band was doing exactly this during their performance as the cameras were rolling. Then, for some reason that no one is quite sure of anymore, a live chicken ended up on stage. Some, especially Alice in interviews, suggested that the chicken was thrown on stage from the audience. Others have suggested that the chicken had been found backstage and was determined to be a prop in the show. Either way, when the chicken appeared on stage, Alice threw it out into the audience. As Alice would later relate in his autobiography, ME, ALICE:

> "At [the] Toronto concert somebody handed me a chicken from the audience. I thought chickens could fly. Really. It had wings, and birds fly. Now I ask you, how many chickens do you think I came across growing up in trailers in Detroit and Phoenix? The only chickens I ever saw were on a plate. So when this chicken was handed to me at the finale of the show, I held it tightly so it wouldn't fly away. The pillow was broken and feathers were already flying out over the audience. I held the chicken out to the audience and threw it up in the air, expecting it to soar off above the stadium and fly away like a dove. Instead it screamed and squawked and did a nose dive into the audience. Twenty or thirty hands went up to catch it. Some kid grabbed a wing and another person got a leg and suddenly the kids were pulling it apart, much to the bird's dismay. One wing ripped off and blood began to spray all over everyone, then another wing, and the head went sailing up in the air. A thousand flashbulbs went off in the audience."

At first, one would think such a story couldn't be true – that Alice, who has been known to color his stories up to make them sound more impressive, had made the whole thing up. The thing is, there is proof of the incident as filmed by famous filmmaker D.A. Pennebaker, who was there to film the festival much as he had earlier with Monterey Pop. The film clearly shows Alice throwing a live chicken into the audience, and portions of the film can be seen (along with commentary by Alice and others) in the Alice Cooper documentary, PRIME CUTS.

It is from this story that all of the others have sprung – the concept of Alice throwing an animal out to the audience, waiting for them to kill it before proceeding with the show; the killing of baby chicks on stage; and just the general manhandling of animals and babies on stage. Because of the true story, the idea of other animal killings during shows has become a normal urban legend for many artists in rock music over the years, and we have Alice to thank for that.

Source: Cooper, Alice and Gaines, Stephen. ME, ALICE. G. P. Putnam's Sons, New York. 1976.

3:   Vincent Damon Furnier was born on February 4, 1948 and grew up mainly in Detroit, Michigan and Phoenix, Arizona (moving to Los Angeles in between and finally staying in Phoenix when he was 13). While in Phoenix, Vincent got together with a few friends and started a band that would eventually become Alice Cooper. By 1968, the band had relocated to Los Angeles and was performing as The Nazz, but became aware that a band already existed called The Nazz and this other band had a record coming out from a major record label. To avoid any confusion, Vincent's band needed a new name.

The band had started going in for a look that was outrageous for the time, even in the hippie culture that populated the places they were was playing in the late 1960s. Vincent himself had taken to wearing a women's mini-skirt outfit as a shirt for the shock value, while the other members were experimenting with their look as well, often going for bizarre costumes and makeup. In keeping with the look and with their shock-value appeal, the band decided to call themselves Alice Cooper. The name change was mainly a gag – the name sounded so normal and sweet that the band anticipated people to come to the show expecting to see a lovely young female folk singer, and instead would get five grungy looking guys playing hard rock music. At first, some of the other guys in the band were not exactly happy with the name, but when nothing else sounded even as good as "Alice Cooper" to the others it was decided to go with the name (as Cooper himself confessed to Headley Glitter in the book ROCK 'N' ROLL ASYLUM). The name stuck and they remained Alice Cooper when they signed up with Frank Zappa's experimental label, Bizarre in 1968 (although there were stories that Zappa wanted to change the name of the band to Alice Cookies as a further joke on the name).

To make the name sound spookier and more odd, the band – in particular Alice himself – passed around a story that the band had once tried to contact a spirit on an Ouija board and the name that was spelled out was Alice Cooper. Vincent decided to research the name a bit more and found that it supposedly belonged to a girl born on the February 4 (Vincent's birthday), 1623. The girl would learn witchcraft from her older sister, and after her sister was burned at the stake, would die at her own hands when she was 13 years old.

It was a completely bogus story. There was no girl named Alice Cooper and some have even denied that they ever were around an Ouija board, much less that they spelled out Alice Cooper on it. Still, it sounded like a great story to Vincent at the time and the band stuck with it in order to give themselves some background.

One problem that was set in place with the name change was that people assumed (much like the problem Pink Floyd ran into) that the name meant someone in the band, not the band itself. Because Vincent was the lead singer of the group, he was in the spotlight and thus it was assumed that he was Alice Cooper.

For Vincent, this was exactly what he wanted. He had growing concerns that if he did become famous in such a crazed, rock and roll band, that it might hurt his family's reputation back home in Phoenix – particularly that of his father who had become a minister in the Church of Jesus Christ, a church not commonly thought of as liberal in their understanding towards rock music, particularly at that time. So, if people assumed that he was Alice Cooper that was fine by him. He told the rest of the band his decision and they were fine with the idea as well, so from that point forward, Vincent Furnier became Alice Cooper. Vincent would begin to use the name in interviews and stuck with it long after its original usage as the band's name had been forgotten.

Source: Sherman, Dale. THE ILLUSTRATED COLLECTOR'S GUIDE TO ALICE COOPER. Collector's Guide Publishing, Toronto. 1999.

4: The rumor that Alice Cooper had played Eddie Haskell on the old situation-comedy LEAVE IT TO BEAVER was started by Alice himself back in the early 1970s. As mentioned in the previous entry, Alice had shied away giving people information pertaining to his past, in consideration for his family. Because of this, when people asked where he came from or what he had done before being in the band, Alice would typically make up something in order to confuse the press and the public about his past. The Eddie Haskell rumor was probably the best known of the various stories Alice has told about his past, which also included saying he was the illegitimate son of baseball player Jimmy Piersall and that he was actually Liza Minnelli.

The Haskell rumor probably stuck to Alice (and vice-versa) the strongest because it seemed to click so well in people's minds. The nasty, smarmy kid on LEAVE IT TO BEAVER turning out to have grown up to become the nasty, horrifying rock and roller Alice Cooper – how could you make the story any better?

Eddie Haskell was actually played by Ken Osmond, who was born five years before Alice in 1943. Osmond was out of the public eye after the 1960s when he joined the Los Angeles Police Department, but would return to acting in the many LEAVE IT TO BEAVER sequels that occurred in the 1980s and 1990s.

If it is of any help to those disappointed to find out that a kid from LEAVE IT TO BEAVER was never in a hard rock band, there was one fleeting child actor in the series who did end up in rock music, albeit in a parody form. Harry Shearer, who went on to play Derek Small in the heavy metal parody group Spinal Tap, was a child actor and played "Frankie" in an episode of the series from 1957.

Source: Morgan, Hal and Tucker, Kerry. RUMOR!. Penguin Books, New York. 1987. Page 75.

5: One consistent element in Alice's concerts has been the use of large balloons during the encore. These balloons are four to five feet in diameter and are pushed out into the audience one by one as the band performs the encore. Usually four or five of these balloons make it out into the crowd, sometimes reaching all the way to the back of the arena or hall before breaking.

The balloons, once broken, usually dispense some type of confetti on to the people below them. There have been occasions where stage-blood (a concoction used as a special effect to make it appear that someone is bleeding) has been put into the balloons and, once popped, covered the audience members pretty thoroughly – a situation that sometimes made having a front row seat at an Alice show not such a good thing unless you had a change of clothes with you.

Typically it was confetti, and because the spotlights would catch the light colored confetti falling on the crowd, some audience members from a distance would have no idea what exactly was being dropped from the burst balloons and came to their own conclusions. Never have the balloons held maggots and with the exception of the stage-blood, never have the balloons held anything other than confetti.

6: Because Alice has been selective over the years in discussing his personal and family life, fans have wondered about his background. As discussed previously, some of this had to do with Alice wishing to distance his performing career – where he played this demented character named Alice Cooper – from his family life, which was quite different.

As the 1970s wore on and Alice began to demonstrate that the character on stage was not at all like he was in reality, he eventually began to open up a bit about his parents. He even had his father, Ether Moroni Furnier, write the introduction to his autobiography, ME, ALICE, in 1976. From all of this information, it became clear that Alice's father was a minister; and with Alice stating in his autobiography, "we studied the Bible and the Book of Mormon backward and forward," it was clear that the family had some type of Mormon background.

Alice's father actually was a minister in the Church of Jesus Christ, a denomination of the Church of Latter Day Saints, and therefore the standard scripture of the church would be the Bible and the Book of Mormon. Alice's grandfather, Thurmond Furnier, was a minister and president of the Church of Jesus Christ in Allentown, Pennsylvania, very close to the world headquarters of the church in Monongahela, Pennsylvania. Alice's father had left the church when he was a teenager, but eventually found his way back years later, rejoining the Church of Jesus Christ when Alice was nine years old. A few years later, Ether Moroni Furnier would become a minister in the church.

This is where the urban legend comes into play. Because of the patchwork deduction needed to learn more about Alice's family, some people latched on to the fact that Alice's grandfather was a president of the church and that Alice's father had left the church when he was a teenager. Since many people assume all Mormons going on "missions" when they are teenagers, and that Alice's father left the church when he was a teenager, it was assumed that Alice's father left the church and was on his mission. From there the story grew to be that Alice's grandfather was not just a minister and president of the Church of Jesus Christ in Allentown, Pennsylvania, but that he was a Mormon Bishop – making him more important in the hierarchy of the religion. For someone now conceived as being so important, the son's mission had to be more important as well, so Alice's father was conceived to be on his mission in England when he dropped out. Over all, it is simply a case of trying to make the true history of Alice's father more flamboyant than it actually was.

This urban legend links itself to a common discussion among fans – that of Alice's religious belief today. Many have tried to downplay Alice's Christian beliefs, but as he grows older, Alice had made an increasingly public display of his beliefs in interviews and (some would say, at least) on his albums. He has even been directly involved with a Christian youth organization called the Solid Rock Foundation and engages in events in support of the organization on a regular basis in his hometown of Phoenix, Arizona.

For some people, such public display of his faith has been looked upon as detrimental to his history as the "evil" Alice Cooper of lore. Some have viewed it mockingly, as if to prove that Alice has become a "wimp" because of his beliefs and cannot be taken seriously anymore. Those who feel this way are missing a vital part of Alice's performance objective – to put on a show and have a good time presenting a theatrical "horror show" to a rock audience. The Alice Cooper on stage and on the albums was never more than a character that Alice played, not the person he was in real life.

Source: Cooper, Alice and Gaines, Stephen. ME, ALICE. G. P. Putnam's Sons, New
York. 1976.

7: Alice has repeatedly told a story over the years about an airplane trip that he took to England with his band in the early 1970s. As Alice tells the story, he was seated on the long trans-Atlantic flight next to an older woman. At one point during the flight, the woman decided to take a nap and asked Alice to tell the flight attendants not to worry about serving her food during the trip.

Alice agreed to this and the trip went well, ending with the plane landing in England. As the passengers rose from their seats to leave the plane, Alice noticed that the old woman had not stirred from her sleep. Trying to wake her, Alice discovered that she had died in her sleep during the flight.

After talking with authorities about the incident on the plane, Alice left as the old woman was being put into a waiting ambulance. The press had been notified and many were waiting as Alice left the plane, circling him after he descended the stairway. He told the story about the old woman dying in her sleep next to him on the flight, whereupon, as Alice told it, the press descended on the body, "looking for teeth marks on the neck."

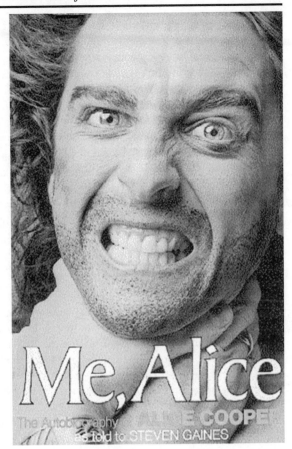

As stated, Alice has told this numerous times in interviews, in his autobiography and in the video documentary, PRIME CUTS. It was also referred to in Michael Bruce's autobiography, NO MORE MR. NICE GUY. It's a good story, but one that has some problems that fans have yet to remedy. First off, the date of the flight has never been established. Alice refers to it in his autobiography as occurring on a flight to England where the band ended up being banned by the government. However, while a suggestion was made later in the 1970s that the band be banned from performing, there was never any actual ban. A proposed Australian ban of Alice in 1975 did lead to him not touring that country (he would eventually tour in 1977), but there was never anything more than some discussion of a ban in England during the early 1970s. The Alice Cooper group performed in England in 1971 and 1972, with Alice facing a bit of an uproar in '72, so quite possibly it happened then, but still no firm date has ever been established in any of the interviews or books discussing the event. Considering the unusual nature of the story, it can safely be assumed that the story would have been covered in the newspapers and magazines at the time. Instead, the only reference that can be found has been in interviews. Perhaps some documentation of the event is out there, but if so, fans have had trouble locating it.

Source: Cooper, Alice and Gaines, Stephen. ME, ALICE. G. P. Putnam's Sons, New York. 1976.

Creedence Clearwater Revival

> *1. John Fogerty was so insistent on his vision of the music being done that he would rerecord all the other musicians' parts after they had left the studio.*
> *2. The song Fortunate Son is about David Eisenhower.*
> *3. The song Bad Moon Rising is about Richard Nixon or astrology.*

1:   This rumor evidently has derived from the position that John Fogerty WAS Creedence Clearwater Revival. When asked about this urban legend in ROLLING STONE (February 4, 1993 edition), Fogerty stated that "99% of the tracks we did as a quartet are played live with all four guys playing at the same time." As reported on Electric Bayou (http://www.cc.jyu.fi/~petkasi/ccr-jcf/trivia.htm), Stu Cook appeared on the Bayou Moon internet mailing list in 1996 to clear up the rumor as well. While Cook would surmise that Fogerty himself had made it sound as if rerecording the norm, Cook could tell readily from listening to the tracks that they were not rerecorded.

The major thrust of this legend really stems from Fogerty having gone on record several times in stating that he not only arranged the music in the studio, but also showed the other musicians how to play the parts. He would also work on the recordings after the band had finished the basic tracks – embellishing to make the material richer in tone. As time progressed, his influence in this area became greater; and once he had become a solo artist, it was evident how strongly his style had influenced the music of CCR. This does not detract from the fact that what was heard on the final product did represent the band recording as a whole. Nevertheless, such additional production work by Fogerty on the albums naturally led to such an urban legend being created.

2:   While the song is directed more at a group than a specific person, John Fogerty told Ben Fong-Torres of ROLLING STONE in 1969 that he came up with the song after seeing a newscast of David Eisenhower with Richard Nixon's daughter, Julie. It clicked in his head at that moment that some individuals were never going to have to worry about having to fight in the Vietnam War because of their family background. The song progressed from there.

3:   One of the most popular songs by the band was *Bad Moon Rising*. In addition, the song has had different interpretations, depending on the listener. Of course, taken literally, "Bad Moon Rising" would suggest some type of celestial warning. Because of this, it is no wonder that some people believe it to be a song dealing with astrology in some form, or even some type of horror film or science fiction movie reference. The song certainly was put to good use in this fashion during the ending credits of the movie, AMERICAN WEREWOLF IN LONDON. At the same time, because of the political atmosphere at the end of the 1960s, it is no wonder that some saw the song as a political statement about Nixon's presidency. As it turns out, the image of the song is definitely one of impeding danger, and with the ongoing Vietnam War at the time, it took little to take the song as a political message. John Fogerty, however, stated that the image of a "Bad Moon Rising" did not represent astrology (as he told Harold Steinblatt and Chris Gill in an interview with GUITAR WORLD magazine back in 1997), but rather an image from the 1941 movie THE DEVIL AND DANIEL WEBSTER. In the film a storm hits at night and destroys a neighbor's corn crop, but doesn't touch Webster's crop because it is protected by the Devil. Fogerty took the image of a "Bad Moon Rising" to mean the first signs of a horrible storm, much like a hurricane. This lead directly into the warning given in the song to "don't go out tonight; it's bound to take your life." Thus, the astrological interpretation of the song is not true. As to the Nixon rumor, *Fortunate Son* is a song more pointedly directed at Richard Nixon than is *Bad Moon Rising*.

Sources: Bordowitz, Hank. BAD MOON RISING. Schirmer Books. 1998, pages 59-
60, 69, 80.
Electric Bayou, http://www.cc.jyu.fi/~petkasi/ccr-jcf/trivia.htm
Fong-Torres, Ben. "Creedence Clearwater Revival at the Hop." Rolling
Stone. April 5, 1969.
Steinblatt, Harold, and Chris Gill. "New Moon Rising." Guitar World.
July 1997.

Dave Matthews Band

> As a boy, Dave Matthews appeared as Billy, the owner of two hunting dogs, in the motion picture WHERE THE RED FERN GROWS.

Matthews did appear in a movie called WHERE THE RED FERN GROWS, based on the popular children book of the same name, but it was not the 1974 version that most are familiar with. The role of Billy in the 1974 film was played by Stewart Petersen. Dave Matthews, born in 1967, would have been between 6 and 7 years old when the 1974 film was made, too young for such a role even if he had been a child actor.

Matthews would play the character Will Coleman in a remake of the film in 2000. The film was left uncompleted due to money problems and probably will never see the light of day (or the dark of the theater).

Death (and the Conspiracy of Life)

The story goes that Elvis didn't die while in the bathroom back in 1977. He faked his death, with the cooperation of the authorities, in order to have a normal life again. He even left behind clues so that his loyal fans would know that he was still somewhere out there instead of being long gone. He must have taken a cue from Morrison, knowing that Jim had faked his death as well and got clean away with it. For Morrison it was not only to have a normal life again, but also because he was hiding out from a government conspiracy that claimed the life of both Hendrix and Joplin. It was obvious that Joplin's death was done by "men in black" in order to control the voice of the hippie population, while Hendrix was left to drown in his own vomit because it looked more "natural" that way. As for Elvis, the faking of his death was purely personally motivated – at least some fans believed so. Others thought there was a more sinister edge to his hiding in plain sight, as if he needed to in order to avoid criminals that wanted him dead after his turning over state's evidence about drug deals. Of course, that just made his escape from one life to another even more daring and adventurous. More recently, Tupac Shakur is rumored to be alive and hiding out from the mob (or record producers, depending on the stories you hear), and just like Elvis, he's leaving clues around left and right to prove he's still out there somewhere.

If a rock star didn't somehow fake his death, then his death is usually attributed to some type of conspiracy. In a way perhaps, it is also fitting that the more controversial the person was in life, the more controversial their death becomes as the years go by. Take Brian Jones of the Rolling Stones for example: His drowning in that pool on the Winnie the Pooh estate has been restaged so many times in numerous books and articles over the years, and with so many players, that people remember him more for his death than his life. Rumors abounded for years that Mick Jagger and Keith Richards had drowned Brian Jones in his swimming pool because they did not like his "pretty boy" looks and ability to attract more women than they did. Meanwhile, others have suggested that it was another close associate of Jones, or even another case of a government conspiracy to eradicate the world of the "rock prophets" who preached "peace, love and understanding."

Government conspiracy theorists have for years suggested that a vast campaign by the CIA, FBI or even more sinister (and invisible) organizations has been wiping out musicians for reasons never quite refined between theorists. The biggest use of this type of theory deals with the accidental death of the "big three" (Morrison, Hendrix and Joplin) who were thought to be controlling the minds of the nation's youth. Of course, this is proposed by the same people who believe that the government was also involved in the assassination of John F. Kennedy and/or Martin Luther King, Jr. Even John Lennon's death at the hands of a deranged fan has led to theories about it all being a government conspiracy of some sort. Conspiracy theories have even given birth to books and movies about the subject (although usually so contrived that only the most desperate of conspiracy theorists would give them much serious thought).

At other times, a rock star's death is clouded with mystery – why did their death suddenly occur, or what were the reasons behind their sudden death. This certainly plays into the theories about Elvis being alive even though it was clear at the time of his death that he was not in good health. Nevertheless, people still believe that they see Elvis at the local convenience store, getting pop-tarts and drinking Pepsi; never mind that such continuing theories fly in the face of all the evidence. More recently, Kurt Cobain's suicide had been part of a conspiracy theory pointing the finger at his wife, Courtney Love, who supposedly wanted Cobain to die in order to protect her own career. Of course, this kind of thinking is just vicious rumor propagated by some fans in order to preserve a "victim's" persona for Cobain, while demonizing Love, but that doesn't stop the theorists from having a field day with it.

Even the most mundane of deaths have some story created around them in order to make the final acts of those stars spectacular or at least interesting in some way. One of the best known urban legends of rock music is that Mama Cass Elliott died not from a heart attack, but because she choked to death on a ham sandwich (and what better way to make her sound like a pig then making it a ham sandwich?). A gun found among the wreckage of Buddy Holly's plane gave root to stories, no matter that the plane crashed due to the weather. Even Sid Vicious' death and that of his girlfriend Nancy Spungen have been twisted into a story of conspiracy, with Vicious as the poor sap drawn into the middle of a drug deal gone sour.

Why do such legends about a person's death end up being remembered more than what they did in life? Would a person who wasn't already a fan be able to say anything more about Vicious, or Cobain, or Shakur, or even Elvis than how they died? Do most people born in the 1980s and thereafter know anything about Mama Cass beyond that "ham sandwich" story? Yet the stories remain and are repeatedly retold, over and over.

Why? Because they were our heroes and heroes are not supposed to just die a normal death. In fact, they're not supposed to die at all. That's the key to understanding why so many people live in hope that Elvis is out there somewhere, or that Tupac is still in hiding – either one ready to come back at a moment's notice in order to prove to the naysayers what the fans knew to be true all along. Elvis couldn't have died while sitting in the bathroom, drugs coursing through his veins like some type of common junkie; Jones was too good a swimmer to let any drug or drink cause him to drown that night in July 1969, it had to have been someone else; Hendrix would have survived if only the people trying to save his life were not incompetent; and onward and onward it goes. To believe that our heroes are mere flesh and blood is to believe that there is an end to their messages as well, that time is finite for everyone eventually, even for the gods. Those fans who admit to the death of their heroes still want to be comforted by the thought that their hero's death is at least of some significance, contains some meaning.

At least let them die in thunder, the fans say, if they have to die at all;. or at least with a wink to the crowd. Otherwise the story has no ending.

Thus the ending always must be larger than life; and in becoming so, the legends sometimes become larger than the lives of the performers themselves. Either way, the legends live on.

Chris DeBerge

> *In the music video for DeBerge's hit Don't Pay the Ferryman, former DOCTOR WHO, actor Tom Baker portrayed the Ferryman. You can tell by the grinning teeth and wide, staring eyes of the Ferryman at the end of the video.*

At the time of DeBerge's 1982 hit, Don't Pay the Ferryman, it was rumored that actor Tom Baker (probably best known for playing the fourth incarnation of the Doctor on the British science-fiction series DOCTOR WHO) played the Ferryman in the music video. The video shows a Ferryman frequently throughout the video, wearing a hooded cloak with his face hidden from view. At the end of the video, there is a brief shot of the Ferryman, with the hood blowing back to reveal a wild-eyed, grinning man.

While such a mistake is easy to make (the image is very quick in the video and Baker is known among his fans for his wide-eyed, grinning facial expression), but it is not Baker in the video. A fan asked Baker point blank about this particular rumor at a DOCTOR WHO convention and he seemed quite familiar with this particular urban legend. Baker stated that he could never understand the error on the part of viewers as it is "obviously" DeBerge as the Ferryman in the video and DeBerge is quite a bit shorter than he is.

Source: Video of Tom Baker's appearance at Chicago Doctor Who convention, 1985.

Def Leppard

> 1. *The opening words of Def Leppard's hit Rock of Ages is an incantation picked up from ancient times. Some say it is actually a message praising Satan.*
> 2. *At the end of the song Love Bites, you can hear someone saying "Jesus of Nazareth, go to Hell."*

1: The line heard at the beginning of Rock of Ages is commonly written as "Gunter Glieben Glauten Globen." While many want to chart it up as some type of incantation or perhaps even German, it is actually producer Mutt Lange counting off the song without having to say, "1, 2, 3, 4." In other words, what sounds like gibberish actually is gibberish.

2: This band seems to have a preoccupation with having gibberish misinterpreted in their songs, and mainly thanks to producer Mutt Lange. What is actually said at the end of the song is "Yes it does, it does . . . Bloody Hell." This is said by producer Mutt Lange using an electrical device called a vocoder, along with a fake accent.

John Denver

> *Sunshine On My Shoulders is John Denver's ode to his successful days as a sniper for the U.S. Army during the Vietnam War.*

Although every biography about John Denver (including his autobiography, TAKE ME HOME) clearly points out that Denver never served in the military, this legend continues to make the rounds even up to the present day. As pointed out by the writers at Snopes.com (the Urban Legends Reference Pages), such a legend persists because of the irony involved – Denver was perceived, and in reality was, a longtime environmentalist and peaceful person. To expose him as a sniper for the U.S. Army during a war that many considered to be wrong (especially in the 1970s when Denver's career was at its peak, and the public's perception of the Vietnam War was at an all-time low) fulfilled the goal of many people who did not like Denver.

This urban legend is typically told as a stand-alone sentence and nothing more. However, as time has passed, more and more has been added to the legend in order to make it sound epic in scope, especially as reviews of the Vietnam War and the soldiers involved become increasingly less hateful and more respective. The longer version of the story goes that Denver became an expert marksman and sniper, leading to him developing a technique called the "Denver Method" when out on patrol. The Denver Method involved hiding in a high position, like a tree or building, and waiting for the enemy to come into range. He would then attract their attention to his position by whistling. The enemy would look upward, only to be blinded by the sun; whereupon John would pick them off, one by one.

Returning home to the U.S. as a decorated war hero, Denver began to have second-doubts about his military past. Escaping into music, Denver brought forward a peace-loving side of his persona to the public, yet he was still haunted by his past. The hit ballad *Sunshine On My Shoulders* was actually an ode to his previous life as the happy sniper who waited for his enemies to be blinded by the sun.

Of course, the story is pure poppycock. A sniper would have no need to make his position known to the enemy, and would actively try to avoid giving away his position for as long as possible, as such advantage points were susceptible to return gunfire. Also, the shadow caused by the sun being behind Denver in such a position would either highlight him for return fire, or shadow him, thereby making him impossible to see anyway. There also is no Denver Method used in the U.S. armed forces.

Besides, the only direct military history in Denver's immediate family involved his father, Henry John Deutschendorf, who served in the U.S. Air Force, retiring as a lieutenant colonel. Denver did receive a draft notice in 1964 and would have been eligible to fight in the Vietnam War, but was classified 1-Y and never served due to having lost two toes in a lawnmower accident when he was younger.

Sources: Denver, John. TAKE ME HOME. Harmony Books, New York. 1994
"Denver Sniper," Urban Legend Reference Pages, http://www.snopes.com/music/artists/denver.htm, January 20, 2000.
Roeper, Richard. URBAN LEGENDS. Career Press, New Jersey. 2001, Page 266.

Thomas Dolby

> *Dolby, being a technical and musical genius, created a noise-reduction sound system called "Dolby Stereo" and made a mint off of the technology.*

Surprising how often this story goes around, considering that Thomas Dolby's name was involved in a prominently recognized lawsuit in the 1980s.

Dolby was born as Thomas Morgan Robertson in Cairo, Egypt on October 14, 1958. The "Dolby Stereo" system, which helped to reduce noise on audio, was created in the mid-1960s at Dolby Laboratories, Inc., meaning that Thomas Dolby would have been about seven- or eight-years-old at the time of its creation – clearly a sign of genius if this was true. Of course, it wasn't; the inventor was the founder of Dolby Laboratories, Inc., Ray Dolby.

While growing up, Thomas Robertson had taken an interest in electronics, while also studying the guitar and synthesizer. Because of his varied interest in the electronics side of music, friend had nicknamed him "Dolby" and the name stuck. By 1981 he had begun a successful career as a musician and then earned a greater level of success as a solo artist with the success of his single *She Blinded Me with Science*.

Dolby Laboratories, Inc. in 1981 demanded that Thomas Dolby stop using the name, but he continued and there were no further objections from Dolby Laboratories until 1985 when Thomas Dolby began contributing music to motion pictures. Because of his work on the flop movie HOWARD THE DUCK, Thomas Dolby's name appeared in close proximity to the Dolby Stereo trademark. This was enough to force Dolby Laboratories' hand and they sued Thomas Dolby in order to stop him from using the name due to what they deemed to be possible confusion on the part of the public between the musician and the company.

Thomas Dolby fought the case, fearing that a forced change in name would do harm to his career. The United States District Court for the Northern District of California decided that confusion was possible between the two, but felt there Dolby had used the name in good faith so far and could continue to do so as long as he did not partake of any thing that could be seen as detrimental to Dolby Laboratories, Inc. in the eye of the public. In other words, Thomas Dolby could not endorse an inferior sound-system that Dolby Laboratories felt was below their standards, or perform material that could be seen as hurting the company in some fashion.

Thus, the common urban legend about Thomas Dolby may have both helped and hurt his career overall.

Source: Litowitz, Robert D. and Traphagen, Mark. "The Song Remains the Same," Legal Assistants Division / State Bar of Texas. http://www.lad.org/TPJ/18/song_same.htm. 1999.

The Doors

> 1. During the March 1, 1969 concert at the Dinner Key Auditorium in Miami, Florida, Jim Morrison exposed himself to the audience.
> 2. Jim Morrison did not die on July 3, 1971 and there are plenty of clues around to prove that he faked his death and is living in seclusion somewhere, waiting for the right moment to come back.

1: By 1969, Jim Morrison was on his way to a meltdown in front of an audience that consisted of too many enemies just waiting for him to make a mistake. He had already been arrested twice before since becoming famous as the lead singer of the Doors, including an infamous on-stage arrest during a December 9, 1967 performance in New Haven, Connecticut. At the New Haven show in 1967, Morrison had a run-in with a police officer before the show and ended up being maced by the cop. Disgruntled by the incident, Morrison brought up the incident during the concert. His tirade eventually brought the police out on stage and he was arrested and charged with "breach of the peach" and resisting arrest.

Morrison's legend preceded him by this point in the band's career, so when the Doors were set to perform in Miami in 1969, the police were prepared to stop Morrison and/or the show if anything "lewd" or "dangerous" occurred. Morrison was also reaching a state with his alcoholism and drug-use where he was more than willing to do anything he wanted to on stage without fear of what repercussions may occur. Due to missing his flights for the trip out to Miami, Morrison spent most of his time in the airport lounges getting drunk, and arrived in Miami so intoxicated that he could barely stand on his feet.

Still, a show was a show and the band tried performing, although Morrison did little to help the other band members. Frequently stopping songs, shouting abuse at the audience, and finally taking his shirt off, Morrison then went into a long, unfocused monologue about giving the audience something they "wanted to see."

This is where the stories go in different directions, depending on who you talk to. For the police and the fans that want to believe, Morrison then unzipped his pants and pulled out his penis. From reports made by the band members and people working with the band at the time, Morrison did no such thing. It has also been questioned if Morrison really had asked the audience if they wanted to "see my cock?" as reported in many sources.

In drummer John Densmore's book, RIDERS ON THE STORM, he mentions that by the time Morrison was threatening to disrobe completely, Densmore was already leaving the stage (along with the rest of the band). Therefore, it would be hard for them to say that they saw everything that happened. However, Vince Treanor, a roadie for the band, stated in Densmore's book that he got behind Morrison and held on to Morrison's pants in such a way that he would not have able to unbuckle or unsnap them.

No matter, by that time, the auditorium was in complete chaos. The band was gone and Morrison eventually jumped into the crowd and lead people in a "snake dance" through the auditorium. The police were unhappy and the press-coverage made it appear that Morrison had stripped naked and run through the audience by the time they were done. On March 5 the police were in a bind – the press and public demanded satisfaction about the crazed rock star that was "exposing" himself to kids in the audience – and had little choice but to issue a warrant for Morrison's arrest. The charges were one felony count of lewd and lascivious behavior and three misdemeanor counts of indecent exposure, open profanity, and drunkenness.

Morrison and the band were in Jamaica at the time of the warrant. He finally returning to the U.S. on April 4, 1969 and turned himself in to the FBI in Los Angeles, California. The jury found him guilty of indecent exposure and profanity, both misdemeanor charges. Nevertheless, the judge in the case, Judge Murray Goodman, sentenced Morrison on October 30, 1970 to six months of hard labor and a $500 fine for public exposure. It was an extreme sentence for such a minor crime, which many protested had never even occurred. Morrison was appealing the case at the time of his death in July 1971.

Sources: Densmore, John. RIDERS ON THE STORM. Delacorte Press, New York. 1990.
Marsh, Dave and Bernard, James. THE NEW BOOK OF ROCK LISTS.
Fireside Books, New York. Pages 539-540.

2: Like him or hate him, it has to be admitted that Jim Morrison was one of the icons of
the late 1960s rock movement. He was controversial, over-the-top, inconsistent, and
had flashes of brilliance in both his public life and in his music with the Doors.
Therefore, when Morrison died, it was little wonder that there was some speculation
about his death – there likely would have been even if he had been hit by a car driven
by a little old woman while crossing the street. That he died under clouded
circumstances in a foreign country, with his burial somewhat odd as well, it's no wonder
that people created legends about what really happened to Morrison on July 3, 1971.

Morrison was living in Paris with his constant companion, Pamela Courson, in July
1971. Returning to their apartment after going to a movie, the couple went to bed,
but Morrison woke up later in the night complaining about chest pains. He went to
take a bath and was found dead there by Courson at around 5 AM on July 3. The
death certificate stated cause of death as being "heart failure," but no autopsy was
done to prove what might have caused such heart failure. This lead to speculation
that Morrison may have died from a blood clot thanks to a respiratory illness, or that
he may have died from a drug overdose. Many, including John Densmore in his 1990
book RIDERS ON THE STORM, lean towards the second theory, figuring Morrison to
have confused Courson's stash of heroin as cocaine and snorting enough to kill him.

Morrison's body was buried on July 8, 1971 in a closed coffin ceremony at Pere-
Lachaise cemetery in Paris, France. Some have stated since that they felt the coffin
was a bit small for Morrison's body, as well as his grave. This would lead to
speculations about Morrison's death, which will be discussed further on in this entry.

There are two main theories about Morrison's death and both really fall into a
conspiracy setting: One is that Morrison did not die from "heart failure," but rather
he was murdered. Leading on from this, the conspiracy theories lean towards
Morrison being murdered by the French authorities as part of an international multi-
governmental plot against the young rock stars of the day who were the "leaders" of
the 1960s hippie culture. Fans and conspiracy theorists concentrated mainly on the
belief that Morrison was not the type to overdose. They also wonder about the delay
in having the authorities brought in and the fact that no autopsy was done. Because
of these elements, it was felt that the authorities were hiding something from the
public. Compounded by the fact that the woman who found Morrison, Courson, died
two years later from an overdose herself, and the theorists were gleeful in being able
to put two and two together and come up with murder.

The problem with this theory is that it negates several facts about Morrison: first,
Morrison had increasingly shown signs of drug and alcohol dependency long before
his trip to Paris, reaching a point where it was greatly affecting his concert
performances, his public appearances, and his personal life. While some theorists have
stated that Morrison was shown to be in perfect health at the time of his death (thus
leading to wild speculation that he couldn't have died from an overdose), it was
obvious that his health was failing him. Maybe not to the point where he was

obviously going to die if he didn't try to clean himself up, but still noticeable. It was also known by some that Courson was using heroin, which many now believe that Morrison snorted while presuming that it was cocaine and died as a consequence of his error. Courson would later admit to writer Danny Sugerman, the co-author of the Morrison biography, NO ONE HERE GETS OUT ALIVE, that she felt responsible for Morrison's death because it was "her stash." Since Courson would be dead within two years from a heroin overdose herself, it is easy to see that her guilt led her to her own death.

The conspiracy theory that Morrison was killed also fails when the fallacy is proposed that the French government considered him some type of threat that had to be dealt with. The thing is, Morrison's star was on the decent by 1971, even though the Doors were still considered a popular group (and would even have posthumous hits sung by Morrison). Morrison's public display of general recklessness was starting to eat into his fan base, painting him more as an overweight, drunken clown by the end of his life. Indecent exposure and a couple of swear words were hardly the things that would upset the French government, and so the logic behind that theory really falls flat, no matter how romantic it may seem to the fans and conspiracy theorists.

Oddly, there has never been much momentum in the idea that Morrison was killed by others – say a drug dealer, or by Pamela herself. All conspiracies dealing with murder make it sound as if Morrison had been held down in the tub on July 3 and murder by government agents.

The other leading urban legend about Morrison is the one that seems to adhere to all of the great rock and roll legends who die suddenly and out of view of the public – faking his own death. The reasons why this theory has long been held by many fans is discussed in more detail earlier in the book (see the entry for Death [and the Conspiracy of Life] for more details), but the details behind the rumor are simple. Morrison, wishing to escape the image that the press and he himself had created over the years, decided the best way to do so was to fake his own death. Once this was accomplished, he would then be free to do as he wished without worrying about people scrutinizing everything he did. A variation of this reasoning also plays into the above conspiracy theory – that Morrison knew of the government attempts to kill him – just as they had Joplin, Hendrix and Jones before him – and wanted to vanish before he could be assassinated. This version of the legend was even given as the reason for Morrison faking his death in the fictionalized biographical film, BEYOND THE DOORS (a.k.a. DOWN ON US).

With Pamela helping, Morrison was able to obtain a fake death certificate. Since all that was seen by others was a closed casket with what was supposed to be Morrison's remains, Pamela Courson went through with the burial while Morrison hid out somewhere. Because some who witnessed the burial stated that Morrison's coffin and burial site were a bit small for the size of the man they knew, it has been speculated that this proved Morrison's body was not inside the coffin and that he was actually hiding out somewhere. With Pamela Courson's death a couple of years later, Morrison decided to stay hidden away and is still somewhere in Europe, living off of his royalties and living a simple life.

Such a theory may be a pleasant ending to the life of what is considered one of rock's early madmen. It also led to many years of jokes about Morrison still being around, much like those told at Elvis' expense, another rock icon who supposedly faked his own death. Nevertheless, all evidence points to Morrison dying in 1971, most probably from a drug overdose that stopped his heart.

As to rumors that Morrison was killed via "black magic" – if you wish to believe in such things, go for it.

Sources: Densmore, John. RIDERS ON THE STORM. Delacorte Press, New York. 1990. Pages 290-291.
Stallings, Penny. ROCK 'N' ROLL CONFIDENTIAL. Little, Brown and Company, Boston. 1984. Pages 198-199.

Bob Dylan

1. In 1969 Bob Dylan recorded an album with Mick Jagger and ¾ of the Beatles called THE MASKED MARAUDERS.
2. Blowin' in the Wind was actually written by a high school student and Dylan plagiarized the material.

1: THE MASKED MARAUDERS is a case where fiction became reality. More appropriately, where a joke no longer was a joke.

To find the underlying cause of the legend, we have to go back to 1969 when a new rock music (news print) magazine was being published called ROLLING STONE. It was also the year when bootleg albums first came into public awareness. Bootlegs, as many readers may know, are albums released from non-official sources and contain material not officially released. Usually this comes down to live concert recordings, but sometimes these albums contain studio tracks that were scrapped. In 1969, what is typically viewed as the first true bootleg album to spark the interest of the public had been released: GREAT WHITE WONDER, an album of unreleased Dylan material. ROLLING STONE featured an article about the bootleg album's sales. In response, writer Greil Marcus wrote a review, under the pseudonym of T. M. Christian for a fictitious album called THE MASKED MARAUDERS.

The review stated that the album was recorded by a "supergroup" of musicians. The term supergroup was a common name thrown around, referring to situations where popular musicians get together to either jam in concert or record together for an album. In this case, the supergroup was made up of what many at the time would have seen as the ultimate in supergroups – Mick Jagger of the Rolling Stones, Paul McCartney, George Harrison, and John Lennon of the Beatles, and, of course, Bob Dylan. The album was supposedly produced by renowned recording artist / producer Al Kooper, which would have seemed like a "cherry on top" of the production.

As the review stated, the album was recorded by the group, but released without the true musicians listed because they were contracted to other record labels at the time.

This explained why fans had not heard about the album until the review, as the whole production was done in secret. (A variation of this legend would actually work its way into the famous "Klaatu is the Beatles" legend. See the Klaatu entry for more details.)

Any delirious hopes that readers had upon reading the review should have been dashed as they got further into the review itself. It was obvious that the review was a joke, thanks to the parody nature of what the musicians were supposed to be doing on the album (for example, Dylan doing a Donovan song, *Season of the Witch* – which was a reversal of the common joke that Donovan was always trying to write like Dylan). Even so, that did not stop some fans from completely missing the point and trying to track down the album.

Marcus, seeing a good thing when it presented itself, got together with fellow writer Langdon Winner and a group of Berkley musicians to record an album that matched the review. This album eventually was released in November 1969 by Warner Brothers Music, under their Reprise label. To give a degree of authenticity to the album, it was actually released with the label being listed as "Deity," a name found only in the review. The album can still be found, but the legend pretty much died off soon after people had a chance to hear the album itself. It was then that fans knew they had been party to a joke taken to an ultimate level.

Incidentally, a Dylan site, http://www.searchingforagem.com, has a page dealing specifically with additional songs and albums that Dylan supposedly worked on that have turned out to be no more than just rumors.

Sources: Urban Legends Reference Pages: Music (Unmasked Marauders), http://www.snopes2.com/music/artists/masked.htm
Red Herrings, http://www.searchingforagem.com/RedHerrings.htm
Marcus, Greil (as T. M. Christian). "Masked Marauders," Rolling Stone. October 18, 1969

2: *Blowin' in the Wind* was a song that was first made famous by Peter, Paul and Mary back in 1963. It was also the song that not only was a cornerstone of the coming protest movement of the 1960s, but the song that would seal Dylan's place as a songwriter / performer. As most people (and certainly Dylan fans) know, Bob Dylan had written the song while performing in New York during the folk music phase of his career. What many people have forgotten now, however, was that for a time a persistent rumor followed Dylan and the song around. You see, the story went that Dylan did not write this important song of the 1960s, but rather had stolen it from a high school student who never received credit for his work.

How did such a story come about? It's a case of a kid's wish to create something important snowballing completely out of proportion until he could no longer control the actions of his statement.

The kid was Lorre Wyatt, a student going to Millburn High School in Millburn, New Jersey. In 1962, Wyatt's senior year in high school, he had a chance to audition for the school's singing group, the Millburnaires. A budding songwriter and guitarist, Wyatt was thrilled for the chance to try out and wanted to make good by showing off his collection of songs he had written. Wyatt also had another song running through his head – one that he had seen in a magazine called SING OUT! The song was *Blowin' in the Wind*, and – as was a common practice at the time for folk songs – the song appeared in print months before it turned up on a commercial release.

Wyatt was stunned by the lyrics and music to the song. So much so that when he finally had a chance to perform for the singing group, he decided that the song he had found in the magazine would get him over more than even his own song would. In a split-second decision, Wyatt performed *Blowin' in the Wind* for the group.

The students were stunned. Wyatt had known he had made an impression, and was happy with the results. Then the problems started. Everyone wanted to know if he had written it. Thinking the chances that a song he found in a magazine and never heard anywhere since would become popular, Wyatt thought he would be fine in claiming ownership to the song. That was not enough, however. The teacher and students were not only happy with Wyatt, they loved the song and ecstatically wanted to perform it at the Thanksgiving assembly for the school. Wyatt attempted to weasel out of the performance – first by saying that the song wasn't ready to be performed, then by demanding that if they did perform it, it would be just the one time and no mention be made as to who wrote it.

Wyatt believed that the whole thing would be over after the assembly. The only problem was that he was announced at the assembly as the writer of the song. After that, there was no turning back for Wyatt. When asked the following week why he didn't want to do the song anymore, he fibbed that he had sold the rights to the song for $1,000 and given the money to the charity organization, C.A.R.E. Even that was not enough for people to forget, and Wyatt would be reminded of the song in person and in print constantly thereafter.

Then the reality hit. In May 1963, Bob Dylan recorded the song as part of his album, THE FREEWHEELIN' BOB DYLAN. It was also recorded by the folk trio, Peter, Paul and Mary, and their version became a major hit in mid-1963. With the national attention, people in Millburn wanted to know what was up. Wyatt repeated the story of selling the rights to the song, but that didn't set well with some people. A conspiracy had to be the explanation for it, and those in the press that didn't care for Dylan found Wyatt's story an easy one to mistranslate into a case of thievery on the part of Dylan.

It is from here that the urban legend branches off in to variations. The easiest and most remembered version is that Wyatt sold the rights to the song; Dylan recorded it and then bought the rights so he could be credited as the songwriter instead of Wyatt. Wyatt had no choice in the matter and that was it. Other variations of the legend are far more sinister:

Dylan was visiting a sick Woody Guthrie at Greystone Hospital in New Jersey and overheard Wyatt singing the song to patients in a large room. Dylan then plagiarized the song and never paid Wyatt a cent for it.
Dylan recorded the song, then found that it was not copyrighted. So, he copyrighted the song in his own name; again never paying Wyatt a cent for his creation.
Wyatt wrote the lyrics as a poem in the Millburn high school yearbook and Dylan paid for or stole the poem for the song, never giving Wyatt any credit for his work.

Dylan wrote a song called *Blowin' in the Wind* which was terrible; he then heard Wyatt's song, knew it to be better, and copyrighted Wyatt's song as his song. Again, as the story goes, Wyatt never received a cent.

One thing that all of these variations have is an attempt to show Dylan as an untalented hack who did not write the song that some say changed the thinking of a generation. As the song gained national attention, the papers caught wind of Wyatt's story and used it as a way to expose Dylan as a charlatan. In November 1963, NEWSWEEK went so far as to print the rumor, and it was picked up nationally from there. Although by that time Wyatt denied any involvement with the song, it was too late.

In 1974, Wyatt wrote an article for NEW TIMES magazine where he explained how the whole thing got started. Nevertheless, the urban legend persists to this day.

Sources: "Blowin' in the Wind," Urban Legends Reference Pages.
http://www.snopes2.com/music/songs/blowin.htm. January 27, 2001.
"Did Bob Dylan Lift "Blowin' in the Wind" from a High School Yearbook?" The Straight Dope.
http://www.straightdope.com/mailbag/mblowin.html, April 23, 2001.
"I am My Words," Newsweek. November 4, 1963, pages 94-95.

Eagles

Hotel California, both the song and the album, are about Hell. There is even a Satanic message hidden backwards on the title song. Or maybe, Hotel California *is about drug addiction. Or, perhaps* Hotel California *is about a house of prostitution.*

Since all three urban legends deal with the same song, it is easily to cover them at the same time. The first legend goes like this: The album is a series of stories about people who are on their way to eternal damnation or are already in Hell for their sins. The title song deals with a man's journey from death into Hell where he realizes that he can "never leave." Even more sinister, this legend states, is that the photo in the gatefold cover shows a shadowy figure that is actually Satan.

For people who were wanting to find satanic elements in rock music anyway, this was a gold mine of opportunity, and additional elements of the legend were simply tacked on. The most common of these were:

The song and album are called *Hotel California* in reference to First Church of Satan leader (and all around spooky guy) Anton LaVey. After all, LaVey had been established in San Francisco and the band was from California, so there was bound to be a connection. It was also rumored that LaVey started his church on California Street – an obvious link to the song.

Lyrics such as "They just can't kill the beast," "This could be Heaven or this could be Hell," and "We haven't had that spirit here since 1969" are all supposed to be references to LaVey and the church (the "1969" line supposedly in reference to the year LaVey established his church).

The building seen on the cover is the LaVey's home in California.

LaVey can be seen on the back cover of the album.

There is a backmasked message on the title song during the lyrics, "This could be Heaven or this could be Hell." The message is supposedly this piece of bizarre gibberish, "Yes, Satan, he organized his own religion . . . it was delicious . . . he puts it in a vat and fixes it for his son and gives it away."

It had also been suggested that the song is not about Satan or LaVey at all, but rather about drug addiction. The urban legend told is that the song tells the story of a man going to a rehabilitation center, a.k.a. the Hotel California, in order to get over his cocaine or heroin habit. As part of this legend, the building seen on the cover of the album is actually a mental institution in Santa Barbara. The main variation of this story is that it tells about a man becoming addicted to heroin or cocaine.

This could certainly be seen in the lyrics: "How they dance in the courtyard . . . some dance to remember, some dance to forget," was rumored to mean a group of addicts using drugs to achieve the happiness of a forgotten memory or forget a tragedy that they cannot get out of their heads. "They stab it with their steely knives, but they just can't kill the beast" – a line used above to suggest Satanism, was viewed here to mean that the drugs were no longer able to help the addicts; in other words, that the addiction had gotten the better of them. Of course, the final line, "You can check out anytime you like, but you can never leave," suggested to some that even if one left the Hotel California, their addiction would never be completely over.

Seeing the song as being about addiction certainly seems logical in relation to some of the other tracks on the album. Although one of the band's biggest successes, it is one depressing group of popular songs. *Life in the Fast Lane* is about love and addiction and most probably the one that ties in with the best with this version of the urban legend; meanwhile, such tracks as *New Kid in Town*, *The Last Resort*, *Victim of Love*, and *Wasted Time* all deal with love gone wrong. Oddly enough, people are correct in thinking that the song does deal with some type of addiction, but it is not necessarily about drugs, but also dealing with the need for love and "love gone wrong."

As stated in Marc Eliot's book, TO THE LIMIT – THE UNTOLD STORY OF THE EAGLES, Don Henley wrote the lyrics to the song (with Glenn Frey, while Don Felder wrote the music) as a statement about looking for the perfect woman. In using a composite of women in his own life as references for the song, Henley was referring frequently to Loree Rodkin, a woman who he had a long-standing relationship and rather nasty break-up with before the album was recorded. Henley even is quoted in the book as stating that the lyrics, "Her mind is Tiffany twisted, she got the Mercedes bends; she got a lot of pretty pretty boys that she calls friends . . ." as being specifically about Rodkin, and – obviously – not in a nice way.

Meanwhile, Frey had gone on record to say that the song dealt specifically with the cocaine-driven world they were living in at the time.

Yet, could the song be about a house of ill-repute? Going back to such lines as "mirrors on the ceiling" and "they stab it with their steely knives" would suggest some type of sexual innuendo. While this could be suggested in a few lines, it does not seem to match up other images from the song, as mentioned above.

With this, the song all falls into place. The song is not about drug addiction, Satanism, or strictly about sex. Instead, it is rather a mixture of what was happening with the band members at the time of the song's writing – the rock star party scene out in Los Angeles and falling in and out of love with a woman. More importantly, how there is always the wish to return to simpler times in the relationship, or to even go back to a point before it began. Still, the ending is always the same – "check out anytime you like, but you can never leave" such yearnings behind.

Thus, the song still has a very dramatic element that has to be read into the lyrics, just not one that suggest a vision of hell in either drug or religion-assisted ways.

As for the building seen on the cover of the album, it is not a hotel in Todos Santos, Mexico as had been rumored for a number of years (there are similarities in the structure of the building). Instead, as pointed out by the cover's photographer, David Alexander, in an interview with the BBC in February 2001, it is actually the Beverly Hills Hotel in Los Angeles.

Sources: BBC. "'Hotel California' for Sale." BBC News.
http://news.bbc.co.uk/hi/english/entertainment/newsid_1180000/
1180206.stm. February 20, 2001.
Eliot, Marc. TO THE LIMIT – THE UNTOLD STORY OF THE EAGLES. Little,
Brown & Company, NY. 1998, pages 125, 149-151.
Godwin, Jeff. THE DEVIL'S DISCIPLES. Chick Publications, Chino, CA.
1985, pages 152-153.
Peters, Dan and Steve. WHY KNOCK ROCK? Bethany House
Publishers, Minneapolis, MN. 1984, page 172.

Mama Cass Elliott

1. Mama Cass Elliott choked to death on a ham sandwich.
2. The "ham sandwich" story was just a cover-up for the real reason of Elliott's death – a heroin overdose.

1: One of the most famous urban legends of rock and roll, this has been around so long that some people today know the legend who have never heard any of the songs Elliott made famous as a solo artist or as a part of the 1960s folk-rock band, The Mamas and the Papas. The story even made an appearance in the first AUSTIN POWERS movie, and has been the punch line to numerous bad-taste jokes over the years.

Elliott, a rather large woman who had an extraordinary singing voice, died of a heart attack brought about most probably from obesity. The rumor of her dying due to asphyxiation caused by choking on a sandwich does relate to something reported in both the NEW YORK TIMES and ROLLING STONE magazine soon after her death, however, which stated that her physician reported such a finding. However, this turned out to be incorrect.

There was also a very short-lived rumor that Cass Elliott was pregnant at the time of her death, with John Lennon being the expectant father. This rumor never caught on quite the way the "ham sandwich" story did though.

Source: Morgan, Hal and Tucker, Kerry. RUMOR!. Penguin Books, New York. 1984. Pages 80-81.

2: In 1981, former member of the Mamas and the Papas, John Phillips, was involved in a trail for his life. He was facing a possible prison term on the charge of "conspiracy to distribute narcotics." When discussing his problems with drugs over the years, Phillips invited reporters to examine everyone's life around him. This included a statement by Phillips that Cass Elliott had not died of a heart attack several years before, but rather from a heroin overdose.

Not only does the coroner's report clearly state that her heart had given out due to obesity, but friends and family of Elliott had also refute Phillips' story. It was also suggested in some quarters that Phillips had told the story as a way to steer questions away from his own drug abuse when talking with reporters. Either way, there has been no evidence beyond the statements by Phillips to prove that such a cover-up occurred with Mama Cass Elliott's death.

Source: Stalling, Penny. ROCK 'N' ROLL CONFIDENTIAL. Little, Brown and Company, Boston. 1984. Page 207.

Faith No More

> *Faith No More got their name from the name of the horse that won a horse race the band members had bet heavily on. Because of the win, the band members were able to buy new equipment and pursue their musical career full-time.*

The story is sometimes told that instead of a horse race, the band won the money betting on a greyhound race, with the winning dog being named "Faith No More." Instead, the true story is a bit more mundane, although with some humor attached.

The band was originally called Faith No Man, with Mike Bordin on drums, Wade Worthington on keyboards, Billy Gould on bass and Mike "The Man" Morris on guitar and vocals. When Mike "The Man" Morris left the band, it was decided to make fun of the fact that "The Man" was gone, so they changed the name from Faith No Man to Faith No More.

It should also be pointed out that Faith No More was one of the many bands that both the "Gross-out Contest" and "Killing Puppies On Stage" urban legends have been attributed to during their careers. See entries under Alice Cooper for more details on these two urban legends.

Source: Dolgins, Adam. ROCK NAMES. Citadel Press, New Jersey. 1998. Page 72.

Marianne Faithfull

A drug bust during a Rolling Stones party found Jagger's then-girlfriend, Marianne Faithful, with a Mars bar stuck up her vagina.

The urban legend that Mick Jagger was found by the police eating a Mars bar out of Marianne Faithful's vagina during a drug bust has so many fallacies that it should never have been taken seriously. The "party" was actually a weekend get-together of a group of people at the Redlands Estate in West Sussex, England. In addition, only two members of the band, Jagger and Keith Richards, were present; all the other members of the Stones were busy elsewhere that weekend and did not attend. More discrepancies will be discussed below.

The bust occurred on a Sunday evening, February 12, 1967. The night before someone called the newspaper NEWS OF THE WORLD – a paper that Jagger at the time was suing over allegations made in a story printed about drugs – and informed the paper that a party was occurring at the Redlands Estate with a couple of members of the Rolling Stones. The informant, refusing to give his name, stated that the police should be informed about the party. A senior executive at the newspaper passed on the information to Scotland Yard, who contacted the police in West Sussex.

After a warrant had been issued, nearly 20 police officers converged on the estate, arriving at 7:55 that evening, just as the nine guests had finished dinner and had moved into the drawing room to watch television. All the guests were in the room when the police arrived, thus negating the legend that Jagger and Faithful (whom Jagger was in a highly publicized and notorious romantic relationship with) were found in another part of the house "going at it" with a Mars chocolate bar. There was also no evidence that Faithful was found dazed in a bathtub with only a fur coat covering her naked body.

Faithful, instead, was with the rest of the guests in the drawing room, wrapped up in a fur-lined bed sheet as she had gotten out of a bath soon before dinner and did not want to redress. This is probably were the idea that Faithful was in a bathtub wearing only a fur coat came from. The story the police told later at the trial was that Faithful was under the influence of something and repeatedly dropped the bed sheet, displaying her naked body to everyone in the room. The guests disagreed with the police's version of the story, but it was too late, the damage had already been done to Faithful.

Although many in the press and in the court tried to keep Faithful's name out of the picture, especially when the gossip turned to the get-together being an all-out drug-laced orgy, it was very obvious who the girl was at the "party." Faithful was already known to have been dating Jagger and Faithful's continuing appearances at the trial and visiting Jagger in prison were an obvious tip-off that she was the "girl" who was at the "party." To some, it was a perfect opportunity to make Jagger, and to a lesser extent Richards, out to be "evil incarnate" taking innocent, young girls like Faithful (who only three years previously had debuted on the music scene as the 16-year-old girl shyly singing the Stones song *As Tears Go By*) and turning them into drug-crazed nymphomaniacs.

To do this, it wasn't enough that Faithful was at a get-together where drugs were found (mainly marijuana and amphetamines, although one guest was found to have a form of heroin in his possession). It wasn't even enough that Faithful was found wearing only a fur-lined bed sheet. Instead, the rumors began that Faithful had indulged in an orgy with the men at the party, or had been found in one of the bedrooms with Mick not just having sex with her, but in the process of eating a Mars candy bar out of her vagina. As with most urban legends, even after the truth came out, Faithful was forever branded in some circles as the "Mars-bar Girl."

Faithful didn't hear about the candy bar story until after the Redlands trial had occurred. As Faithful explained in her autobiography, Faithful:

The first time I heard about the Mars Bar was from Mick, shortly after the trial. Mick said, "You know what they're saying about us in Wormwood Scrubs, they're saying that when the cops arrived they caught me eatin' a Mars Bar out of your pussy."

"I laughed it off, but my amusement began to wane when the damn story established itself as a set of British folklore. The Mars Bar was a very effective piece of demonizing. Way out there. It was so overdone, with such malicious twisting of the facts. Mick retrieving a Mars Bar from my vagina, indeed! It was far too jaded for any of us even to have conceived of. It's a dirty old man's fantasy — some old fart who goes to a dominatrix every Thursday afternoon to get spanked. A cop's idea of what people do on acid!"

Faithful would go on with her career, eventually leaving her relationship with Jagger, going through a period of downward-spiraling heroin addiction herself, before finally returning in the 1990s as an artist again in her own right. Even so, the urban legend of her past continues to follow her.

Sources: Faithful, Marianne and Dalton, David. FAITHFUL. Little, Brown and Company. 1994. Page 113.
Stallings, Penny. ROCK 'N' ROLL CONFIDENTIAL. Little, Brown and Company, Boston. 1984. Pages 236-237.
Wyman, Bill and Coleman, Ray. STONE ALONG: THE STORY OF A ROCK 'N' ROLL BAND. Viking, New York. Pages 404-447.

Grand Funk Railroad

A man heckling the lead guitarist of Grand Funk Railroad is challenged to come on stage and do a better job playing guitar. The heckler? Eric Clapton, who proceeds to blow the entire, embarrassed band off the stage.

See the entry for Eric Clapton for more details.

Jimi Hendrix

> 1. Purple Haze is a song about drugs. In fact, Jimi wrote it while under the influence of a drug that was purple in color or LSD.
> 2. Hendrix was kicked off the Monkees tour by the Daughters of the Revolution in 1967.
> 3. While being interviewed on the TONIGHT SHOW back in 1969, Jimi Hendrix stated that Phil Keaggy was the best guitarist he had ever heard.
> 4. Jimi died of a heroin overdose / Jimi committed suicide / Jimi was murdered / Jimi would have survived if not for the carelessness of the ambulance workers.

1: According to the book HENDRIX – SETTING THE RECORD STRAIGHT by John McDermott and Hendrix's engineer Eddie Kramer, Purple Haze was written on December 25, 1966 before an afternoon press function at a club called the Upper Cut Club. In the book, Chas Chandler, a bassist for the Animals and long-time supporter of Hendrix, states that he heard Hendrix playing around on the opening guitar riffs of the song and told Jimi that he had a good song in the makings. The song's original extended lyrics dealt with spirituality rather than drugs, and included lyrics such a "Purple Haze, Jesus Saves." However, when it came time to record the song, Hendrix had second-thoughts about the nature of the lyrics and edited them down to the multi-interpretational lyrics that would become famous.

Source: McDermott, John and Kramer, Eddie. HENDRIX – SETTING THE RECORD STRAIGHT. Warner Books, New York. 1992. Pages 31-32.

2: Always described as one of the weirdest tour pairings ever in rock history, the Jimi Hendrix Experience did actually open up for the Monkees on their 1967 American tour (see entries for Monkees for more details about the group and their other urban legends). Jimi Hendrix was just on the verge of becoming world-known, thanks in part to his show stopping performance at the multi-show stopping music festival, the Monterey Pop Festival (featuring the best-known and best-documented incident of Hendrix setting his guitar on fire at the end of his performance). Drummer and sometimes lead-vocalist of the Monkees, Micky Dolenz, already knew of the man long before then. He had first seen Hendrix at a club in Greenwich Village, playing guitar with his teeth as the lead guitarist for the John Hammond Band. In Spring 1967, the cast from the television series appeared in England on a promotional tour. It was there that Dolenz was again transfixed by Hendrix's guitar work and stage presence, leading to Dolenz going with Peter Tork to see Hendrix in June 1967 at the Monterey Pop Festival (in fact, Dolenz can be seen enjoying the show in the documentary made about the festival). From there it was decided that Hendrix would be the perfect opening act for the group when they toured the US in July 1967.

The reasoning behind such a decision by the Monkees? Because they could. The television series had become hugely popular during its first season and the tour was bound to be a success no matter who was opening for the group on their tour. The Monkees also saw two benefits from having the Jimi Hendrix Experience as one of the opening acts for their tour (two other opening acts were part of the bill, although rarely acknowledged when the story is retold): one, it would demonstrate to the audience some very good up-and-coming, adult talent; and, two – and most importantly – it would allow the Monkees to watch Hendrix every night of the tour and get to know him. Everyone in the group liked Hendrix's playing and visual performance on stage, although Mike Nesmith of the Monkees was hesitant about trying to play guitar after having Jimi out-perform them all for a half-hour ("What? You mean, we're supposed to go and play after him? Naw!"). For Hendrix, the decision to tour with the Monkees was a bit harder to fathom. He had given an interview to the British magazine, MELODY MAKER, where he had compared the Monkees to "dishwater." Now, he was opening a tour for them.

Hendrix's management, in particular Michael Jeffery, saw the tour as a chance for Hendrix to be seen by a general audience, as opposed to the cult-status he was already enjoying. Yes, Hendrix was already known in the England thanks to a number of Top Ten hits there, but he had yet tot put a dent into the American market at that time. The tour was an opportunity to do so and Hendrix agreed.

The tour became a nightmare for Hendrix and the Monkees had a guilty consciences about the situation afterwards. While the Monkees enjoyed the opportunity to hear him play, the group had forgotten what their audience was made up of – mainly hysterical, typically screaming, young girls. Although some of the older fans may have gotten into the psychedelic feel of Hendrix's playing, to the kids in the audience that were there to see their television idols, it was boring and insufferable to have to sit through Hendrix's performance. After a handful of performances, including a final disastrous one in Forest Hills, New York where Hendrix split his pants on stage and was drowned out by an audience screaming, "We want the Monkees!" and "We want Davy!", everyone involved knew that Hendrix had to get off the tour.

The question was how. Although some type of statement had to be made, neither the Monkees nor Hendrix was thrilled with a statement that made either look bad. Eventually it was decided by everyone just to make up an excuse that sounded good. Thus, it was reported that the Daughters of the American Revolution – a well-known conservative group – had found Hendrix to be obscene and too racy for the young audience appearing at the Monkees' concerts. A press release was put together by writer and music critic Lillian Roxon (who was traveling with Lynne Randell, one of the opening acts on the tour) with the help of everyone involved. From there, the story was printed and an urban legend was born out of necessity. While there have been many reports that Hendrix finished that last performance on the Monkees tour by making an obscene gesture to the audience ("flipping the bird"), only some of the participants claim it was so.

Sources: Baker, Glenn A. MONKEEMANIA. St. Martin's Press, New York. 1986. Pages 71-72.
Lefcowitz, Eric. THE MONKEES TALE. Last Gasp, San Francisco. 1985. Pages 41-43.
McDermott, John and Kramer, Eddie. HENDRIX – SETTING THE RECORD STRAIGHT. Warner Books, New York. 1992. Pages 75-81.

3: Phil Keaggy is probably best known as a guitarist for the band Glass Harp. Although the rumor has been around for years that Hendrix said this on a nationally seen television show, it has never been verified. A variation of this tale has Eric Clapton as the guitar legend who gives such praise to Keaggy. Either way, Keaggy stated in an interview that he has never been given any proof of Hendrix or Clapton saying such a thing and found the whole story highly unlikely.

Source: "Interview with Phil Keaggy," True Tunes News. Volume Five, Issue Seven, page 43.

4: Jimi Hendrix's death has been one of the most confused and conflicted of accounts in rock and roll history. This is due partly to what people wanted to believe about the way and the reason why Hendrix died. As stated in an earlier entry, there had to be a reason for Hendrix's death other than merely choking to death on his own vomit (a rather unglamorous way for a handsome, young "god" of rock music to die). So, stories went around quickly after his death that he died form an heroin overdose, although friends and associates knew that Hendrix was never a "hard" drug user, with LSD being the hardest of the substances that Hendrix would indulge in (and even at that, not on a regular basis). Nevertheless, when the press found out about his death, they naturally assumed that his death was due to some type of illegal drug, and when the coroner's report mentioned his death being one related to an "overdose" it was even easier for the newspapers to suggest that it was heroin that killed Hendrix. From there, the urban legend simply grew.

When it became clear through the coroner's report that Hendrix had actually died on September 18, 1970 from choking to death on his own vomit, thanks to an overdose of Vesperax – a form of sleeping pill – people then jumped to the next (oddly) "heroic" out for Hendrix: suicide. It was then suggested that Hendrix was depressed, anxious, and unfulfilled with his musical work, and was taking the drugs as his "way out." This common legend was further intensified by comments made by former lead vocalist of The Animals and friend of Hendrix, Eric Burdon. On a BBC television program called 24 Hours, Burdon flatly stated that Hendrix committed suicide, using the drug as a way "to phase himself out of this life and go someplace else." Burdon even produced a piece of poetry Hendrix had written that had been given to him after Hendrix had died. The poem was only a few lines: "The story of life is quicker than the wink of an eye; the story of love is hello and good-bye; until we meet again." Nevertheless, it was enough to convince Burdon and some fans that Hendrix

Jimi Hendrix

was addressing his suicide in the poem and read it as some type of suicide note instead just a snatch of forgotten poetry Hendrix had been working on at the time. Burdon would later recant the story in his autobiography many years later, but the damage had already been done.

Suicide also became a common pronouncement of Hendrix's death due to him taking nine (some sources say seven) of the Vesperax pills given to him by girlfriend Monika Dannemann during the morning hours of September 18. However, Dannemann had given Hendrix a full bottle of 45 tablets, leading Dannemann, the authorities, and many others to conclude that if Hendrix really wanted to kill himself he would have taken all the pills and not just nine. It was also known that Hendrix was an insomniac and thought little of taking more then the recommended dosage of a sleeping pill if he thought such pills ineffective. It had not been a problem in the past, so he probably thought nothing about taking more when he found he couldn't sleep. It's also quite common for people to have overdosed on such pills after taking more in a groggy state – forgetting the number they have already taken and swallowing more, leading to an overdose.

This conclusion was the one that many of the people around Hendrix believed to be the case. It was also the conclusion of the coroner's report as well – cause of death being from an inhalation of vomit and barbiturate intoxication. While the coroner went on to suggest that there was "insufficient evidence of circumstances" to come to a complete conclusion about Hendrix's death, there was never any reason to question the way Hendrix died.

At least from those around him. Conspiracy theorists, however, had a field day with the death, especially in light of the number of deaths (overdose and otherwise) of rock stars within a short number of years, Janis Joplin, Brian Jones and Jim Morrison being the big three always mentioned with Hendrix. Paranoia about the US government naturally leads to conspiracy theories, linking all of these deaths as a series of assassinations to silence the voices of the younger generation. It has also been suggested at times that Hendrix's manager, Mike Jeffrey, had much more to gain financially from a dead Hendrix than a live one, and had Hendrix killed. Since Dannemann reported soon after Hendrix's death that Jimi was planning to fire Jeffrey as his manager, it would be a logical connection in people's minds. So, the next legend was that Hendrix was murdered. Jeffrey, for his part, was in another country at the time of Hendrix's death and had no knowledge of any plans by Hendrix to fire him. Also, and ironically, Jeffrey himself turned out to be one of the few that at first believed Hendrix was murdered and did his own investigation into the death before he could be confident that it was accidental in nature.

The facts known about Hendrix's death are as follows: Dannemann stated to the coroner at the time of Hendrix's death that the couple had returned to her apartment at 3:00 a.m. on the morning of September 18 and went to bed around 7 that morning. When she woke up a bit after 10 in the morning, she checked on Jimi and believed that he was sound asleep. After going out to buy cigarettes, she came back to discover Jimi still in bed, only now she discovered he had been sick and could not wake him. She then discovered that Hendrix had taken a number of the prescribed sleeping pills she had.

From there, the story gets a bit confused. Dannemann stated that she called someone who suggested she call for an ambulance. However, other sources say that Dannemann spent some time actively trying to locate Hendrix's personal doctor, even calling others to see if they knew who his doctor was. When it became clear that Jimi was not waking up, she was told to call for an ambulance. By the time she called for an ambulance the time was about an hour later than when she first left – 11:18 a.m. While doing so, she left Hendrix upright in his own vomit for nine minutes until the ambulance arrived. In Dannemann's report, she stated that Hendrix was alive when she called the ambulance and was told that he would be okay as he was being taken to the ambulance. She would later go on to suggest that Hendrix even tried moving in the ambulance, but the rescue workers kept forcing him to sit upright and not allowing him to cough up vomit. By 11:45 that morning, it was announced that Hendrix was dead.

Because of this story, some fans have concluded that Hendrix would have survived if the ambulance workers had left him alone – allowing him to cough up the vomit that slowly choked him to death. However, one major problem with this story is that Dannemann was not in the ambulance with Hendrix and therefore could not have seen Hendrix trying to struggle. Moreso, Hendrix was without medical aid by Dannemann's own account for at least 30 minutes before the ambulance arrived.

For the majority of people, the conclusion regarding Hendrix's death was that it came about due to an accidental overdose of sleeping pills. Some speculation has also fallen on Dannemann's account that Hendrix was still breathing normally when she arrived back at the apartment, since interviews with the ambulance personnel stated that when they arrived at the apartment there was no sign of Dannemann, and clearly Hendrix was dead when they entered the bedroom and found him.

The obvious reasoning behind people's belief that Hendrix was essentially killed by the ambulance attendants is that it points to outside circumstances, rather his own actions. "Oh, if only the authorities had left Hendrix alone, he would have been fine." So, Hendrix was not responsible for his own death, thanks to this and the various other legends surrounding that day in September 1970.

Sources: Henderson, David. 'SCUSE ME WHILE I KISS THE SKY. Bantam, New York. 1996. Pages 389-390.
McDermott, John and Kramer, EDDIE. HENDRIX – SETTING THE RECORD STRAIGHT. Warner Books, New York. 1992. Pages 277-291.

Buddy Holly

1. *Buddy Holly named his band "The Crickets" after crickets were found living in the makeshift studio the band was recording in.*
2. *The pilot of Buddy Holly's plane was accidentally or intentionally shot in the head during the flight that killed Holly, The Big Bopper and Richie Valens.*

1: One problem with the movie THE BUDDY HOLLY STORY is that the majority of the film is a fictional account of Holly's life and career. One early story in the film has the band recording a song and playing it back, and hearing a cricket chirping on the recording. From this, Holly decided to call his band the Crickets and the rest was history.

It turns out that this story was made up specially for the movie. The name of the band actually came about because of contractual problems that Holly was facing in 1957 when trying to get a new speeded-up version of his song *That'll Be the Day* past the record executives and a new contract with a record label. The problem was that Holly had recorded the song in 1956 for Decca under a one-year contract that went nowhere. Although Decca passed on the song, the contract Holly signed stipulated that he could not rerecord the song for five years.

Not wanting to wait, Holly decided to record the song and send it around to the record labels. To do so, he had to come up with a new name for himself in order to hide his connection to the rerecording. Trying to come up with a name for the band, the group sat around reading from an encyclopedia. The group decided on a name of an insect and chanced upon the name "cricket." Since the insect made a music-like sound and seemed like a more cheerful name than some of the other names tossed around, the Crickets was used for the recordings.

As it turned out, the band was contracted to Brunswick, a subsidiary of Decca. The connection was discovered by Decca before the record was released, but since it was all "in-house" as it were, nothing came of the brief attempt by Holly to cover up his association with the band.

Source: Mikkelson, Barbara and David P. "The Crickets," Urban Legends Reference Pages. http://www.snopes.com/music/artists/crickets.htm. May 9, 2000.
Dolgins, Adam. ROCK NAMES. Citadel Press, New Jersey. 1998. Page 65.

2: Just a few years ago, a gun was found at the site where Holly's plane had crashed on February 3, 1959. The gun, a .25 automatic belong to Holly, was reported to have been found by Albert Juhl, the owner of the farm where the crash site was located. In discussing the gun with reporters, Juhl mentioned that the gun still worked, leading to the press statement that the gun had been recently fired.

Readers of the story misread the statement, assuming that saying the gun had been "recently fired" meant that the gun was fired during the airplane flight itself. This lead to further speculation that the pilot, Roger Peterson, had been shot during the course of the flight and this was the reason for the crash.

Of course, this conflicts with all the evidence ever reported. Coroner's reports showed that all individuals on the flight died due to injuries sustained in the crash. No bullet wounds were found on any of the bodies, nor were there any bullet holes found in the wreckage. While it surprised some that Holly carried a gun, there is no evidence that someone used it in the flight, although some conspiracy theorists are sure to find some type of twisted story to play up in all of it.

There is also no truth to the story that the plane was called "Miss American Pie" or that Holly survived the crash and is still in hiding.

Sources: Hendrix, Randy. "Buddy Holly Frequently Asked Questions," http://members.door.net/hollyweb/wtmc/wizzv.htm. 2001.

Michael Hutchence

> *The lead singer of the Australian band INXS died while attempting autoerotic asphyxiation.*

On November 27, 1997, fans of the band INXS were shocked to find out that the lead vocalist of the band, Michael Hutchence, had died. To compound that shock was the rapid global reach of a rumor that Hutchence had strangled to death while engaged in a masturbatory act sometimes referred to as autoerotic asphyxiation.

The reason for the rumor became clear when it was revealed that his naked body had been found in his Syndey, Australia hotel room. A leather belt was wrapped around his neck, while the buckle of the belt hung from door hook, obviously having broken away from the belt. To some, it read like many stories that had been passed around about the unfortunate individuals who had died while attempting autoerotic asphyxiation and Hutchence fit the bill for the moment.

For some, including his fiancée, Paula Yates, any possibility was better than the idea that Hutchence had committed suicide, although the idea that people would assume Hutchence was involved in something that was conjured up in the urban legend about his death did not sit well with her. Yet, suicide as a possible reason was one that Yates refused to believe in, and by 1999 she was willing to go with the "autoerotic asphyxiation gone wrong" theory as well, saying so in a television interview on Channel 4 in the UK. As she stated there, "He could have done anything at any time, but the one thing he wouldn't have done was leave us."

Other fans and conspiracy theorists insisted that Hutchence was killed by the government for his political stance, or even thugs hired by Yates' ex-husband, Boomtown Rats vocalist and creator of LIVE AID, Bob Geldof. Although Hutchence was having bouts of depression in connection with a custody battle he and Yates were pursuing against Geldof, along with an on-and-off dependency on drugs such as Prozac and Cocaine, fans and Yates refused to believe that he would opt for suicide. So stupidity and/or conspiracy were heavily favored by the fans and Yates as alternatives to suicide.

February 1998 was the release of the coroner's report on Hutchence's death. There, NSW Coroner, Derek Hand, concluded that Hutchence committed suicide alone in his hotel room. This was backed up by several witnesses, including bystanders, Yates, his family and even Geldof (who received two overseas phone calls from Hutchence) that showed him to be depressed over the possible outcome of the custody battle. The coroner also found traces of Cocaine, Prozac, alcohol and other drugs in Hutchence's body during the investigation.

Even with the evidence, theorists continued to believe that there was more to the story, while many people not aware of the findings continue to this day to believe that Hutchence accidentally killed himself during a rather embarrassing sexual act. As for Yates, she was never happy with the results of the Coroner's report and fought it for quite some time afterwards. In the end, Yates never got over the death of Hutchence and on September 16, 2000 would die herself, a victim of a heroin overdose.

Sources: "The Coroner's Report – Full Transcript," The IZINE. http://www.thei.aust.com/music98/hutchcor.html. 1998.

Herman, Gary. ROCK 'N' ROLL BABYLON. Plexus, London. 2002. Pages 241-242.

Thompson, Dave. BETTER TO BURN OUT: THE CULT OF DEATH IN ROCK 'N' ROLL. Thunder's Mouth Press, New York. Pages 146-149.

Michael Jackson

1. *Michael Jackson is actually the singer on many of Diana Ross' songs.*
2. *Michael Jackson and Janet Jackson (or LaTonya Jackson) are the same people.*
3. *Michael Jackson has a shrine to Elizabeth Taylor in his home.*
4. *Michael Jackson has had plastic surgery done in order to look like Diana Ross.*
5. *Michael Jackson has had plastic surgery and skin-whitening done in order to become white.*
6. *Michael Jackson has had so many surgeries done on his nose that it has caved in.*
7. *Michael Jackson tried to buy the bones of the Elephant Man.*
8. *Michael had a chimp named Bubbles that he eventually got tired of and locked away. The chimp eventually went insane and died of loneliness.*
9. *Etc., etc., etc.*

If every urban legend about Michael Jackson were listed here, there would be no room for any other stories in the book. Michael Jackson has had more urban legends written about him tan any other artist, including such notables as the Beatles, Ozzy Osbourne, and Alice Cooper. Probably even more than all those other artists combined.

What is it about Michael that has elevated him to this infamous level? When Jackson started with the Jackson Five as a little boy, no one could have expected that he would end up becoming the poster child for Rock 'n' Roll Urban Legends that he is today. Oh, there were the early rumors – that he did all the singing on Diana Ross' albums, and that his family had taken him to South America for "surgery" in order for him to keep his high voice; yet those were nasty rumors directed at the adults, not really at Michael himself. In fact, he seemed to be a perfectly likable, though internationally famous, kid all through his childhood and into his teenage years. Even that popular 1972 song about the rat, *Ben*, could be forgiven – the song didn't necessarily have to be about a rat, after all. It wasn't like the song had lyrics that were, "Ben, you're a rat and I love you," it was simply a song about friendship and companionship.

Then things started getting weird. Jackson hit beyond big with the 1979 release of his album OFF THE WALL. It was the turning point in his career, as he was no longer just the lead singer of the family musical group; he was now a superstar in his own right. Jackson was 21 years old and had proven that he could make the jump from childhood stardom to adult pop star, a feat that was not completely uncommon, but definitely one not seen since the 1960s. The public embraced him and there he was on the cover of the album, looking confident and cool in his tux. Everything was fine. The nose was different, but only slightly and, well, who could tell him that he couldn't have a tuck done to his nose? Everyone in Hollywood did that kind of thing.

Then came the follow-up album, THRILLER, in 1982. The world was presented with a new Michael Jackson. Still dark and handsome, his hair had become a slicked-down stringy affair and his nose looked somewhat different, again (obviously different this time around). The hair could be readily explained since it was a style that had come and gone and come again, so no one thought much about it. Even the military-like costumes could be explained, appearing at a time when flashy outfits were becoming the norm for performance attire. The nose, though, which would change even again in 1984, was starting to send up flares to the public that something was a bit off with Michael Jackson. The joke became that he was trying to make himself look like one of his sisters or even Diana Ross. Then the jokes became rumors, until it reached the point that Jackson had gotten so many surgeries done on his nose that his face had caved in (one of the reasons for wearing the surgical mask all the time, no doubt, some people would speculate).

Then he started hiding his face and looking paler. Rumors started going around that he was having his skin "altered" so that he could "pass for white," an obvious slam against Jackson's ability to cross over musically with a mutli-racial fan-base. Jackson publicly stated that he had a (real) skin disorder called vitiligo that would cause pale blotches on the skin, which were very sensitive to light (a more logical reason for the surgical masks over the past several years when in public). Even so, there was no appeasing the public, who wanted to believe that Jackson had something not physically wrong with him, but rather mentally wrong with him.

Then came the other stories: that his friendship with Elizabeth Taylor extended to having a shrine to her in his home; Better yet, that he had asked her to marry him; That he slept in an oxygen chamber in order to stay "forever young"; That he tried to buy the Elephant Man's bones for his own personal collection. None were exactly true, but there was enough evidence of Jackson's involvement in such things that people naturally jumped to the wrong conclusions. For instance, Jackson did have a picture taken of him inside of the hyperbaric chamber he had bought for a medical center; some even say that he had the picture forwarded to newspapers under the express hope that an urban legend would be created about him sleeping in it. He would deny that later when interview by Oprah Winfrey in 1993, but it was a bit late for the story to die after that.

Why did people believe that Jackson was getting "weird?" Because he was a recluse who lived in a secluded world of his own making. He didn't like to associate with many adults, preferring the company of children. He even had an amusement park set up on his estate and a zoo. He never seemed to date; or if seen out with a woman, it was always someone that seemed to be a "friend" and not a romantic relationship at all. His interviews became flakier, with him giving answers through his sister Janet or skipping interviews and photo sessions completely. He seemed preoccupied with trying to present himself as a tough guy (as with his album BAD), when the world knew he was pretty much a 99-pound weakling with a somewhat effeminate manner.

Essentially it came down to this: Jackson had dug himself into a public relations hole where he came off as a harmless freak who wrote good songs. Because he didn't fit into the norm of what was expected of a rock performer, people assumed he had to be weird. Jackson was as much to blame for this as the public and the press. He delighted in being seen as "different" and "timeless." Like a musical, modern-day Peter Pan.

The problem was, Peter Pan was just a character in a children book. Jackson was flesh and blood. When allegations went around that Jackson was doing more than just staging slumber parties for the little boys that stayed at his house, the public automatically grabbed on to the idea that Jackson was a pedophile. Didn't matter if he was or not, it just seemed like another logical step in his crazed devolution in the public's eyes. By that time, Jackson really did have to make a public stand about himself, but his rushed marriage to Lisa Marie Presley in 1994 seemed like a vain cover-up of the charges being made against him in 1993. Even their public smooch on a television program did nothing to help; in fact, it backfired, with both Presley looking a bit stoned and their kiss conveying all the warmth of cold fish. Nor did it help that after the allegations were made, television commercials for his "best of" album, HISTORY, would prominently feature a young boy screaming, "I love you, Michael." It was just creepy. Jackson had become creepy. Didn't matter if any of it was true – in fact, most people knew it probably wasn't – Jackson had just become too odd to be looked upon as "cool" any longer.

So, the boy who had rumors forced upon him and then sat quietly by as people continued to make jokes at his expense during his rise to fame and power in the 1980s found himself fighting back weakly against the legends when they turned ugly. It was no use, however. Michael Jackson had become the Perpetual Urban Legend Machine.

Jimmy Eat World

> *The initials of Jimmy Eat World spell out J.E.W., standing for their collective religious beliefs.*

As told by Zach Lind on the official Jimmy Eat World FAQ, the name of the band came about from an incident in Tom Linton's family. One time two of Tom's younger brothers – Ed and Jimmy – got into a fight and Jimmy locked his younger brother Ed out of their room. To get back at his brother, Ed drew a picture of his "chubby" brother trying to cram what appeared to be the Earth into his mouth. At the bottom of the picture Ed wrote, "jimmy eat world," then stuck the picture up on the refrigerator. The band thought it was funny and decided to name themselves with the caption on the drawing. It has nothing to do with any acronym that anyone can make from the name.

Source: "Frequently Asked Questions," Jimmy Eat World Official Web site, http://www.jimmyeatworld.com/history/faq.html#5.01. 2002.

Elton John

> *John once had to be rushes to the hospital to have his stomach pumped of semen after a party with a group of football players.*

See the Stomach Pump Entry.

Janis Joplin

> *1. Joplin's hit* Me and Bobby McGee *was written by Janis about her lesbian girlfriend Bobby. When the record company heard the song, they requested that she change the lyrics so that it was about a boy instead of a girl.*
> *2. Joplin was murdered as part of an international governments-based conspiracy to silence the voices of the musical leaders in the "hippie generation."*

1: Me and Bobby McGee was written by Kris Kristofferson, who wrote the song from a male perspective about a girlfriend named Bobby (and it was recorded this way by Gordon Lightfoot). When Janis received the song, she merely changed a few words in order to switch the sex of the character. There was no lesbian girlfriend named Bobby.

2: Joplin, a known abuser of alcohol and drugs, died on October 5, 1970 in the Landmark Hotel in Los Angeles, California. Her death was ruled accidental due to an overdose of heroin. As would happen to Sid Vicious eight years later, the overdose was due to the drug being too pure, leading to Joplin's body shutting down, unable to process the drug.

As with the deaths of Brian Jones, Jim Morrison, and Jimi Hendrix (in fact, Hendrix died less than three weeks before Joplin), conspiracy theorists have tried to tie their deaths together to form some type of international conspiracy to "silence the voices of the younger generation." However, no one has ever come forward with any evidence that this was the case. Nor has there been a significant link between the deaths to prove that they were related any fashion. Conspiracy theories also pale when you consider that all four individuals were known drug and alcohol users (perhaps Hendrix to a lesser extent than any of the others, but still a common user), and that all four deaths were accidental in nature (for more detail, see the entries under each artists' name).

The best question to ask in relation to these deaths is, of course, why would the government wish to murder these people? Granted, all were people well-known to the youth of the day, but none was overtly political beyond comments that were being made by many young people at the time. Moreso, there were certainly much more violent reactionaries in the U.S. that were of greater concern to the government, yet many of them lived full lives. If Jones, Hendrix, Joplin, and Morrison were murdered, why not the others? In addition, how were these alleged political murders achieved by the U.S. government when three of the deaths occurred overseas (only Joplin's occurred in the U.S.)?

The "coincidence" that so many famous young musicians died in a span of three years would be difficult for fans to take. Even so, there is no evidence to support any conspiracy theories unless you're the type who'll believe everything you're told by other theorists and refused to look at the facts. One thing is for sure, government conspiracy theories will not be the last of the theories put forward for the deaths of many rock and roll stars.

Judas Priest

> *Much like Ozzy Osbourne's* Suicide Solution, *Judas Priest recorded a song,* Better By You Better Than Me, *that had a subliminal message which drove teenagers to suicide.*

On December 23, 1985, two young men, 18-year-old Raymond Belknap and 20-year-old James "Jay" Vance, attempted suicide with a shotgun blast to the head. Belknap succeeded in his attempt, killing himself instantly; Vance slipped as the shotgun went off, disfiguring his face, and later died of complications resulting from his attempted suicide.

The event itself would be seen as unfortunate, yet it took on the air of urban legend when the families decided that a Judas Priest album the two had listened to repeatedly that night, STAINED CLASS, had a subliminal message on it that told the boys to "do it." If it had not been for the message, the families claimed, the boys would not have attempted suicide. They decided to sue Judas Priest and CBS Records in May 1986.

At first, the suit was based around the lyrics of one song called *Heroes End*, which featured the lines, "Why do you have to die to be a hero? It's a shame a legend big as that would sin." The suit claimed that the lyrics, along with the beat of the music and the style of music itself (heavy metal) created an "uncontrollable impulse" in the young men to want to kill themselves. Why these particular lyrics would prompt suicide is a question only the family could answer, especially since the lyrics could be taken to be anti-suicidal if anything. Still, the problems with the suit rapidly became apparent when the plaintiffs in the similar Osbourne case were dealt a blow by the California 2d District Court of Appeal in July 1988. In that case, it was decided that the lyrics were covered under the First Amendment.

The loophole that presented itself to the plaintiffs in the Judas Priest case was the concept of "subliminal messages" found on the album that led to the suicide attempts. The reason for this change in tactic was that it was ruled by the Judge in the case, Justice Jerry Carr Whitehead, that "subliminal speech" did not deserve protection under the

First Amendment because it was "forced" upon the recipients without their knowledge and therefore an "invasion of privacy." Because of this, the plaintiffs moved on from the audible lyrics to supposed "subliminal lyrics" on the song *Better by You Better Than Me*. The supposed phrase on the song was "Do it," which led many to ask what "it" was supposed to be. Nevertheless, it was accepted as the main phrase that led the two men to attempt suicide, while the plaintiffs also stated that several backward messages were hidden on the album as well, including the phase, "Fuck the Lord, fuck all of you," on the song *White Heat, Red Hot*, and the phrase "Sing my evil spirit" on the song *Stained Class*.

The case went to trial on July 16, 1990, with members of Judas Priest arriving to take part in the trial. One of the lawyers for the plaintiffs had hoped to prove "through science" that the subliminal messages had forced the two men to attempt suicide. The defense went forward with their own witnesses to prove that there were no subliminal messages on the album and that even if there were previous experiments in "subliminal messages" had been faulty and proved little as to whether people were influenced by such messages even if they were actually present.

The case was eventually decided by the judge who ruled that, while he believed the words "Do it" can be heard on the album – albeit by unintentionally – the plaintiffs failed to establish that the words were the cause of the suicide attempts, especially in light of testimony from a clinical psychologist who showed both having a history of drug abuse, petty crime, school failure, unemployment and violence. Belknap was also shown to have attempted suicide before and right before his death had made comments suggesting another possible suicide attempt. In the end, no proof was ever made to show that the album by Judas Priest had subliminal messages, although the court backed away from coming to a conclusion about the allegation. Why wasn't there a national epidemic of suicides if such a thing were true, instead of just the two mentioned here? But nothing about this was followed up by the courts.

See the entry for Backmasking and Subliminal Messages for more details concerning this type of urban legend.

Sources: Moore, Timothy E. "Scientific Consensus and Expert Testimony: Lessons from the Judas Priest Trial," Skeptical Inquirer. November/December 1996.
Soocher, Stan. THEY FOUGHT THE LAW. Schirmer Books, New York. 1999. Pages 153-170.

Kingsmen

> *The Kingsmen's version of* Louie, Louie *has obscene lyrics.*

The legend that Louie, Louie has obscene lyrics has been around nearly as long as the song has. The song was written in 1956 by a musician named Richard Berry, who recorded it that year with a band called the Pharaohs. The song's lyrics dealt with a sailor's thoughts about the girl he left behind in Jamaica as he "sailed the sea." It should be pointed out that the sailor's thoughts had nothing to do with sex at all. It was just a simple little ballad about a sailor wanting to see his girl again.

In 1963, the Kingsmen recorded the song and had a national hit with it. Because of the popularity of the song and the difficulty in understanding what the singer, Jack Ely, was singing, many came up with their own lyrics. As teenagers are prone to do, they created lyrics for the song centered on sex. As parents are prone to do, they snooped around, found said lyrics, and blew a gasket. The legend would escalate to the point that J. Edgar Hoover would have the FBI investigate the song in order to find out what the "dirty" lyrics were. As it turns out, after a 30-month-long investigation, they never could figure out what the lyrics were and could only guess that they were obscene.

The version of the song recorded by the Kingsmen was not obscene, however. Hard to understand, yes; obscene, no. Still, the legends grew to the point where whole books and web sites would be based on just the one song.

Source: Marsh, Dave. LOUIE LOUIE. Hyperion, New York. 1993.

KISS

> 1. *The name KISS stands for Knights In Satan's Service and the band was made up of Satan worshippers.*
> 2. *Bassist Gene Simmons had a cow's tongue surgically grafted on to his own so he could waggle a long tongue at people in concert.*
> 3. *Gene Simmons' hand gestures during the concert are "devil horns," which he uses to demonstrate his devotion to Satan.*
> 4. *The makeup was created in order to hide the features of Ace Frehley, as he was actually singer Jim Morrison, hiding out from his supposed death by taking on a new persona.*
> 5. *Gene Simmons spits pig's blood during the concert.*
> 6. *The KISS Army was created when a group of fans circled a radio station in Terre Haute, Indiana, demanding to hear KISS songs on the station.*
> 7. *The band once did a concert where they crashed a car on stage as they played* Detroit Rock City.
> 8. Beth *was a love song written about Peter Criss then-wife, Lydia Criss.*

> 9. KISS once met Andy Gibb at a concert backstage and members of KISS proceeded to beat Gibb up using a method that was of their own design.
> 10. When Peter Criss left the band, KISS planned to replace him with a woman.

1: In 1976, KISS was becoming a household name in the US after struggling for three years (and three studio albums and one live album). The makeup and spectacular stage shows had hooked some fans, but album sales were what keep the band on their record label. Seeing their albums starting to move and their names in the papers showed them that all the "extras" they were doing were finally starting to pay off.

The problem was that the band was beginning to reach a market slightly younger than the one they had previously attained. With a conscious effort to promote themselves heavily, KISS began making appearances on television shows, selling merchandise, and even appearing in comic books (such as the March 1976 appearance in the Marvel Comic, HOWARD THE DUCK). Sure, the comic book appearance was actually in a comic that was considered more adult-oriented than many at the time, but the general public just viewed it as a comic book appearance and therefore for little kids.

Because of all this, younger fans were being created and some parents, as well as conservative religious figures, were worried about what the band might be trying to "preach" to their kids. With KISS refusing to be seen without their makeup and the suggestive lyrics of many of their songs, some felt that the band was bent on poisoning children with evil messages. The members of KISS and their management at first saw it as "same old, same old" and played off the stories in order to get more press. As some in the band were inclined to say, "any press is good press," so even the urban legend was just another way to advertise the band to the public.

In this context, the urban legend best remembered about the band was that KISS was an acronym that stood for "Knights In Satan's Service." Some variations of the legend appeared elsewhere, such as the name meaning "Knights In Service of Satan," Kings in Satan's Service," and even "Kids In Satan's Service." There was also evidence found by those making this claim that the band's lyrics on their new album at that time,

DESTROYER, were satanic. Gene's character being a demon that spit blood and fire during the concerts only added fuel to the fire.

The band's response to the press was bemused indifference at first, although privately both Ace Frehley and Peter Criss were upset about the accusation (in particular Criss, who had been raised a Catholic). The band really did not start addressing the issue of the rumor until 1982 when the legend had a strong comeback at a time when the band was struggling to reestablished their careers after Criss had left (in 1980) and their experimental "concept" album, MUSIC FROM *THE ELDER*, had bombed (in 1981). By that time, the band had started displaying a "shocked" preoccupation with the urban legend, hoping to generate publicity just as the rumor had in the 1970s.

As it turned out, they did rejuvenate public interest, starting in 1983/84, but that was because they had taken off their makeup and were producing more middle-of-the-road, commercial albums. Meanwhile, heavy metal had become a huge phenomenon during the mid- to late 1980s and KISS was able to sail on that crest of popularity for quite some time.

But all of this is getting away from the story about the band's name. No one is really quite sure where the urban legend came from, although 1976 was the first public discussion of the legend within fandom. In reality, the band's name had nothing to do with any type of acronym at all.

In 1972, Paul Stanley and Gene Simmons had broken up a band they were in called Wicked Lester. Eventually they met up with drummer Peter Criss and formed a new band under the old band name. As 1972 rapidly drew to a close, the threesome struggled to come up with a new name. While they were driving in Stanley's car one day, Criss made mention that one of his last bands before joining the others was called Lips. Paul Stanley was then hit by a brainstorm, as he explained to Adam Dolgins in Dolgins' book, ROCK NAMES:

> "We were at the point where we were already rehearsing songs, and very clear on what the band was about and who we were. That's the point where you have to come up with a name to kind of reflect that. I was driving my '63 Plymouth Grand Fury on the long Island Expressway, and the name suddenly came to me. I remember thinking to myself, 'God, I know this is the right name, I hope I don't get any grief from the other guys.' I told them I thought the band should be called KISS and I held my breath, waiting for some sort of response, and everybody went, 'Yeah, that sounds pretty good.'"

The name felt right to Stanley and the others because it was a name that could mean different things to different people, therefore the band would not be trapped into just one style of music (although they soon would be anyhow). It was also short and easy to remember. It was not, however, supposed to stand for anything other than just the name of a band.

The urban legend about "Knights In Satan's Service" still gets tossed around, resurfacing about every five years or so, typically along with any resurgence in interest about the band and normally paraded around by uninformed church-goers as an old stand-by when discussing bands that are evil.

Source: Dolgins, Adam. ROCK NAMES.
Sherman, Dale. BLACK DIAMOND: THE UNAUTHORIZED BIOGRAPHY OF KISS. CG Publishing, Toronto. 1997.

2: One of the first things noticed about KISS when seen in photos, on television or in concert was Gene Simmons waggling his tongue at the audience and the other band members.   Because of his longer-than-normal tongue (not to mention his preoccupation in displaying it), many wondered if he had somehow had something done to it in order to stick his tongue out so far.

Rumors usually fell into two explanations: one, that Simmons had surgery in order to have his tongue stick out further; and two, that he had some type of bizarre Frankenstein-like human / animal plastic surgery done that grafted a cow's tongue onto his own.

The first solution was really reaching for an answer, but the second was way out in left field. Surgery of the tongue would take months to a year to heal and would be quite costly – an impossibility for a musician struggling to make it on a teacher's salary in the early 1970s; and upon achieving success, the band was so busy that there would not have been the time necessary to have any type of surgery done as suggested by the rumor. Such a surgery would have been impossible anyway, and only a quack would even attempt such an operation, even if given all the time and money in the world to do it. Such an operation would have also left scarring that would be detectable in photos and on television, which – of course – Simmons doesn't have.

While others may find it hard to believe, some people are just born with longer tongues, Simmons being a good example. A rumor has also gone around that Simmons could stick out his tongue so far because he was double-jointed in the jaw, but this rumor was short-lived.

3: Along with the band's name meaning "Knights In Satan's Service," one of the most common arguments of the religious fanatics who believed KISS to be Satan worshippers was Simmons' usage of the "Devil Horns." This hand gesture that the righteous were complaining about was where Gene would take one or both hands and raise them up with the thumb, index finger and little finger extended, while the other two fingers were pressed to the palm.

Gene began using the gesture back in the early days of the band. Simmons gives two reasons for the gesture. The first was that one night while performing with the band on stage, he wanted to wave to the crowd while at the same time not losing his guitar pick. To do this, he placed the pick into the palm of his hand with his middle fingers, and then extended his fingers out in a "wave" motion. After seeing how it looked, he decided to start using it on a regular basis.

The second story was one that Gene told interview Marty Herzog in the magazine, COMICS INTERVIEW:

"You know, I started doing a hand signal like this in live concerts that everyone is now doing. I didn't even know what it meant. Then I found out it means, 'I Love You,' in sign language. And, of course, the idiots in the Bible belt thought that it was devil worship stuff . . . Then I found out that subconsciously, I must have been doing Dr. Strange."

Dr. Strange was a comic book character created by Stan Lee at Marvel Comics. The character was a mystic sorcerer who defended Earth against demon forces and evil magicians. When Strange would chant an incantation, he would raise his hands up in the exact same manner as Gene. The artist on the comic, Steve Ditko, has never explained why he used this gesture for Strange (or the same gesture for the other major comic book character he created, Spider-Man), but to suggest that "love" was the power behind Strange's incantations certainly did give the comic a hidden layer of charm.

The true genesis of the gesture is most probably a combination of the two stories; in essence, Gene made the hand gesture in concert, thought it looked "cool," and decided to use it from that point forward.

Gene's quote from COMICS INTERVIEW perpetuates a common myth about the gesture – that it became the popular hand gesture of many fans and musicians in the 1980s (especially those who attended heavy metal concerts). That gesture was slightly different, with the index and little finger sticking up, while the thumb and middle fingers were clasped to the palm as if forming a fist. It was actually this hand gesture that would be prominently featured in all types of anti-rock religious pamphlets and books as the "Devil Horns." The hand-gesture Gene made, however, would be easily confused with the other. Ironically enough, once Gene stopped wearing the makeup and performing as the "Demon" on-stage, he dropped the hand gesture, and only once in a great while has he used it since the early 1980s.

Sources: Herzon, Marty. "Interview with Gene Simmons," Comics Interview. 1984.
Sherman, Dale. BLACK DIAMOND: THE UNAUTHORIZED BIOGRAPHY
OF KISS. CG Publishing, Toronto. 1997. Pages 83-84.

4: The band's insistence on not being seen without their makeup during the 1970s (and up until 1983 when the makeup finally came off with the release of their album LICK IT UP) led to all types of strange rumors explaining why this was done. Some of the rumors were like the following, and nearly all were just as bizarre:

The band was really a franchise, where studio musicians were sent out in several parts of the country at once in order to make more money for the record label. The makeup would hide the facial differences.
The band members had the makeup tattooed on their faces so that they would never have to bother with putting it on or taking it off.
Some of the band members were so horribly scarred from some type of accident that it was the only way to make them presentable to the public.
Behind the makeup were really some of the best known names in the business, all too embarrassed to be linked to the band's success.

This last rumor was the one that stuck in people's heads, especially in the mid- to late 1970s. With the continuing rumors that musicians who had died were actually still alive and hiding out in various parts of the country, it took little for people to tag the band's refusal to take off their makeup as a continuation of an earlier death conspiracy. One of the most popular musicians to have had such stories told about him was Jim Morrison of the Doors, thanks to the mystery of his death and burial (see entry for Jim Morrison for more details). Two mysteries combined here and became one where people deduced that Morrison had decided to come back to music and joined (or even started) KISS as a way to do so. In some versions of the legend Paul Stanley was the man who secretly was supposed to be Morrison. The KISS member that was most commonly proposed (especially during the band's earlier popularity) was Ace Frehley. Frehley had a reputation as a drinker, just as Morrison; but more importantly, Frehley did not commonly do any talking or sing solo in the band – at least on the early albums. This was gold to the believers of the legend, but it led them to believe that Frehley / Morrison did not speak because he would be found out once his well-known voice was heard.

This rumor has a few problems, as anyone who thought about it for more than a second or two would see. Although Frehley wore makeup, he physically did not look anything like Morrison – Frehley was thin and scrawny, with long, flat, straight hair; Morrison had a physical build that left him trying to keep weight off near the end of his life, with thick hair that naturally curled as it got longer. Morrison was also not known for being a guitarist, while Ace was then and still is now considered one of the better guitarists of the 1970s – quite a leap musically within a short period if Morrison truly was Frehley.

Of course, the game was up once Frehley got over his natural shyness and started singing songs in the band as well as doing television interviews. There was no way that the same man with the thick New York accent and high-pitched squeals of laughter was Morrison.

Source: Sherman, Dale. BLACK DIAMOND: THE UNAUTHORIZED BIOGRAPHY OF KISS. CG Publishing, Toronto. 1997.

5: Besides spitting fire during the show, Gene Simmons also incorporated another visual effect into the solo he performed when the band was in-concert. This second visual was commonly referred to as spitting or vomiting blood. It was certainly effective, since it is something that people still remember seeing when the band played in the 1970s. Of course, kids being kids, it wasn't long before stories started going around that Gene spit actual human blood on stage during his solo. When people were not readily convinced of that version of the legend, it became pig's blood or cow's blood.

While even the animal blood story did not win over many fans, people did wonder what he was spitting up during the solo. Simmons actually experimented for a time to come up with something that would be effective, yet not dangerous for him to use. Old fashioned blood capsules did not have much visual effect, especially from a concert stage, while chemical products (there was a rumor at one time that he had helped to develop such a product with chemical industry company 3M) were too watery and fake-looking.

Gene finally settled on a recipe of his own. While he has never gone into full details what is in the recipe, he has admitted that he uses a type of red dye along with raw eggs in the recipe in order to give the blood a thick consistency that could be seen in the dim lighting of the concert hall.

At least, that's his story.

Source: Sherman, Dale. BLACK DIAMOND: THE UNAUTHORIZED BIOGRAPHY
         OF KISS. CG Publishing, Toronto. 1997.

6: The KISS Army was a collective term used to describe both the band's fans and the band's official fan club back in the 1970s. What made the KISS Army so special to the band was the story told about how it was created.

The story goes that on November 2, 1975, a KISS fan named Bill Starkey was fed-up with his local rock radio station in Terre Haute, Indiana. Although Starkey and several of his friends would call the station, WVTS, and request KISS songs, the Disc Jockeys at the station would refuse, feeling that the music was beneath them to play. On that day, Starkey called up the station and gave them an ultimatum: either play KISS on the radio right that minute or he and his friend would make sure that nobody left the station. The DJ who answered the phone thought the kid on the other end of the line was making a prank call and laughed. His laughter turned to shock however, when several employees at the station let him know that there was a large group of teenagers stationed outside, encircling the building. WVTS played their first KISS song just a few minutes later. The DJ also called the local television stations and newspaper, realizing what a publicity story the incident was. The reporters called the group of intimidating teenagers "the KISS Army," and the rest, as they say, is history.

In reality, it was not really history, it was a publicity stunt. In fact, it was a publicity stunt that the band latched on to and elaborated upon in order to make it sound even better than what actually occurred.

In 1996, Starkey was interviewed by the INDIANAPOLIS STAR newspaper, and he explained in detail what had actually occurred with the radio station back in 1975. At the time, Starkey and a friend by the name of Jay Evans began requesting KISS songs from the DJs at the radio station. WVTS refused until another radio station in town, WPFR, began playing KISS songs and their ratings start to pick up. With this, the management at WVTS asked Starkey and Evans to help with a publicity stunt to generate interest in the station again. Starkey and Evans agreed and began by submitting a "KISS Army Letter of the Day" to the station for the DJs to read and ridicule. This continued until the band actually took notice while touring through Terre Haute, Indiana and invited Starkey to help put together the official fan club for the band. From there, the official KISS Army began.

It's true that the KISS Army was started in Terre Haute, Indiana in 1975 and that Bill Starkey was the creator of the KISS Army, thanks to the help of the radio station, WVTS. Yet, the rest of the story is just simply a story made up to make the fan club look more exciting. There was never an assault on the station, nor were there threats of violence against the DJs if they didn't play KISS that November day in 1975 — that was all just made up.

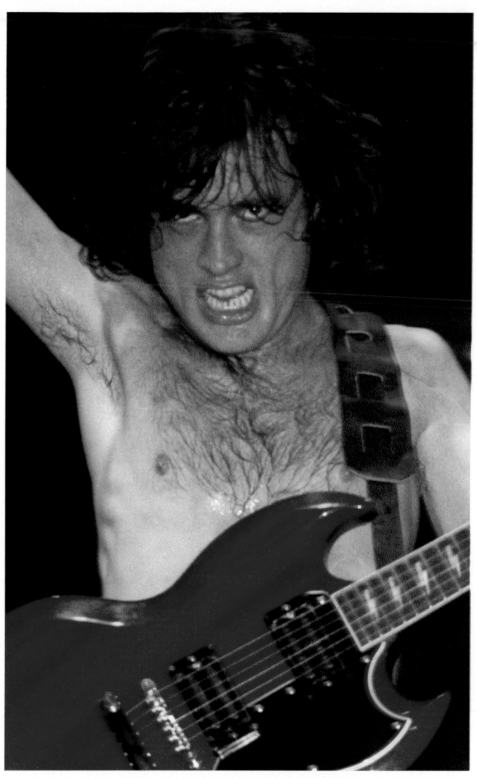

Angus? A child of the devil? This innocent face? See page 12.

Does Eric Clapton look sorrowful for blowing
Grand Funk Railroad off stage? See page 37.

Alice Cooper or Eddie Haskell? Only his
hairdresser knows for sure. See page 41.

Does Sarah MacLachlan write songs for FBI agents? See page 97.

Was Madonna TV's Tabitha? See page 98.

Did Marilyn Manson have ribs surgically removed
for sexual reasons? See page 98.

Is Stevie Nicks enchanting in more ways than one? See page 106.

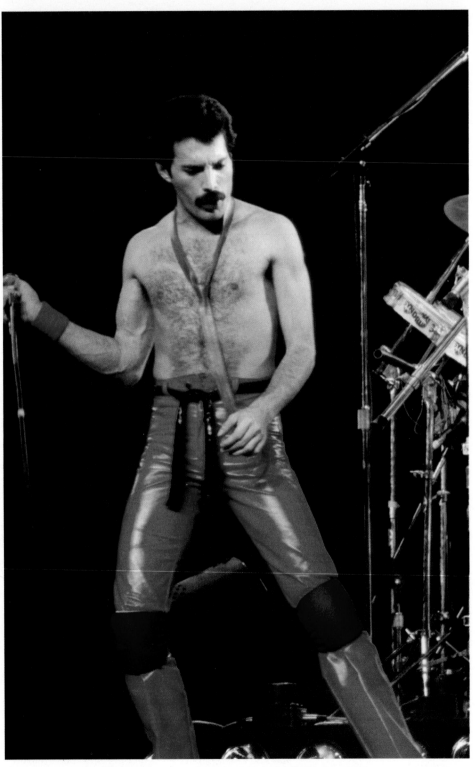

Have you seen this man's teeth? See page 131.

Still, the story was told for so long that many people started believing it and it has been reported that way in several biographies about the band over the years. Even the band members believed it eventually, as Bill pointed out in his newspaper interview in 1996. In 1995 Bill had run into Gene at a KISS convention and they were talking for a couple of minutes when Gene asked for a copy of the photo taken outside the radio station that day in November 1975. Starkey had no idea what Gene was referring to until Gene went into more details, describing the photo as the one that showed all the kids encircling the WVTS radio station. Starkey was taken aback, as he explained in the newspaper interview: "I didn't know what to say. I didn't want to say, 'Gene, no such picture exists.'"

After telling the story for so long, even one of the band members thought the publicity story they had made up was true.

Source: Sherman, Dale. BLACK DIAMOND: THE UNAUTHORIZED BIOGRAPHY OF KISS. CG Publishing, Toronto. 1997.

7: KISS released an album in 1976 called DESTROYER. The album contained a song that was released as a single called *Detroit Rock City*. The song, one of the most popular among fans, dealt with a teenage boy who is driving fast in his car, trying to make it in time for a concert. Eventually he loses control of the car and crashes it, killing himself instantly. The song on the album starts with a little "mood setting" featuring the sounds of someone getting into a car, starting it up, and turning the car radio on. An announcer on the radio (actually the voice of Gene Simmons) can be heard as the song begins. As the song ends, there's a squealing of tires and a crash can be heard.

Because the band was known for outlandish stage productions, they were always trying to come up with new gimmicks to put into the show. In fact, a machine that created lightning on stage was tried for a time during the early part of the DESTROYER tour, but was ultimately scrapped as being too heavy and dangerous to use on a regular basis. One idea tossed around and even sketched out in an ad for the tour that appeared during the year was having a car simulate a crash on stage. This was only ever seen in the ad, however, and never went beyond the drawing board. Still, for years after, fans constantly would ask if the band really did crash a car on stage during the tour and the rumor has been one of KISS' most consistent urban legends over the years.

Speaking of tours in support of albums, there is also no truth to the long-held rumor that the band went on tour for their 1981 concept album, MUSIC FROM *THE ELDER*. Sketches and plans were made for the tour, but were dropped when dismal sales and high costs kept the band from touring for the album.

Source: Sherman, Dale. BLACK DIAMOND: THE UNAUTHORIZED BIOGRAPHY OF KISS. CG Publishing, Toronto. 1997.

8: When *Beth* became a big hit in late 1976 (oddly enough, as first the B-side and then the A-side of the song *Detroit Rock City*, which generated its own rumor as listed above), people were taken with the melodic song that seemed so different from the type of hard rock music performed by the band. The song's lyrics tell the story about a relationship between a man and a woman where the man is in a band and has to spend time away from the woman when practicing with the band. That's pretty much all there is to the song, with the man resigning himself to working with the band, knowing that his wife or girlfriend is sitting at home alone.

For years it was assumed that the song was written by drummer Peter Criss (who also sings the song) and Stan Penridge as a tribute to Criss' wife at the time, Lydia Criss. Peter had even said so in some interviews at the time. While it makes a good story, this is not the case.

The song was actually written by Penridge and Criss back in 1970 when they were both in a band called Chelsea. Another member of the band, Michael Brand, had a wife named Becky who was, as Penridge would say in an interview with the author in 1994, "continually calling up and interrupting our rehearsals." With the phone nearby, the others in the band could hear Brand's side of the conversation, with Brand typically upset that his wife had interrupted their rehearsals once again. After a time, Penridge and Criss started writing down some of the things Brand was saying to his wife and decided to put them into song.

The song, however, did not contain the sweet, sentimental lyrics of the version recorded in 1976 for the DESTROYER album. Instead the lyrics were originally written as a put-down of the woman for constantly interrupting their rehearsals.

After writing the song, which they titled "Beck" after Becky Brand, Penridge and Criss put the song into their files and moved on to other material. In 1976, KISS was working on their new album with producer Bob Ezrin when Criss decided to offer the old song to the group. Depending on who tells the story, either Gene Simmons or Bob Ezrin told Criss that the song was okay, but the title didn't quite work. The title was then changed to *Beth* and the lyrics were changed slightly to make them less of an insult to the woman that the song is directed towards and more of a song about resignation and loneliness.

We can imagine that the rewritten lyrics may have sparked from Peter's own feelings of loneliness when being away from his wife, Lydia, but the origin of the song had nothing to do with Lydia Criss at all.

Source: Sherman, Dale. BLACK DIAMOND: THE UNAUTHORIZED BIOGRAPHY OF KISS. CG Publishing, Toronto. 1997. Page 74-75.

9: This is a story that obviously came from the school yards of the late 1970s. Andy Gibb was the younger brother of the Gibb Brothers of the Australian band the Bee Gees. Andy had achieved success on his own in the late 1970s and had become a pin-up boy for many teenage girls in the late 1970s / early 1980s. He was also packaged as a pop singer who sang sappy love songs, and between that image and his designation as a young girl's favorite, many teenage boys pretty much hated Gibb's guts.

So what do you do in a case where there's a rich, famous singer that all the girls like and you can't stand? You knock him down to size by reveling in a story that supposedly shows the man getting what should be "coming to him." And, who better to knock this "star" down to size than a band that many teenage boys at the time thought was one of the coolest bands in the world – KISS?

Thus an urban legend sprang forth from the school yards. The legend went that the band met Andy Gibb backstage at an awards ceremony (some versions of the story make it just backstage at a KISS show). Gibb takes little notice of the band and starts hitting on the women backstage, whereupon KISS decides to pound some manners into Gibb. To do this, they don't just beat him up, but use their musical instruments to beat on Gibb – Peter with his drumsticks, Gene with his bass, Paul and Ace with their guitars, turning him into a bloody mess by the time they're finished. Gibb then requires several weeks in the hospital to recover, having learned his lesson.

While the story is ludicrous enough as it stands – the idea that major celebrities like Andy Gibb and KISS could have a fight backstage at a television award shows and it's not subsequently featured in the gossip shows and tabloids – the story is sometimes expanded further. Not only does each member of KISS use his musical instrument to beat on Gibb, but they also patiently wait their turns, queuing up to take their swings at Gibb who lets each of them knock him around with a quarrel, and there's no interference from anyone else standing backstage.

There's no point in even going further with this legend; it's quite obviously not true.

10: In May 1980, KISS announced that Peter Criss was leaving the band in order to take some time off and then pursue a solo career. With Criss' departure, they also announced plans to hire a new drummer for the band soon. In July 1980, they decided on a man by the name of Paul Caravello to replace Criss. In keeping with the band's history, and to help distance Caravello from his earlier professional career as a drummer (he had played in several New York bands and even recorded an album with one a few years earlier), Caravello's name was changed to Eric Carr.

When KISS' management announced the name of the new drummer, some reporters misunderstood the name and thought that the new drummer was named "Erica." With this misinformation, it took little for people to assume that if the drummer's name was "Erica," it mean that the band had hired a woman to replace Peter Criss. Because of this, and the fact that the band was not heavily promoted in the US during 1980 and 1981, the rumor of the drummer being a woman persisted for quite some time.

There was also no truth to the rumor that the lead guitarist of the band in 1982-83 was a women. Much like the "Erica" rumor, this rumor was about the new lead guitarist, Vinnie Vincent, when he joined KISS in 1982. This was mainly due to the effeminate makeup and physical stance of the guitarist, and once the makeup came off in 1983, the rumor died a quick death.

Source: Sherman, Dale. BLACK DIAMOND: THE UNAUTHORIZED BIOGRAPHY OF KISS. CG Publishing, Toronto. 1997.

Klaatu

> *Klaatu, a band on Capitol Records back in the 1970s, was really the Beatles using fake names.*

In February 1977, the PROVIDENCE JOURNAL newspaper in Rhode Island published Steve Smith's article called, "Could Klaatu Be the Beatles Mystery Is a Magical Mystery Tour." While Smith may not have been the first to say it, his article was at least close to ground zero for one of the best-known rumors of the 1970s rock-world. It was also a legend that would help build and destroy the growing career of the musically talented Canadian trio that made up Klaatu.

Klaatu was made up of three musicians – John Woloschuk, Terry Draper and Dee Long – who had signed a deal with Capitol Records in the mid-1970s. Their first album, the self-titled KLAATU, was released in August 1976 and got some decent notices by the press. Unfortunately, a good album with fair reviews does not always translate into sales. The album was drifting toward the discount racks when the rumor hit in February 1977.

One version of the legend goes like this: the Beatles had recorded an album in 1966 that had been mysteriously lost until recovered in 1975. When found, it was decided to release the album on the Beatles' American label, Capitol. The only problem was that the Beatles wanted the music to stand on its own, and with their continuing legal problems at the time, it would make sense to avoid drawing attention to themselves. Thus, to avoid the press and fans coming to immediate conclusions about the music if it was known that they were involved, the Beatles requested that the album be released with no personal credits as to who played on the album or who wrote the material.

The rather awkward part of this legend is that, while the Beatles did not want their name or personal names connected with the album, they wanted "clues" to be presented on the album to prove it was the Beatles. While this makes little sense, it was nothing to dissuade Beatle fans from reviewing the album intensely, looking for clues that could support the myth. By the time the fans were done, the number of "clues" read like a list of "clues" to the supposed "Paul is dead" legend (see the Beatles entry for more details on that particular legend), which is ironic in itself, as one further extension of the Klaatu rumor was that the "lost album" was supposedly put into the vaults in the first place when Paul "died" back in the 1960s.

Of course, some of the clues were immediate: Klaatu had their album released through the Beatles' American label, Capitol; no individual credits are given for anyone on the album (suggesting someone or a group of people not wanting to be known); nor were there photos of the band on the album or in any promotional material. Of course, the music had a brilliant musical quality reminiscent of the Beatles, while the lyrics had the fanciful, clever imagery that repeatedly showed up in McCartney and Lennon's whimsical Beatles songs. After that, however, the "clues" became a bit of a stretch, or to put it bluntly, downright insane. As pointed out in David Bradley's brilliant article about the Klaatu / Beatles legend on the official Klaatu web site (http://www.klaatu.org), the clues reach into references of song titles (Klaatu's *Sub-Rosa Subway* being a takeoff of

McCartney's *Red Rose Speedway*) to the album cover (8 trees pictured right at the very bottom of the front cover . . . only 7 have roots showing . . . there are 7 letters in the name Beatles) and beyond. By the time a fan had wrapped his or her head around all the "clues" it was little wonder that they thought Klaatu might have been the Beatles.

Ironically, the rumor that the musicians on the album purposefully did not use their names on the album so that the "music could do the talking," is exactly what the three band members in Klaatu had in mind. As John Woloschuk told Dave Bradley in an interview for the above-mentioned web site:

> "We said all along, from day one, before we even put the first note to tape, we had always said that we wanted to remain anonymous. Not because we were trying to fool anybody; just because we wanted the music to speak for itself. And we were young, and idealistic, and we thought that was the way to go because at the time that was the beginning of the glamour-rock era when everybody was wearing outlandish clothes and makeup, and the music seemed to be taking a secondary seat to what it was ten, fifteen years prior to that."

While the band must have been flattered to be mistaken for the Beatles and the rumor did wonders for their sales at first, they repeatedly denied the rumor through their spokesman, Frank Davies. In retrospect, what may have hurt them the most, however, was their determination for a time to keep the band members names a secret. In doing so, the rumor back-lashed against the band just as readily as it had helped them, for many people not duped into believing the legend thought that the band and the record label were intentionally keeping the identity of the band members secret in order to sell albums. As Woloschuk stated in the Bradley interview, the band's "silence was misinterpreted as complicity." As they struggled to survive, the press refused to support the band, leading to the band members being listed as songwriters on their fourth album, the 1980 release, ENDANGERED SPECIES. But it was too little, too late. The legend persisted and the band had become a joke to the music critics through guilt by association and nothing more. Klaatu broke up after one final album – the Canadian-only release, MAGENTALANE – in 1981.

The band is still remembered by fans today, and the original albums have even been reissued on CD over the years. Even so, no matter how good the music was, Klaatu will always be best remembered as the band that people thought was the Beatles.

Sources: Bradley, David. "Klaatu Identities and Beatles Rumors," http://www.klaatu.org.

Bradley, David. "John Woloschuk Interview," http://www.klaatu.org, September 20, 1997.

Led Zeppelin

> 1. *The infamous "mud shark" groupie story.*
> 2. *The band was heavily involved in black magic, and all, with the exception of John Paul Jones, sold their souls to the devil in order to become famous. Troubling situations that faced everyone but Jones in the 1970s (including Bonham's death) were connected with this pact with Satan.*
> 3. Stairway to Heaven *is a satanic song that has a subliminal hidden message celebrating Satan.*

1: Groupies, the young men and women who follow bands around in order to have sex with them and then move on to other bands, have been around since the dawn of celebrity and certainly long before rock music itself was created. The only thing different after rock music came along was that the groupies came out, in a sense, and were publicly seen and heard, sometimes worshipped as much as the celebrities they were sleeping with.

The publicity about groupies began in the late 1960s and continued for some time, reaching a peak in the mid-1980s before the AIDS scare made many groupies scuttle back away from the limelight. With their emergence in the 1970s came the notorious stories about bands and their escapades with the groupies, and one of the best known was the "mud shark" story dealing with Led Zeppelin.

The story goes like this: a groupie had made her way into the inner sanctum of the band's hotel room floor after a concert during the height of their popularity in the 1970s. The groupie, doped up and willing to do anything, was thrilled to be with the band in one of their rooms. The band, bored with groupies, couldn't have cared less, and decided to use the groupie as an experiment in order to see what they could insert into the orifices of her body. A camera was nearby and the proceedings were filmed for the band's enjoyment as they proceeded to insert a variety of objects into the groupie who was either willing or, in some darker versions of the story, had been tied down to the bed by the band. The proceedings climaxed with someone pulling a mounted shark or swordfish off the wall and shoving the stuffed fish inside the woman as far as possible. In some variations of the story, the fish was actually alive, but the results were the same. After this was done, the band again became bored and moved on to other rooms on the floor, forgetting the groupie as quickly as they had become interested in experimenting with her. The groupie then stumbled out of the hotel in severe pain and a bit wiser concerning the violent tendencies of the band.

A shocking story, of course, and one of the most famous groupie stories every told. In fact, Frank Zappa used the incident as the basis of a song after hearing about it, called *Mud shark*. The problem was that some of the facts had been changed in order to make the story more interesting. The following appears to be what actually occurred, according to most accounts:

In 1968 (not mid-1970s as many versions of the story have been placed), Led Zeppelin had played a festival in Seattle, Washington, and were staying at a hotel called the

Edgewater Inn. The hotel was unique in that it was, just like the hotel's name, right on the edge of the water in Seattle. Because of this, guests could actually fish from the waterfront window of their rooms and a fish and tackle shop was located in the lobby for people to rent equipment. Because of this, it was a favorite spot for touring bands and the fishing gave the musicians something different to do besides sitting in a hotel room and watching test patterns on the television and being bored.

Richard Cole, a tour manager for the band, was sharing a room at the hotel with John Bonham. Fishing from the window of the room, the two had caught a number of small sharks from the waters below and had hung them up in the room's closet, using coat hangers as hooks. With a groupie entering the room, Cole proceeded to have his way with the woman, and while Bonham watched and Mark Stein from Vanilla Fudge (who was touring with Zeppelin at the time) filmed them. Cole took one of the sharks from the closet and inserted the nose of the fish into the willing girl on the bed. The girl was unhurt, according to Cole, and she left soon after.

That's the whole story. Some have suggested in later years that Cole was never a good source for accuracy about the band, but the story seems to match that told by others about the event. Besides Bonham, who just watched and did not participate, no other members of the band were involved in the "mud shark" incident (although some seem to recall Plant and Page entering briefly to see what was going on, only to become bored and move on quickly). While there remain rumors as to whether the fish was dead or alive at the time of the insertion, we can assume, since Cole clearly points out that the fish had been hanging up in the closet for some time, that it was dead. Ultimately, however, the story grew into an urban legend because fans wanted to put the band at the center of the action. It was also used as a cautionary tale directed at young girls to show that the life of a groupie was dangerous, both physically and mentally (which explains the more horror-oriented versions of the tale that have the girl needing medical attention or in one variation, or even dying). These variations of the tale are not true at all.

Source: Davis, Stephen. HAMMER OF THE GODS. Berkley Boulevard Books, New York. 1985. Pages 79-80.

2: Much of the speculation about the band being Satanic, involved in black magic, or having sold their souls to Satan has to do with Jimmy Page's publicly known fascination with the world of black magic. In particular, Page was known for his study of the life of Aleister Crowley, famous (or rather, infamous) practitioner of black magic (some would say con man). Because of Page's interest, it was assumed by some that the band itself had to be involved in such practices, and that their success rested entirely on their deal with the devil and not at all with their popular music and performance abilities.

The rumor went on to suggest that certain horrible accidents and problems that faced the band members in the 1970s were simply repayment by Satan for their success. The retribution came, as the rumor went, through such things as physical injuries and ultimately to the death of Jon Bonham in September 1980. Jones, however, was supposedly not linked to any horrible events because he supposedly never sold his soul as the others did.

This rumor, of course, has no basis in reality. Although Page did have a keen interest in the study of black magic, he was also up-front about his lack of interest in Satanism and was not a Satanist. None of the others really showed much interest in any such nonsense either; and the implication that terribly tragic events in the band members' lives were somehow their own faults and inevitable was a despicable element of the rumor. Still, many religious fanatics had rambled on about the evils of Led Zeppelin for years and these "incidents" made them gleeful. It satisfied some people to believe that these "Satan worshippers" (as the fanatics believed the band to be) had received their comeuppance, making the tragic events even worse in a way.

3: The idea of "backmasking" on *Stairway to Heaven* has been around for years and had typically been used as one of the main examples of "Satanic" backmasking by religious fanatics. The message is supposed to appear, cleverly enough, during the passage in

the song where Robert Plant sings, " . . . because you know sometimes words have two meaning." This is supposedly a clue to listeners that there really is a second message hidden underneath for them to hear. Of course, if this was true, it would negate the whole purpose of backmasking – to place subliminal messages backwards in the music so that the subconscious mind will pick them up and the listener will not be any wiser. To give everyone a clue that says, "hey, we have a secret message here," is hardly the way "backmasking" is supposed to work.

The message that is supposedly found, once the song is played backwards is the following:"There's no escaping it . . . Here's to my sweet Satan. No other made a path, for it makes me sad, whose power is Satan." Others have suggested that the album continues with at least two more backward messages:"There was a little child born naked . . . now I am Satan," and "I will sing because I live with Satan."

The main problem with "backmasking" is that you not only have to be looking for the messages in order to find them, but also know ahead of time in many cases what was supposedly said in order to distinguish the message from the gibberish heard. For some, they will swear that the messages supposedly found are clear and distinctive; for others, it will always sound like gibberish. In other words, we hear what we want to hear, whether it's really there or not.

The band's reaction to the "suppressed messages" on a song that is so immense in symbolism forward that no one knows exactly what it means was surprise, and the artists and the band's label both expressed repeatedly that the charges were false.

Simply put, Led Zeppelin never recorded backward messages on their albums. Of course, any response to the accusation is automatically suspect by the religious fanatics, as they just know that the band would lie if there was "backmasking" on the album. So, it's a losing battle, and one that has frustrated the band over the years, as Plant said himself in an interview with ROLLING STONE from the early 1990s:

> "I mean, who on earth would have ever thought of doing that in the first place? You've got to have a lot of time on your hands to even consider that people would do that. Especially with *Stairway To Heaven*. I mean, we were so proud of that thing, and its intentions are so positive . . . I found it foul, the whole idea . . . but it's very American. Nowhere else in the world has anybody ever considered it, or been concerned or bothered at all about that. I figure if backward masking really worked, every album in the store would have 'Buy this album!' hidden on it."

Source: Peters, Dan and Steve. WHY KNOCK ROCK? Bethany House, Minneapolis. 1984. Pages 172-173.

Sarah MacLachlan

> 1. *MacLachlan's song* Possession *was about a true incident in MacLachlan's life when a fan began to stalk her. The fan eventually sued MacLachlan over the song, and when he lost the case committed suicide.*
>
> 2. *MacLachlan wrote the song* Building a Mystery *about Agent Fox Mulder, a character on the popular television series, X-FILES.*

I: The song is about stalking and written from the stalker's point of view. Sarah has stated in several interviews that she wrote the song after an incident with a fanatical fan. The story from there is a bit twisted, however, as a fan from Ottawa, Canada presumed that the song was written about him. The fan, Uwe Vandrei, believed that MacLachlan had taken several phrases out of his past letters to her and used them not only in *Possession*, but several other songs as well. After trying to contact MacLachlan directly about the song with little result, Vandrei sued MacLachlan's management to help clarify that he was not the stalker of said song. Meanwhile, MacLachlan insisted that the song was not about him but another man. In fact, the song was written about a different fan that had gotten so obsessive that MacLachlan had to obtain a restraining order. It was at that time that she wrote *Possession*. Ironically, it sparked a lawsuit from another obsessed fan who thought he was being labeled unfairly through the song. In September 1994, an intent of settlement was evidently reached between Vandrei's and MacLachlan's lawyers, but Vandrei was discovered dead from carbon monoxide poisoning soon after and the case was dropped by his family after that. Unlike the legend told, no restraining order was ever issued against Vandrei, the case was not dropped before his death, and evidence points to another man as having been the basis of the song all along. In a way, Vandrei did get what he wanted – he wanted some type of association with MacLachlan, and in the end he got exactly that distinction.

2: According to MacLachlan herself during an appearance on VH1 (a cable music channel connected with MTV), the song is about how people hide their true selves behind "masks" in order to present what they wished they were like to the world. She also stated the same when asked in an interview with the magazine ROCKET in 1997. It has nothing at all to do with the X-FILES television series.

Sources: MacLachlan, Sarah. VH1 Storytellers. July 1999.
         "Sarah MacLachlan," Rocket. No. 256, July 1997.

Madonna

> *Madonna played Tabitha on the television series, BEWITCHED.*

The main point of this legend is to take a child actor and suggest that they grew up to become a famous musician. This kind of rumor has been associated with artists such as Alice Cooper, Billy Corgan (of Smashing Pumpkins), and Marilyn Manson over the years, so Madonna is no exception.

The part of Tabitha on BEWITCHED was played by Erin Murphy. Madonna, a good six years older than Erin Murphy, would have been too old to play the part on BEWITCHED, even if she had been a child actor at the time. Nor did Madonna play Tabitha in the short-lived sequel series, TABITHA. That series ran from 1977-1978 and featured Lisa Hartman in the role. Madonna first appeared in films in 1984.

Marilyn Manson

> *1. Manson took part in a "gross-out" contest with Ozzy Osbourne backstage at a concert.*
> *2. Manson kills puppy dogs on stage during his show.*
> *3. While a teenager, Manson joined a Christian youth group, but was so shunned by the other kids that he denounced Christianity and became Marilyn Manson as a way to get back at the kids who picked on him.*
> *4. When Manson was a kid, he played Paul Pfeiffer on the television series THE WONDER YEARS.*
> *5. Manson had ribs surgically removed so that he could fellate himself as part of his ongoing quest for the next perversion.*

1: See the entry for Alice Cooper.

2: See the entry for Alice Cooper.

3: Here's how the legend goes, as told in one variation or another over the years: Brian Warner was a teenager who moved to a new town with his family and joined a youth group at a local church. Shy and awkward, Warner had problems mixing in with the kids already established in the group and the presiding pastor for the group did little to encourage his participation.

After an incident at an amusement park, where none of the kids in the group wanted to be paired with him, Warner left the group and never returned. No one thought much about it until years later when the pastor, who had become the head of a seminary by that time, heard from one of the former participants in the group. The person asked the pastor if he remembered a kid called Brian Warner from the youth group so many years before. The pastor vaguely recalled the name, but couldn't really place the face. The person then informed the pastor that Warner had become the "evil, satanic" pop star, Marilyn Manson.

The purpose behind the story can have been interpreted in a couple of ways by tellers of the legend. The first is that Warner was just a "mama's boy" who became this "evil, horrible, anti-Christian" character on stage merely because he wasn't picked by anyone in the Christian youth group so many years before. So, the point of all his musical work is simple – petty revenge over a piddling little event in his youth – making Manson out to be a brat, essentially.

The other and more commonly proposed purpose of the story is to teach people involved in church organizations to reach out to all members of the group or else some may fall by the wayside. In essence, if only the pastor and the kids had reached out to Brian Warner, he wouldn't be the "evil, horrible, anti-Christian" character that he is today. So, a lesson had been learned, although much too late to save Warner's soul from the fires of Hell (or so those who tell the story in this fashion would like to believe).

The problem with the story is that it never occurred. Warner was born and raised in Canton, Ohio, where he went to a Christian school, Heritage Christian School, until the 10th grade. After that, he went to a public high school, Glen Oak, until he graduated in 1987. From all reports, Brian was never impressed by Christian school, found it oppressive and was more than happy to leave it behind him when he could. There are also no reports that his family was religious. Reports state that the Christian school was chosen for Brian specifically because it was considered a good school in Canton and not for any religious reasons.

The story also suffers from "collective amnesia," as there are no published reports of Warner ever attending a Christian youth group while going to church. Nor are the names of the pastor, the church, or even the city ever mentioned (or they're changed with every new telling of the story). No one has ever come forward as remembering Warner in their youth group and Manson himself has never mentioned the story in any interviews or in his autobiography.

Therefore, while it's an interesting story, it's nothing more than a story told for the entertainment of the teller and listener, and nothing more.

Source: Mikkelson, Barbara and David P. "Greener Pastors," Urban Legends Reference Pages. June 30, 2000.
www.snopes.com/music/artists/marilyn3.htm

4: Another variation of an old Alice Cooper urban legend that was updated for Manson. As discussed in the Alice Cooper entries in this book, Cooper himself circulated a rumor that he had played Eddie Haskell on the comedy series LEAVE IT TO BEAVER (a situation-comedy that, oddly enough, dealt with the adventures of a young boy growing up in the 1960s). Manson, of course, would have been too young to be Eddie Haskell, so another series had to be found in order for the urban legend to work. THE WONDER YEARS worked perfectly in this regard; and to have the young actor who played the geeky friend to the main character turn out to be this heavily promoted "scary monster" of the 1990s music scene was too good to pass up.

The story may sound great, but there is no truth to it. Paul Pfeiffer was played by Josh Saviano, who has moved away from acting and is pursuing a career in law. Manson also did not play Kevin Owens on the situation-comedy MR. BELVEDERE. That part was played by Rob Stone. Marilyn Manson's real name, as mentioned in the above entry, is Brian Warner, and he was born and raised in Canton, Ohio. He never performed on television while growing up.

Source: Roeper, Richard. URBAN LEGENDS. New Page Books, New Jersey. 2001.
Pages 253-254.

5: Rumors have abounded for years about Manson doing horribly perverted things to himself and others on and off stage. In many cases, these rumors were merely variations of earlier legends told about other artists. The killing of small animals on stage (or throwing kittens out to the audience and refusing to continue the show until the audience members have killed the animals) had been around for years and commonly associated with such artists as Ozzy Osbourne and Alice Cooper. In fact, Manson seemed to have taken on the mantle of many of the Alice Cooper stories from over the years, as can be seen in this book. If Manson is frustrated that he has merely be inserted into old stories the predate him, he can at least be comforted that the "Ribs" urban legend is one that he can claim as all his own.

The urban legend goes that Manson wanted to be able to perform oral self-gratification, and decided that surgery to remove a couple of ribs would be the only way to obtain his objective. While this certainly brings to mind rather humorous ideas of how the interview with the proposed surgeon would be conducted, the story is patently false. Manson never had such surgery done, and as seen previously in a review of the rumor that Cher had such surgery done in order to make her waist look slimmer, such surgery is not done nor has it ever been done for cosmetic reasons.

The rumor about Manson obviously came about due to the public image of the man as being like his stage character, and thus a perverted, twisted soul who would have such surgery done because no one would dare want to be around him. Knowing Manson's preoccupation with dating a variety of women, one would think that he would not have to worry about sexual gratification, however. Manson is also physically quite thin, which no doubt led credence to the rumor when heard. Still, in the end, the rumor was simply that, and just another element that made Manson appear even more freakish to the public.

Finally, stories that Manson performed sex with his brother and/or farm animals on stage, had breast implants, or took LSD and pulled out his own eyeball with a fork (among other rumors even more obscene than this) are merely stories added by fans and detractors to make Manson appear demented and perverted.

Source: Roeper, Richard. URBAN LEGENDS. New Page Books, New Jersey. 2001. Pages 253-254.

Meat Loaf

> 1. *Meat Loaf got his nickname from friends in high school after he allowed them to run over his head with a car.*
> 2. *A millionaire who loved listening to Meat Loaf's BAT OUT OF HELL album found out that the sole family member and beneficiary of his will could not stand the album and berated it every time the rich man played it. When the millionaire died, the family member found out that the millionaire had changed his will so that the beneficiary would only receive his monthly inheritance check as long as he listened to BAT OUT OF HELL in it's entirely every day for the rest of his life.*

1: Does this legend even seem likely? Still, we can't blame people for having a tendency to believe this story, since the man who told it was Meat Loaf himself. In fact, the former Marvin Aday had told many different variations of how he got his famous name, including the following:

The above variation, where Aday bet he could have a Volkswagen run over his head. When he won the bet, a classmate told him that he was "as dumb as a hunk of meat loaf."
That he stepped on the foot of his football coach and the coach told him to "get off my football team, you big hunk of meat loaf."
Kids at school called him that just due to his general attitude.

However, in his autobiography, TO HELL AND BACK, Meat Loaf finally admitted that he actually got the nickname from his father when growing up. As he states in the book, his father was calling him that "almost from the time my mother brought me home." From there, the name would follow him throughout his schooling and into his stage and musical career.

And as to the Volkswagen running over his head? Meat Loaf states that the story is true as well.

Source: Loaf, Meat and Dalton, David. TO HELL AND BACK. Regan Books, New York. 1999. Page 35.

2: This one is obviously a joke, a rock and roll variation of Dorian Gray and other urban legends about preposterous stipulations in wills. Although BAT OUT OF HELL is a great album to many fans, it was obviously used in this situation as a "painful" listening event that the beneficiary would have to suffer through forever as ironic punishment for not liking it when the millionaire was alive. Of course, like many urban legends, once someone thinks about the story for a bit, it is be seen clearly that such a stipulation would never hold up. After all, as Richard Roeper asked in his book, URBAN LEGENDS, "who was supposed to monitor the beneficiary's behavior every day to make sure that he listened to the album? For the monitor's sake, I hope he loves Meat Loaf."

Source: Roeper, Richard. URBAN LEGENDS. New Page Books, New Jersey. 2001. Page 181.

The Monkees

> *1. Charles Manson tried out for the Monkees.*
> *2. Jimi Hendrix was kicked off the 1967 Monkees tour after the Daughters of the American Revolutions complained about his "lewd" concert performances.*
> *3. The Monkees never played their own instruments, nor did they know how to play musical instruments. All the music was done by studio musicians.*

1: In 1965, producers Bob Schneider and Bert Rafelson decided to produce a new television series that was an American variation of the Beatles and their first two movies (A HARD DAY'S NIGHT and HELP!). They envisioned a weekly series that would include great songs and madcap comedy, with fast editing and pacing. After looking at a few prospective young men to play the foursome who would make up the group on the show, the duo decided that they wanted to get young guys who were talented and mostly unknown for the roles.

It was decided that the best way to do this was to hold open auditions for the roles. With every young man in Hollywood hearing about the auditions, many later-to-be-famous faces made their way to the studio to try out for THE MONKEES television series. Among them were Paul Williams, Tommy Boyce and Bobby Hart (who were featured in the original pilot and would go on to write music for the series), and even Stephen Stills (who convinced his friend Peter Tork to try out for the series as well). One of the most infamous names on the list was Charles Manson, who would later become nationally known as the leader of a cult that was involved with the Sharon Tate / Helter Skelter murders and who thought the Beatles were sending him hidden messages through their songs.

Manson would be known for spending part of the late 1960s trying to infiltrate his way into the music business – both by writing music and by living in the home of Beach Boy drummer Dennis Wilson – and it was this generally known information that made the story about Manson trying out for the Monkees somewhat believable. Having people who were at the auditions state that they were sure Manson was there also led to the conclusion that the rumor was true.

For years the story was repeated by everyone, including members of the band (in particular Micky Dolenz), and was referred to in some of the late 1980s biographies about the band. However, such a story does not stand up to the facts.

In 1965, Manson was serving time in the United States Penitentiary, located on McNeil Island, Washington, for violating his probation. He would not be released from prison until 1967, making it impossible for him to have tried out for THE MONKEES. He also would have been too old for the role, being 30 at the time of the auditions and with the producers looking for guys between the ages of 17 through 21.

Sources: Baker, Glenn A. MONKEEMANIA. St. Martin's Press, New York. 1987. Pages 6-9.
Bugliosi, Vincent. HELTER SKELTER. W.W. Norton, New York. 1974. Pages 136-157.
Mikkelson, Barbara and David P. "The Music Manson," Urban Legends Reference Pages. September 25, 1995.
http://www.snopes.com/radiotv.tv.monkees.htm

2: See the entry for Jimi Hendrix for more details.

3: One of the most common misconceptions of THE MONKEES is that the foursome not only did not play their own music on their albums, but never even knew how to play their own instruments. Instead, all they did was sing, while studio musicians play all the songs. The truth of the matter was a little more complicated than what the legend would lead one to believe.

When the show was put together, it was decided that the foursome hired should have some type of musical background so that they could at least sing in the show if not do more than that. As it turned out, all four men hired were musicians in some sense of the word, with some having worked as composers of music as well as musicians. The two strongest musicians of the group were Michael Nesmith, a guitarist from Texas who has already done some studio work under the name Michael Blessings, and Peter Tork, who had worked in Greenwich Village as a folk musician before heading out to California to catch the musical scene out there. The other two members of the Monkees had also come from some type of musical background – Micky Dolenz had sung and played guitar in the studio before being hired for the show, and had also been a child actor in the series CIRCUS BOY; while Davy Jones had appeared in the theater, including Broadway, in many musical roles.

So there was certainly enough talent for the four to be able to play music. The problem was that there wasn't enough time for them to learn how to play together when the series was on the fast track to being filmed. Because music had to be supplied as the show was being rehearsed and filmed, the Monkees were told to just let the producer in charge of the music, Don Kirschner, handle the recording of the music. At first, that was fine with everyone involved.

That is, it was fine until the first song from the series, *Last Train to Clarksville*, became a massive hit. When both Tork and Nesmith began to receive congratulations on their musicianship in the song, both felt that they had become phonies. They also felt that they should at least be allowed to do some of the music in the studio since they all knew how to at play something. Nesmith was also wanting to have some of his own material used in the series and was frustrated that Kirschner treated the four more as an irritation than as musicians.

While neither Dolenz nor Jones was greatly frustrated by the situation, they were young and headstrong. With a push from Tork and Nesmith, Dolenz and Jones joined the others to present a united front to the producers of the series that they should be given the opportunity to record their own material and perhaps even play their own instruments for the songs on the show and albums. Eventually, it was agreed that they could do so. The crest of their work as an actual band in the studio came with the album HEADQUARTERS. The album was a success and the system of recording as a band continued with their next album, PISCES, AQUARIUS, CAPRICORN AND JONES LTD. After that, however, the band aspect of the group started falling apart. They continued to record and even toured as a band in 1967 and 1968, but with the demise of the series in 1968 the reason for the group being together became less and less apparent. By 1968, Tork had left and Nesmith followed in March 1970 after attempting to continue as a trio with Dolenz and Jones. Dolenz and Jones would attempt one more album after Nesmith left, but it was too late for the Monkees to continue as a duo and the group ended.

Eventually, Nesmith would have a major hit of his own with *Joanne*, record several albums, and become a major innovator in video productions and music videos. Tork would go back to playing small clubs as a musician of many talents. Dolenz would go on to become a television director, while Jones continued to work in television and on the stage. In 1986, a revival of the television series on MTV led to a concert tour reunion of Tork, Dolenz, and Jones (with Nesmith making a token appearance at one of the last shows of the tour). All showed that they could still play their instruments (although backed up with a large band as well), and occasional tours since then, as well as a 1996 album called JUST US, showed that the foursome were always more than just actors who couldn't play their own instruments.

Sources: Baker, Glenn A. MONKEEMANIA. St. Martin's Press, New York. 1986.
Lefcowitz, Eric. THE MONKEES TALE. Last Gasp's, San Francisco. 1985.

Alanis Morrisette

> 1. *Morrisette's song* You Oughta Know *is about her relationship with actor / comedian Dave Coulier.*
> 2. *Morrisette once had to be rushed to the hospital to have her stomach pumped of semen after a party with a group of football players.*

1: In 1995, Alanis Morrisette's third album, JAGGED LITTLE PILL, was released and became the linchpin to her makeover from popish teenage singer to "hard-edged" alternative singer. Whether she succeeded in doing that is up to listeners, but there is no argument that the album was a huge success for her.

The album, as all of Morrisette's albums since, was written from a personal viewpoint of an "angry young woman," digging deep into personal problems and crises. Because of this, *You Oughta Know* was looked upon as being a personal message to a former lover in Morrisette's past. And Morrisette has stated that the song was directed at someone in particular.

The question remained, who? For a time, Morrisette was involved with comedian Dave Coulier, who was a regular on the popular ABC-network sitcom, FULL HOUSE. The two began dating in 1992 and had a serious relationship growing before breaking up and moving on. To confuse matters further, Coulier himself was unable to state definitively whether he believed the song was about him. This can be seen clearly when asked about the question on his web site (http://www.cutitout.net/html/questions.html):

"I've been asked that question a million times and I still have the same answer – 'No. Yes. Maybe. I don't know.' I apologize in advance, but I'd like to keep my personal life somewhat private"

One factor to keep in mind, however, is that Alanis has made mention in interviews that the relationship discussed in the song occurred before she started dating Coulier. Also, Coulier went on to explain on his web site that he and Alanis have remained friends, which would seem to be impossible considering the vicious, negative tone Morrisette uses in the song. As to who the mystery person is, Morrisette has also gone on record stating that she would never tell.

Source: Dave Coulier, home web site,
           http://www.cutitout.net/html/questions.html

2:   See "Stomach Pump" Entry for more details.

Stevie Nicks

Stevie is a witch.

This rumor has followed Stevie Nicks around ever since she first obtained national attention in the mid-1970s with the band Fleetwood Mac. Although typically articulate and down-to-earth in interviews, Stevie's songwriting and personal appearances are what led to people trying to pigeonhole Nicks into being either a) a witch, or b) a flake who thinks she's a witch.

Stevie's style of dress has always suggested a cross between a ballerina and an earth-mother, a Bohemian look with leather and lace (no pun intended) that was unique, sleek,

feminine, and – in an odd way – somewhat mystical. It seems to call back to an earlier age, while still being modern.

Meanwhile, Stevie's songwriting and in particular her lyrics tend towards mystical references and magical places. Her voice had a breathy, yet solid, undertone that seems to sweep the listener along through the melodic tones of her songs.

These elements form an image of Stevie Nicks that to some suggested an other-worldly creature who could leave them

Alanis Morrisette

spellbound with her songs. The next step in suggesting that she's a witch is pretty simple. To others, especially her critics, her music has been considered simplistic and vapid, like that of a teenage girl writing about unicorns and putting hearts to dot the "I's" in her letters. The suggestion that she was a witch came from these people as a form of abuse – that Steve thought she actually was a witch as suggested by her music and therefore was really a nut. Therefore, the rumor was used in the case of these people as a means to discredit Stevie's work.

While Stevie has stated in interviews that she believes there are things in life that can be seen as magical and make life wondrous, she is by no means a witch and has never been a witch. That ends the rumor right there.

Night Ranger

> *Night Ranger's hit* Sister Christian *is about a drug-dealing nun;* Sister Christian *is about a girl who gets gang-raped.*

One of the biggest hits for this band of the 1980s was *Sister Christian*. The only problem was that some listeners had no idea what the song was about. Because the name "Sister Christian" conjures up a religious element, some thought the song was about a nun. Because kids listening to it wanted it to have a rebellious streak, the story grew that the song was about a nun who sold drugs ("what's your price for flight?").

A more disturbing rumor stated that the song was about a young, wild girl who ends up being in the wrong place at the wrong time and is gang-raped. Looking at the lyrics, one has to wonder where such a thought got into people's heads.

While the song is clearly about a young girl going out, it is not about something terrible happening to or because of "Sister Christian." The song was written by drummer and lead vocalist Kelly Keaggy about his sister. It is essentially an ode a young girl coming of age and the fear of her innocence (not necessarily in a physical way) being lost too soon. The original title was "Sister Christy," but the band thought Keaggy was saying "christian" instead of "Christy," and believed that to be a better name to use.

At no time in the lyrics are rape, drugs or nuns mentioned. Any such labeling is in the mind of the listener and nothing more.

Nirvana

> *Kurt Cobain did not commit suicide, he was murdered.*

Some called it "grunge"; some called it a backlash against the "Glitter" Metal that was all the rage in the late 1980s; some called it "alternative"; some called it the new force in rock music; some called it crap. How ever it was interpreted, a new style of music was gaining popularity in the early 1990s. With the thrashing guitar beat of the 1980s' metal

scene mixed with the rebellious edge, driving drum beat, and anti-everything lyrics of the 1970s punk scene, this music was popular with the teenagers growing up in the early 1990s.

And Nirvana was at the forefront of the wave. Fronted by guitarist / vocalist Kurt Cobain, the band really broke through in 1991, with the release of their album NEVERMIND, on a national scale. They became one of the biggest bands of the 1990s and have usually been looked upon as being certainly one of the most influential of bands of that decade.

From all evidence, Cobain was torn up about the success of the band. From many reports it was clear that he was never the happiest of guys in the first place, and the success that would have propelled most people into feeling a sense of accomplishment, merely dragged Cobain into despair, wondering why he didn't feel any better about himself and if he was just a fraud.

On April 5, 1994, with his wife Courtney Love out of town to work on her next album with her band, Hole, Cobain was at their home in Seattle, Washington. Leaving the house and entering the apartment above their garage, Cobain left a suicide note, lay down on the floor, put a shotgun to his head, and pulled the trigger. He had both heroin and Valium in his system at the time of his death.

His body was finally found three days later by an electrician working on the house. Neither the Seattle police nor a private detective hired by Love had found him before that day, but Love had suspected something had occurred as she had received a phone call from Cobain suggesting that he might try committing suicide. It had become something that he had talked about and many believed he had attempted just that in Rome in early March 1994. Reports that guns were confiscated from their home by the police at Love's insistence went on to suggest that Love was in fear of Cobain attempting suicide.

Within days people were suggesting that Love had mentally and physically abused Cobain to the point of suicide. Angry fans that had never warmed to Love's presence with Cobain went even further, suggesting that Love had hired someone to kill Cobain.

Granted, Love was not the picture of the perfect widow either, but it was obvious with hindsight that she was distraught and conflicted about Cobain's death – knowing that it was probably inevitable; wondering if anything different could have been done to prevent it; angry that he was never convinced people loved him; and angry at herself for allowing it to happen. Nevertheless, her tape recorded reading of Cobain's suicide note, punctuated with her rambling responses in vain, further angered some fans, and the rumors of Love being a vicious gold-digger who helped kill Cobain somehow made them feel better about the whole incident. It didn't matter that it was Cobain's wife trying to appease a group of fans, who didn't know the man personally, by giving them his last message, all they saw was someone trying to "ruin the moment." Their moment.

Several "investigations" have been made into Cobain's death, all trying to prove that somehow Love had wanted Cobain dead for a variety of nonsensical reasons, with the "research" done being as nonsensical and ignorant as the legend. Descriptions of martial problems supposedly sent a red flag up for the theorists, totally negating the fact that many fans had known for some time that the Love and Cobain had a sometimes stormy relationship. It was also known that Cobain had problems with severe depression and suicidal tendencies, which Love had tried to prevent less than a month before, although the theorists would love for fans and others to forget about Cobain's past and instead try to view him only as a happy, positive person who would never become suicidal. There have also been suggestions that Cobain had too high of a dosage of drugs running through his system for him to have pulled the trigger and/or that he would have picked a drug overdose or the gun but not both. However, it is just as likely that the drugs either helped him decide to end his life, or that he took the drugs knowing full-well what he was about to do and wanted to be in a "heightened" state before. As to "witnesses" that were supposedly hired by Love to kill Cobain, none have ever come forward to the police (although they seem to be able to find fans to tell their stories to them all the time, oddly enough).

None of the "evidence" produced has proved anything that has stood up to any kind of test. Even the motivation given for Love to have murdered, or hired someone to murder, Cobain made little sense; based predominately on the idea that Cobain was somehow holding up her career, which was clearly not the case.

There has never been any evidence beyond what was found that day – a man who killed himself in order to end the pain and confusion within him. He wanted it to end without hurting anyone, yet in doing it the way he did, he created the environment for grief, suspicion, and false stories to be told. Moreso, he became an icon so huge that even less than ten years after his death more people know how he died than can name any of the music that he created in life.

It was a sad conclusion to his life, and the way it was twisted after his death made it even sadder.

Sources: Editors of Rolling Stone. COBAIN. Little, Brown and Company, Boston. 1994.
Herman, Gary. ROCK 'N' ROLL BABYLON. Plexus, London. 2002. Pages 205-207.
Thompson, Dave. BETTER TO BURN OUT. Thunder's Mouth Press, New York. 1999. Pages 183-190.

Notorious B.I.G.

> *Notorious B.I.G. was involved in the cover-up involving the murder of Tupac Shakur. He ended up being murdered a few months later, ironically enough, in another cover-up involving the police.*

See the entry for "Shakur, Tupac" for more details.

Ted Nugent

> 1. *Ted Nugent is the son of the actor who played Mr. Greenjeans on the children's television series, CAPTAIN KANGAROO.*
> 2. *Ted Nugent wrote a humorous, conservative essay called "I am a Bad American."*

1: This legend, typically told of Frank Zappa (see the entry for Frank Zappa for more details) seems, oddly, to also have been connected with Nugent.

2: The essay, "I am a Bad American," has gone around the Internet frequently since it first appeared under the title, "I am a Bad Republican" in a message forum on a conservative web site called http://www.freerepublic.com. The essay is a series of statements that are supposed to be the angry voice of a disgruntled American. Of course, the irony of the piece is that all the statements are supposed to be things that are considered politically incorrect, yet readers are bound to find at least a few that they agree with. Therefore, everyone is supposedly a "bad American," which means that they're really normal Americans.

Which just goes to show that sometimes explaining a joke really messes up the joke.

This essay was originally seen in September 2000 and subsequently started being sent around via email to friends and family across the U.S. and around the world. At the time, the title was changed to "I am a Bad American" and to help get people to read it, the author's name was changed from that of an alias on a message forum to a real person – typically someone that the emailer liked. This led to the piece being attributed to such diverse individuals as George Carlin, Rush Limbaugh, Denis Leary and Ted Nugent. As time went by, some of the perceived celebrities have gone on record denying their involvement with the essay (some even quite strongly). Nugent, on the forum of his web site, also denied his involvement with the essay, although he agreed with it (of course, as stated, it is hard not to find something in the essay that one would agree with).

Since 2000, the essay has continued to reappear in people's email boxes, usually with another line or two added to keep it current. As it stands, the essay is now so long and contradictory that it no longer makes much sense as a whole. Nevertheless, it will probably continue to make the rounds for years to come.

Ohio Players

> *In their 1975 hit song,* Love Rollercoaster, *there is a high-pitched scream. That scream was from a woman who was killed in the studio in order to get the desired scream effect for the song.*

Another urban legend that would seem to scream out (pun intended) that there is no way it is true. Still, many people to this day believe the story about the woman who dies as she screams on the Ohio Players hit single. The only difference is which of the many variations of the story one believes.

The most sinister version of the story is one that people probably hear the most – that the band actually killed the woman in the studio in order to get the scream. Of course, such a version is automatically suspect by the resounding illogic of the story: why would a group of people kill someone in order to implicate themselves by putting the murder victim's death rattle on a song? And more importantly, on a song that they hoped to be a massive hit?

One way around the improbability of this story is by adding more to the mix. In an extension of this story, the model on the cover of the Ohio Players' album, Honey, comes into play. The model appearing on the cover of the album is shown naked atop a piece of fiberglass, with honey dripping on her body. This kind of pose was typical of all of the Ohio Players' albums, but that didn't get in the way of a good urban legend. According to the legend, the honey on her body fused with the fiberglass and when she tried to stand up, she torn away several layers of skin. Becoming hysterical after the incident, the model eventually cracked completely and stormed into the recording studio of the band as they were recording (you've guessed it) *Love Rollercoaster*. Pulling out a gun and threatening to kill them all for the honey incident, the band was saved by their manager who supposedly stabbed her with a knife he luckily happened to have in his hands at the time. As she died from the knife wound, she cried out and that was the scream heard on the album. Unfortunately, while such an elaborate retelling adds detail to the story, it does nothing to correct the problems that the earlier version had. It still means that the band watched someone be murdered in the studio, yet there was no police investigation or press coverage of the event.

The next step in logic would be that the band got the recording of the scream from another source and did not know that the scream belonged to a woman being murdered at the time of the recording. When they found out, they were appalled, but the album had already been released and the single was already climbing the charts, so there was no way to stop what had already been put in motion. However, according to this version of the legend, because of the situation, the band refused to perform the song in public in reverence of the dead woman.

Again, the story still lacks much plausibility. If the recording really was of a woman dying, why didn't the band do anything to stop the album from being released or stop the sales of the album? Also, it would seem that someone would have asked where the recording came from and verified who the singer (okay, screamer) was. After all, there are contractual and union rules about such things to consider. One variation of this story (as told by Richard Roeper in his book, Urban Legends) is that the recording was made of a woman as she fell off the Blue Streak rollercoaster ride at the Cedar Point Amusement Park in upstate Ohio. While this certainly does tie in with the band being the Ohio Players, it also means that someone was actually in the seat next to or behind the woman on the coaster itself as she fell to her death with a recorder. Again, another implausible variation.

Probably the last well-known variation of the story is that the band actually recorded the song while the murder of a woman took place in a separate room. This way, the band had no previous knowledge of the murder, but "fortunately" found the scream when mixing the album and decided to keep the scream because it fit the song so well.

As it turned out the scream was actually recorded in the studio by a vocalist hired specifically for the scream in the song. It was not an accident and the whole point was to give the song a feel of being on a real rollercoaster, with the screams of the delighted travelers going along for the ride.

Source: Roeper, Richard. URBAN LEGENDS. New Page Books, New Jersey. 2001.
          Pages 171-173.

Ozzy Osbourne

1. Ozzy is satanic, a practice he picked up while in Black Sabbath.
2. Ozzy took part in a "gross-out" contest with Marilyn Manson backstage at a concert.
3. Ozzy bit the head off a bat during a concert.
4. Ozzy bit the head off a dove during a promotional appearance, driven to do so by his manager and soon-to-be wife, Sharon.
5. Ozzy kills animals on stage during his live shows and throws the pieces out into the audience.
6. Ozzy urinated on the Alamo while wearing a dress and threatened to urinate on the steps of the White House.
7. Ozzy's song Suicide Solution *has backward-masking on it that led to a teenager commit suicide.*

1: See the entry for Satanic Music for more details.

2: See the entry for Alice Cooper for more details.

3: Ozzy did bite the head off a bat during a concert, although he insists to this day that he did not realize it was a real bat at the time.

The incident occurred during a January 20, 1982 concert in Des Moines, Iowa. The tour was for Ozzy's DIARY OF A MADMAN album and the tour had been filled with a variety of mishaps (ultimately leading to lead guitarist Randy Rhoads' accidental death in March of that year). During this tour and the one before, Ozzy had done a stunt on stage where he would throw raw meat out into the audience. In turn, the audience started throwing things back at the stage. At this particular show, someone threw a bat on stage. It's not known now whether the bat was alive or dead, but for a person to be able to throw a bat on stage, one would have to assume that it was dead. Either way, under the lights and chaotic circumstances of a concert experience, Ozzy believed the bat to be a toy.

Thinking it was a toy, Ozzy picked up the bat, stuck it into his mouth and bit the head off. It was then, of course, that everyone realized it was real. Unfortunately, it was too late. Ozzy would end up having to get a series of rabies shots and the incident would become the most famous story of his career – to the point were it has become an annoying topic for Ozzy to discuss; he even commented during the MTV reality series THE OSBOURNES that he wishes he'll never see another bat in his life.

Source: Crawford, Sue. OZZY UNAUTHORIZED. Michael O'Mara Books Limited, London. 2002. Page 89.

4: The bat incident (see the above entry) would suggest that Ozzy either wasn't paying attention to what he was doing, or so out of it that he didn't think about what he was doing until after the incident was already over. For these reasons, many try to find some excuse for his behavior and see it as a legitimate mistake. In other words, fans who know what happened just shake their heads in disbelief and then think nothing more of it. People who are not fans, once they know the history, do much the same.

It was an accident, biting the head off a bat. Surely no one would do it intentionally, no matter how out-of-it the person was.

So, while it's an incident that many remember, people can generally excuse the bat-beheading incident.

However, the dove-beheading is quite another matter.

In March 1981, before most people knew of Ozzy unless they were Black Sabbath fans, and certainly long before the infamous bat-biting incident discussed elsewhere. Ozzy had been invited to appear at a conference at CBS headquarters to promote his solo career and a new solo album. To help make him noticeable to the group of largely disinterested record executives and business people, it was decided that Ozzy should enter the boardroom and produce a number of live doves from his coat pockets. With photographers in the room to record the event, it would be a nice publicity stunt, and perhaps get the CBS executives to notice Ozzy a bit.

What happened next is still filled with confusion, even with photographic proof to bear witness to the event. Ozzy entered the room and did exactly as discussed, releasing a couple of birds from his coat, which subsequently flew around the room. Ozzy, a bit out of it due to having drunk half a bottle of whiskey before entering the room, then proceeded to sit down in the lap of one of the women present, pull out a third dove and bite its head off.

The camera clicked away while the people in the room gasped in horror as Ozzy coughed up a couple of feathers and laid the beheaded dove on the conference table for everyone to see. Ozzy then left the room and the event went down in history as one of the most notorious of Ozzy's career.

Still, questions remain. To the present day, many people who were present felt that Ozzy's actions were not spontaneous but pre-planned. More importantly, they figured that Sharon had talked Ozzy into doing the stunt, with Ozzy being in no state to refuse. There is also continuing disagreement as to if the dove that Ozzy bit the head off of was alive or dead before he did so. The photos give no indication that it was alive, since there is never any indication of movement from the dove. Others at the event swear that it was alive, but also stated that the panic which settled in after Ozzy's snack-attack made it evident that no one was thinking clearly at the time and the bird could have been dead.

Either way, the stunt worked. While the CBS executives were not happy with Ozzy's actions, it did give Ozzy much-needed press and helped kick start his solo career in a big way.

Source: Crawford, Sue. OZZY UNAUTHORIZED. Michael O'Mara Books Limited, London. 2002. Pages 82-85.

5: As previously mentioned, during the DIARY OF A MADMAN tour Ozzy had made it a practice to throw raw meat around on stage during the show. It was also becoming a common practice for people to throw things at Ozzy, such as rubber snakes and plastic rats (leading directly to the bat-biting incident given above). Because of this, an old urban legend attributed to Alice Cooper came back into style, now with Ozzy's name attached to it.

The urban legend was that Ozzy was killing puppies, kittens, and other animals on stage (surprisingly, baby chicks never entered the equation, as it did with Alice). The twist this time around, however, was that Ozzy would not kill the animals themselves, but instead throws them out into the audience and refuse to continue with the show until the audience had killed the puppies, kittens, etc. and threw the carcasses back on stage.

The rumor was preposterous. The chance that Ozzy could have performed such an act – even if he wanted to – without major press and public outcry would be less than zero. For him to have supposedly done such a thing every night of the tour, never have been brought up on charges of animal cruelty or inciting a riot, among others, was completely unrealistic. Still, people believed it because they wanted to believe it; fans who thought that Ozzy was truly demented after the bat-incident were not overly surprised at the thought that Ozzy could do something so crazed and disgusting; some die hard fans no doubt loved it, but people who lived in fear of Ozzy and his music used the story as a basis for even more hate towards him and his fans.

It was enough to propel some officials, particularly those with the Humane Society, to investigate Ozzy's shows. Some arenas even began having security checks, looking specifically for live animals being snuck into the show by concert-goers instead of illegal substances or weapons. Protesters marched against Ozzy outside arenas, as much for his supposed nightly abuse of animals as for the "satanic" motivations of his music. It became a case of people jumping on a bandwagon, with Ozzy being the focal-point.

Ozzy tried to restore some semblance of reality by donating $36,000 to the American Society for the Prevention of Cruelty to Animals. This did little to stop the rumors, however, and for years after Ozzy was presumed to have killed animals on stage and/or forced the audience to do it for him. That is, until Marilyn Manson arrived and took over the rumor in the mid-1990s, probably much to Ozzy's relief.

Source: Crawford, Sue. OZZY UNAUTHORIZED. Michael O'Mara Books Limited, London. 2002. Pages 93-96.

6: Ozzy did urinate on the Alamo while wearing a dress, and there is evidence that Ozzy may (emphasis on the "may") have threatened to urinate on the steps leading to the White House. Perhaps a little background may help to explain how such a thing occurred.

There's no way around the fact: the DIARY OF A MADMAN tour was a low point in Ozzy's solo career. This was not due so much to professional matters – the album had been a huge success, and the tour continued to sell out across the country – but rather to personal problems that continued to plague Ozzy. The unfortunate biting-off of the bat's head during a show occurred on this tour, while continued accusations that Ozzy was killing animals left and right during the shows continued as well. Fringe Christian organizations were also protesting strongly against Ozzy in the long-held, mistaken belief that he was a Satanist. It would be more than enough to drive most people to drink.

Which was a problem in itself, Ozzy was battling alcohol addiction, with his manager and soon-to-be-wife, Sharon, trying to keep him away from alcohol as much as she could physically manage. In a quest to help Ozzy from nipping out to have a drink in the hotel bar or going to a bar somewhere while she was not around to supervise (Sharon had already forbidden the staffs at the hotels they were staying at from providing Ozzy with drinks), Sharon a bright idea. Or rather, an idea that she thought was brilliant at the time.

To make sure Ozzy did not go anywhere, Sharon would strip him and take all of his

Ozzy Osbourne

clothes so that he couldn't leave the hotel room. She did this in San Antonio, Texas while on the tour and thought it would work. The problem was Ozzy's that thirst was too strong, and Sharon's clothes were left in the room. Soon enough, Ozzy was drinking a bottle of Courvoisier and walking around downtown San Antonio wearing Sharon's green evening dress.

Arriving in the dress and with his bottle for a photo shoot at the Alamo, Ozzy decided he needed to relieve himself. Being drunk, he thought nothing of urinating on a nearby wall until he was informed in a rather violently nasty manner that he was urinating on the Alamo itself. He was arrested for the incident and was banned from performing in the city for several years. The ban was finally lifted in 1992, but the incident was still remembered. Which is understandable – a drunken British rock star wearing a green evening dress and urinating on a national monument was not likely to be forgotten by many people.

The only variable element in the story is that Ozzy supposedly did the whole thing either as a publicity stunt or as a way to infuriate Texans and Americans as a whole. Neither variation of the story was true; it was simply a case of a drunken man doing something stupid without thinking beforehand of the consequences of his actions.

As to Ozzy's comment about urinating on the steps of the White House, this supposedly occurred in St. Louis on the same tour. Ozzy would later claim that he doesn't remember saying such a thing, but that perhaps he made the remark while drunk. With no denial, Ozzy found himself faced with even more protests, now from people protesting his supposed "anti-American" comments and actions as well as his "Satanic" values and killing of animals on stage. None of it was true, but it didn't matter and the tour ended with Ozzy relieved to be done with it all.

Source: Crawford, Sue. OZZY UNAUTHORIZED. Michael O'Mara Books Limited, London. 2002. Pages 93-96.

7: When a 19-year-old boy named John McCollum committed suicide with a .22-caliber hand gun on October 27, 1984, he had been listening to Ozzy's SPEAK OF THE DEVIL album. It was this aspect of his suicide that led to McCollum's parents to supposing that the music itself had led their son to suicide, and on January 13, 1986 (more than a year later), the McCollums filed a lawsuit against Ozzy and his record label.

The McCollums and their lawyer, Thomas Anderson, stated in their suit that they believed Ozzy's music not only led their son to suicide, but had contributed to the death of at least twenty other known teenage suicides as well. Moreso, they claimed that Ozzy's "entire attitude, and even his album covers, demonstrate a preoccupation with death." In particular, the suit suggested that Ozzy's song *Suicide Solution* advocated suicide and even had a subliminal message hidden backwards in the song (a practice commonly referred to as "backmasking") which stated: "Why try, why try / Get the gun and try it / Shoot, shoot, shoot."

The lawsuit occurred at a time when many fanatical Christian organizations were pursuing a heavy campaign against rock music in its many different forms (including rap, country and – in particular – heavy metal). The U.S. government also became publicly concerned when the PMRC senate hearings and the lawsuit against Ozzy over the song became national news.

Ozzy himself was torn up about the lawsuit, upset over the suggestion that a song he had written had driven someone to suicide. He also made clear that the song had been written about alcoholism after seeing how drinking had killed Bon Scott, the singer of AC/DC. In essence, the "solution" of the song's title was alcohol, and how alcoholism was a form of slow death. It was never intended to be read as a song about suicide as a "way out," which was the suggestion made by the McCollums and their lawyer.

After several years in court, the verdict came down in favor of Ozzy. The court felt that the McCollums had not proven that Ozzy's music was the source of their son's decision to commit suicide. The court also determined that Ozzy would have had to engage "in an immediate incitement to violence" in order to lose his first amendment right to free speech even if he had suggested suicide as an option in the song as the McCollums claimed. It was also felt that the supposed backmasking on the song was clearly "unintelligible" gibberish and not some clear message that could be understood by the listening. Finally, it was clearly pointed out that the song that supposedly was such a menace to McCollum and others was not even on the album McCollum was listening to at the time of his death (*Suicide Solution* appears on Ozzy's first solo album, BLIZZARD OF OZZ, while SPEAK OF THE DEVIL was a live album featuring only covers of Black Sabbath songs).

Ozzy was relieved, but the song is still proposed by religious fanatics today as a "satanic" song that causes people to commit suicide.

Sources: Crawford, Sue. OZZY UNAUTHORIZED. Michael O'Mara Books
Limited, London. 2002. Pages 142-147.
Soocher, Stan. They Fought the Law. Schirmer Books, New York. 1999.
Pages 158-161.

John Parr

> *John Parr, the musician who had two hits in the 1980s was originally found by a record producer in a graveyard suffering from amnesia and clutching a demo tape of his songs.*

John Parr had two hits in the 1980s: Naughty, Naughty in 1984 and St. Elmo's Fire (Man in Motion) in 1985. The publicity story dreamed up in 1984 for his first album, the self-titled JOHN PARR, was that he had been found by a record producer suffering from amnesia while wandering in a graveyard. Parr supposedly did not remember who he was or where he came from, but he did have a demo tape with him of his music (good thing he ran into a record producer in the graveyard, instead of, say, a psychiatrist or police officer). The tape was played for the producer and Parr was signed to a record deal soon after.

Of course, anyone reading the above would immediately see that the story was nothing more than a publicity stunt. Still, some fans did believe it to be true, and in later concert appearances, Parr would be asked about this rumor by interviewers.

Peter, Paul & Mary

> Puff, the Magic Dragon *is a song about marijuana dressed up as a children's song.*

Although more of a folk group than a rock band, this song did make it into many of the music charts during the spring of 1963 (including the R&B chart, reaching No. 10 there). It was also one of the first modern musical hits of the era to earn itself an urban legend, the story being that *Puff, the Magic Dragon* was a coy way for the folk group to wink at their intended audience by dressing up a song about smoking pot as a children's song. For this reason, the song ended up being continuously brought up by outraged parents who believed the rumor, even ending up as an "example" used by religious fanatics of the evils of rock music and the subversive nature of the music.

Peter Yarrow of the group wrote the song while attending college in 1958 with Leonard Lipton, a fellow student and fraternity brother. The song, originally written as a straight adventure about a dragon, was changed by Yarrow into a song dealing with childhood innocence and how such innocence is lost as people become adults. It, however, was never intended to be a song talking about or even implying marijuana. And when the group performed the song over the years since (and it was so popular that it was a regular part of their concert performances), they sometimes took the time to address this legend in order to clarify the situation.

Still, the rumor grabbed hold after the song became a hit in 1963 and has continued to be a regularly returning urban legend about the song ever since. Paul Stookey, the "Paul" of the group, stated that he eventually found out that Newsweek had run a story where the rumor was first presented. The writer of the piece later admitted to an associate of Stookey that a group of writers at the magazine had created the legend after discussing the reoccurring stories about "hidden messages" in rock music. Wanting to pick a song that was considered by the writers to be the "most innocuous song" they could think of, *Puff* was chosen as their target. Stookey went on to say: "He said, 'We never thought for a minute that it would take hold.' And it's still tearing at us."

Just goes to show the power of the press.

Source: Ruhlmann, William. "Peter, Paul and Mary – A Song To Sing all Over This Land," Goldmine. Issue #410. April 12, 1996. Pages 30 & 44.

Tom Petty

> *Just as the first Tom Petty and the Heartbreakers album was to be released in 1976, Petty got beat up during a bar fight and slipped into a coma, finally passing away about the time of the SHE'S THE ONE soundtrack album. To take his place, an impostor was found, substituting for Petty for many years.*

This is actually a rather shy wink at the old Beatles' rumor about Paul McCartney being dead and all the Beatles' albums having some type of reference to the death and replacement of Paul in the band back in 1966 (see the entry for Beatles for more details). Two college roommates, Bruce Ketcham and Jesse Lavery, in 1996 believed such a rumor could be created using anyone's music and decided upon Tom Petty as their target. Soon, a web site was created called "The Official Tom Petty is Dead" web site and a large amount of comedic and completely bogus information was available for fans to stumble upon while searching the web. Eventually some people would not see the joke and assume that Tom Petty really did die back in 1976; thus, the rumor falls into the urban legend category even though it was only intended as a joke – something people can do too good of a job when trying to pull other people's legs.

Sources: The Merry Cutthroats FAQ.
  http://www.geocities.com/SunsetStrip/Club/8541/mcfaq.html. 1997.
  Lavery, Jesse. Tom Petty is Dead – The Official Page.
  http://www.disraeli.net/petty/. 1999.

Pink Floyd

> 1. *Pink Floyd purposefully recorded DARK SIDE OF THE MOON to be played in synch with the classic children film THE WIZARD OF OZ.*
> 2. *Pink Floyd was asked by Stanley Kubrick to record the soundtrack for his film, 2001: A SPACE ODYSSEY. After recording the soundtrack (or part thereof), Kubrick changed his mind. Instead of trashing what was written, the Floyd decided to release what they had recorded as the song* Echoes *on their album.*
> 3. *Once, former guitarist Syd Barrett showed up at a party in the studio for Pink Floyd after he had been gone from the band for ten years. No one recognized him, as he had gain an enormous amount of weight and was bald.*
> 4. *Syd Barrett played guitar on his own "tribute" song from the Pink Floyd album WISH YOU WERE HERE,* Shine On You Crazy Diamond.
> 5. *Syd Barrett played on the Beatles song* What's the New Mary Jane.

1: It's hard to say when the rumor of Pink Floyd and THE WIZARD OF OZ first appeared – some say they heard about it back in the 1980s, while others say it was about the mid-1990s when the rumor first became known. Either way, everyone wants to be known as the one to have discovered this odd synchronization between the album and the movie. While the idea that such a thing was done intentionally is pretty absurd, one has to admit that the first nearly 45 minutes of the film does work incredibly well with the album as a soundtrack.

Several articles have been written about this game for bored music and movie fans, and several web sites have appeared dealing with the phenomenon as well. All of these give the exact procedure to follow when synching up the movie and the album. The web sites especially give extensive details as to the amazing coincidences that occur when played together (everything from the first "cha-ching" in the song *Money* being heard just as the film changes from black and white to color, to the final "heart beats" heard on the album occurring as Dorothy beats on the Tin-man's chest in the forest).

While it is great fun, was it intentional? When asked over the years about the story (which seems to pop up every time the movie is shown nationally on television), those involved with the album usually have two comments to make: one, that people have way too much time on their hands; and, two, that it would have been impossible, or nearly impossible, to pull off such a stunt intentionally. As engineer (and solo artist himself) Alan Parsons pointed out years later, the concept of recording the album to match up to the film would have been mind-boggling to attempt in the pre-VCR days of the early 1970s. While some fans have gotten around this fact by determining that a print of the film was shown on a large screen in the darkened studio, it merely points out the fantastic nature of the legend. Doing so would have been very complicated, not to mention that it probably would lead to the use and destruction of several prints of the film in order to watch it enough times to record such a "soundtrack." There is also the problem of how the synching would have been possible on a film print that would have a slightly different length than other prints of the film. In fact, one problem fans wishing to try out this stunt run into is that copies of the film released on commercial VHS and DVD since 1989 are from a print slightly longer than pre-1989 commercial releases. In other words, the synching does not work quite as well on post-1989 releases than on pre-1989 releases. If this is true just on the merit of essentially two prints of the film, how could it have been possible to have many multiple prints of the film work for such a soundtrack.

It should be pointed out strongly, that many fans do not believe the band actually did record to the album to be played in synch with the film. Still, the coincidental timing of the two is quite remarkable and does provide a fun game for those willing to go through the trouble of playing.

2: What is it about Pink Floyd that makes people want to synch their albums up to multiple films? First, it was the synchronizing of the entire DARK SIDE OF THE MOON album with the classic film, THE WIZARD OF OZ; now the list has expanded to include tracks connected with movies like CONTACT, PLANET OF THE APES and many others. It certainly appears that there are too many people with VCRs, CD-players and bongs lying around their rooms.

Seriously, while people seem to be having fun with the game of "Floyd synch-up," only two films have gained an urban legend status in connection with the game. The first is that of THE WIZARD OF OZ (as listed above), the second is a slightly more "could they have?" rumor about the classic Kubrick film, 2001: A SPACE ODYSSEY.

The story goes that Kubrick was searching for a composer for his then-upcoming film, 2001. Because of the futuristic nature of the film, Kubrick wanted music that was reflective of the movie's subject matter. To do this, he listened to many different styles of music and types of composers. Eventually, he came across a couple of songs from the new band Pink Floyd, and thought they would be perfect for the movie. The band was asked to do at least part of the soundtrack.

Now, here's where the story goes into two separate directions. In one version of this legend, the band starts work on the soundtrack, but only records a portion before they realize that their recording commitments to their record label will not allow them enough time to finish their work for Kubrick. Thus, Pink Floyd bowed out and Kubrick went on to hire Alex North to score the film.

The other version of the story goes that Kubrick decided that a rock score would be inappropriate for the film and fires the band after part of the score was completed. In either case, the results are the same, music written by Pink Floyd that supposedly was to be used for 2001. As both version of the legend go, the band decided to use the music, retitled as *Echoes*, for the first side of their album MEDDLE. Moreso, if one plays "Echoes" during the film, the two are a perfect match.

As with THE WIZARD OF OZ, there is actually a very odd coincidence in synchron-ization between the "Jupiter and Beyond the Infinite" segment of the film (the final 20-odd minutes of the film) and the music created by Pink Floyd. This ranges from the lyrics, "Overhead the albatross hangs motionless upon the air," matching a shot of the Monolith (the alien object in the film that calls the Earthlings on to higher levels of evolution) in space; to an odd series of pinging sounds heard as the "star-child" appears at the very end of the movie. The song and the sequence in the film end at the same time.

Pink Floyd

Such a finding only leads fans to speculate that perhaps there is some truth to the rumor. However, this is quickly corrected simply by looking at how Kubrick worked on the film itself.

Kubrick was well-known for spending much time in preparation of his movies (moreso in later films in his career than earlier on, yet still a period of some years could go by before his next film was ready to be produced). In fact, it is quite true that Kubrick did spend some time trying to find the proper music to use in the film, searching for something unique and different to separate the film's soundtrack from ones expected from a movie. However, he located his 2001 composer, Alex North, in December 1967, while the film was being completed.

By this time in 1967, Pink Floyd had only recorded two singles and one album, and was only then starting to hint at the heavy orchestrations and alien (not to mention alienated) lyrics that would become their norm later on. Kubrick, as stated in James Howard's book THE STANLEY KUBRICK COMPANION, most likely had never heard of the band, much less talk to them about scoring the film at that time. Nor was the band in a state where doing such a score would have been in their best interest. Things were souring within the group due to problems with guitarist Syd Barrett and it would take some time for Pink Floyd to move on to their 1968 album A SAUCERFUL OF SECRETS.

It is also known that *Echoes* was not written and recorded by the band until 1971, a good three years after the release of the film. Although some fans would suggest that such a delay could have been a case of putting a song on the back burner after being dropped from 2001 and then pulled back out a few years later, this is just speculation from fans wanting to see a connection of some kind between the two. Although both Kubrick and Pink Floyd have had many documentaries and biographies written about them over the years, there has never been any inkling anywhere that the two worked together in any form on 2001, and there certainly doesn't seem to be any reason for hiding such a "fact" from the public if it were true.

Sources: Howard, James. THE STANLEY KUBRICK COMPANION. B.T. Batsford, Ltd., London. 2000.
Munday, Rod. The Kubrick FAQ,
http://www.visual-memory.co.uk/faq/index4.html#slot34. July 1999.
"Pink Floyd & 2001," Psychotronic Film Society.
http://www.psychotronic.com/archive/floyd2001.htm

3: Syd Barrett sightings seem to have become the "Hippie-era" equivalent of Elvis sightings. There are many variations to the reports, but the most typical was one that would be dragged out every time that Pink Floyd recorded a new album – that of Syd showing up for a party in the studio and not being recognized because of the drastic physical changes in him since the late 1960s. As it stands, this story does have a basis in fact. Simply the location and atmosphere of the meeting were a little different than the causal nature of the urban legend.

In June 1975, the band was in the studio to work on a song from the WISH YOU WERE HERE album called *Shine On You Crazy Diamond*. The song, a tribute to Syd, was being completed when a heavy, bald man entered the studio. At first, as in the legend, no one was quite sure who he was, but it was only momentarily and soon people recognized him. However, that recognition did not eliminate the awkwardness of having the former band member in the room, with the physical deterioration and obsessive behavior of Syd (who kept standing up, brushing his teeth with a toothbrush and then sitting back down repeatedly) so bothersome that a few people in the room were on the verge of tears.

Shop talk was also out of the question, as Syd seemed uninterested in the music being worked on and quite bored with his surroundings. Finally, Syd asked when he was to do his guitar part, shocking the band and others in the room. He was then told that the guitar work had already been completed (which it was). After that, he never came back to the studio.

Source: Thompson, Dave. "The Creative Genius – Yet Sad Tale – of Pink Floyd's Syd Barrett," Goldmine. Issue 488, April 9, 1999. Page 122.

4:   See above entry for details on the rumor that Syd Barrett played guitar on the song, *Shine On You Crazy Diamond*.

5:   The rumor went around for years that Syd Barrett played guitar on the outtake that appeared on several Beatles bootlegs (and a few Pink Floyd bootlegs) before finally turning up on one of the Beatles ANTHOLOGY albums. The rumor seems to come in part because the Beatles did meet with members of Pink Floyd in 1967, while Pink Floyd recorded at Abbey Road, the studio best known as the normal recording residence for the Beatles.

As per Mark Lewisohn's book, THE BEATLES RECORDING SESSIONS, John Lennon recorded *What's the New Mary Jane* on August 14, 1968, with George Harrison, Yoko Ono and Mal Evans. This was long after Syd had left Pink Floyd and several weeks after he had finished recording his solo album in 1968.

Sources: Lewisohn, Mark. THE BEATLES RECORDING SESSIONS. Hamlyn Books, London. 1988. Page 148.
Schuetz, David, et al. "Section 4: The Syd Barrett Years." The Pink Floyd FAQ.
http://www.jasongeo.com/gdh/faq/html/section4.html. 1999

Elvis Presley

1. *Elvis never toured overseas because Colonel Parker was an illegal immigrant.*
2. *Presley was supposed to be the Kris Kristofferson part in the 1975 theatrical remake of A STAR IS BORN, but was passed over when Colonel Parker asked for too much money.*
3. *Buying a broken-down Harley Davidson motorcycle led to the discovery that it once belonged to Elvis Presley.*
4. *Elvis faked his own death in order to step away from the claustrophobic life he was leading in the 1970s and just be a normal, "average Joe." Some also believed that he faked his death because of death threats he was receiving from either the Mafia or a gang of drug dealers who were trying to take revenge against Elvis for his assistance to the FBI in breaking up a drug ring.*

1: One of the frustrations foreign fans face is the inability to see a performer live. The expense involved in flying to another country in order to see a favorite performer just isn't realistic for many fans, so they have to hope that the artist will come to them. The problem there is that the cost, logistics and time needed to put together an "overseas" tour can make it impossible for musicians to do so. The options for a performer are to either scale back their production and do something on the cheap – something that may disappoint fans – or become such a successful artist that such headaches as cost, etc. would not pose a problem.

Which brings us back to Elvis. In the 1970s, Elvis had drawn himself into a continuous cycle of tours that would ultimately accelerate his death in August 1977. As time went on, Elvis' performance became pocketier, with highs and lows that made it a flip of the coin whether one would be seeing a good performance or a bad one. Still, the shows were normally selling out because not only was Elvis tremendously popular, but when he was on top of his game, he was extraordinary.

With that in mind, Elvis did get offers to tour other countries around the world. Moreover, Elvis himself had suggested numerous times that he would tour, or would like to tour, Europe. By the early 1970s, offers were arriving for Elvis to do such tours (some of them quite lucrative), but Parker was always turning them down for one reason or another.

To foreign fans, this resistance seemed puzzling. In retrospect, it seems even odder. As reported in many Elvis biographies over the past 25 years, Elvis was feeling a financial crunch as the '70s worn on. Elvis and Parker were both looking for cash, with Col. Parker seeing the constant touring as a means to an end, and Elvis begrudgingly agreeing. Therefore, when some of the foreign offers came through for staggering amounts of money, one wondered why Elvis and Parker resisted.

Then the news hit near the end of Parker's life that he was not an American citizen, but rather an illegal immigrant from Holland, whose real name was Andreas Cornelis van Kuijk. In the late 1920s, Andreas somehow managed to make it to America and, wishing to stay there, joined the army in Hawaii in order to avoid being sent back to Holland. Over time, he adopted the name Tom Parker and eventually followed his ballyhoo career towards meeting Elvis in the 1950s and pushing his career even past Elvis' death.

However, Parker never established his citizenship in the US. This would make some fans suspect that Parker refused overseas tours fearing that this information would eventually leak out and destroy his career. This theory is intriguing, but in evidence full of hot air. Although not heavily reported, Parker's Dutch background had been known among hard core fans since the early days of Elvis' success. Parker would have also been heavily investigated by the US government, especially in light of Elvis' induction into the army. Nor was Elvis ignorant of Parker's background, as evidenced by Elvis writing to Parker about the Dutch language while he was stationed in Germany during his army years. In all, it appears that a lack of citizenship was hardly the focal point of refusing to have Elvis tour in other countries.

If that was not the case, what was it then?

In his biography about Parker, MY BOY ELVIS, Sean O'Neal speculates as to why Parker never allowed Elvis to tour overseas. In doing so, O'Neal asked the question that most fans had on their mind – was it because Parker was an illegal alien and did not want to be found out? As stated above, this question seems highly suspect when a true look at Parker's background is taken. O'Neal does hit upon one factor that could have easily cemented Parker's concerns: control. Even if Parker had gotten a passport and cleared up any lingering nationalization issues (which, as O'Neal points out, considering Parker's military record and his longevity in the US as a successful businessman, would have been easily obtained), Parker would not have been able to control elements pertaining the concerts. In the US, he and his entourage knew the routine. Everyone treated Parker and Elvis with a glowing respect that was hard earned. Parker, no doubt, had heard the horror stories about other musicians who had toured overseas only to run into security risks, money being held back and even equipment confiscated.

In essence, Parker would have had to give up control if they wanted to do an overseas tour. It was a gamble, and Parker didn't like the odds.

As for Elvis, there were assumptions that he honestly did want to tour overseas. Parker's persuasion over Elvis, even though it was evaporating somewhat as the 1970s went on, was still strong enough to kill his desire. As O'Neal reported in his book, Elvis also lost interest when he found out that the Osmond Brothers had been searched for guns when they went on a European tour. Elvis did not want to go without some type of personal protection, and his interest waned after that. Perhaps most importantly, the same report said that the Osmonds were searched for drugs. Knowing Elvis' growing dependence on medication, Parker probably knew it was in Elvis' best interest to keep him where he could still earn money and not have to face any possible scandals.

Source: O'Neal. MY BOY ELVIS. Barricade Books, NY. 1998, pages 239-241.

2: The story goes that Barbra Streisand wanted to remake the classic Hollywood tearjerker film, A STAR IS BORN, and wanted to have a strong male lead for the role. Elvis, meanwhile, had abandoned movies in the late 1960s and concentrated his career solely around touring through the 1970s. At the time of his departure from films it was no wonder he wanted to leave movies behind – the scripts had degenerated into mindless fluff and were on the verge of killing his career as a serious music maker. Still, he had enjoyed the opportunity to act and Elvis would still entertain thoughts of returning to the big screen from time to time.

Streisand, on the other hand, had found her movie career blossoming at the same time Elvis had decided to leave such a career. In fact, Streisand was a certified "movie star." The only problem was finding proper projects for her to work on. Remaking A STAR IS BORN was a sure-fire concept for Streisand. It not only allowed her a ready-made story dealing with a strong central female character, but, with a slight tweaking of the plot, a musical version of the story could showcase Streisand's singing with 1970s pop music material.

The story goes that Streisand actively wanted Elvis for the part – so much, in fact, that she visited him after one of his shows to sketch out the movie concept to him. Elvis was supposedly enthusiastic about the idea and wanted to do the film. However, as the legend goes, Parker did not like the idea of Elvis being out from under his thumb and asked for such an outlandish amount of money for Presley in the film that the studio backed out of the deal.

To some Elvis fans who want to paint Parker with a broad brush as a puppeteer who only used Presley as a money machine, the story told above is just another example of Parker ruining Presley's career in the 1970s. Some would even suggest that doing the film would have led Presley away from his ultimate demise. To say so is only looking at part of the overall picture, however. It also stereotypes of Elvis as not being savvy in the entertainment business and with the people involved.

As pointed out in Peter Guralnick's book, CARELESS LOVE: THE UNMAKING OF ELVIS PRESLEY, Presley's enthusiasm for the project evaporated in the days after the meeting with Streisand. Presley had heard some of the stories about Streisand's strong will on movie sets, of which many stories were told about her less than stellar attitude towards her male co-stars. It was also a project she had developed with her then-boyfriend Jon Peters – a man best known at the time as being a hairdresser. Now he was to direct and produce A STAR IS BORN for Streisand and it was obvious to anyone that the production would be centered on Streisand, and not on her co-star, no matter who got the role. The press was also having a field day with the news that Peters would produce and direct, and the bad vibes of this ridicule rubbed Elvis the wrong way as well. Still, it was a serious role, which Elvis had not been offered in many years by that time.

When Presley did talk about the project with Parker, Parker stated all of the reasons for not doing it that Presley had no doubt also considered. Parker was also offended that Streisand tried to work around him by going directly to Elvis about the project.

To Parker, it seemed that Streisand was trying to get a deal agreed on with Elvis that may not have been the best for him.

Elvis saw the same problems as Parker, yet he was still reluctant to say no. To help, Parker put together a deal that would guarantee Elvis a $1 million salary and additional perks, including 50 percent of the profits and approval of all songs Elvis would do in the film. At this point, negotiations did not so much break down, as stop completely. According to all reports, no discussions took place to try to come to an agreement on a contract. Instead, Streisand, Peters and the studio moved on to other prospects. As Guralnick relates in his book, when no attempt was made to pursue Elvis after that, Presley felt that Parker and he were right – Streisand and Peters were only interested in the value of Elvis' name and thought they could take advantage of him when it came time to sign on.

Although there is only a minor urban legend in Elvis' life, it still points to a common theme that Elvis had no control over the events in his performing life and everything was ruined by the whims and money-hungry engineering of his manager, Colonel Parker. To think such is a discredit to Elvis, since whenever a project came along that maintained his interest, he would follow through no matter what objections Parker had (look no further than the 1968 comeback television special for evidence of this). However, Parker was a good tool to have when Elvis felt unsure about projects and needed a way out. The only problem was that Elvis' need to find new projects dissipated as the 1970s went on and with that also came his decline in health, mentally and physically.

As to Streisand, Elvis is merely a footnote in the story of the making of A STAR IS BORN, and nothing more.

Sources: Edwards, Anne. STREISAND. Little, Brown and Company, New York. 1997. Page 365.
Guralnick, Peter. CARELESS LOVE: THE UNMAKING OF ELVIS PRESLEY. Little, Brown and Company, New York. 1999. Pages 562-565.

3: This is a story that has been occasionally updated over the years, but in all versions the following happens: A person comes across an old, beat-up Harley Davidson motorcycle for sale (usually while traveling along an old country road seldom used). Sometimes the bike is part of a yard sale of some sort, sometimes as part of an estate auction, and other times the bike is just sitting by the side of the road with a "for sale" sign on it.

The bike was a classic from the 1950s, but it definitely needed work and parts, so the price was finally haggled down to $500 (or thereabouts, depending on the teller of the story). The buyer takes it home and realizes that replacement parts needed are not going to be readily available down at the local supply shop. To find out what should be done, the buyer called the Harley Davidson headquarters in Milwaukee.

The buyer describes the bike when asked, and there is a long pause once he is through describing the bike. He is then switched to a person higher up in the company and tells the same story. He continues to be switched until he is finally talking to the CEO of the company.

The CEO asks the buyer to describe the bike once again. After doing so, the CEO then tells the buyer to go out and see if there is an inscription on the back of the bike.

Lo and behold, under the rear fender is an inscription to Elvis Presley from Harley Davidson. Upon verifying the inscription to the CEO, the buyer is offered $4 million for the bike.

What this legend boils down to is a musical variation of the old garage sale masterpiece painting. In that legend, a person buys an old painting at a yard sale, only to discover that the painting itself (or a painting underneath it) was done by a famous artist and the painting bought for a dollar is suddenly worth millions.

While Elvis did ride a Harley Davidson motorcycle, there is no documented case of one being found for sale along the side of the road for only $500 (and, there is still the question of how someone out in the middle of nowhere somehow ended up with Presley's personal HD bike that has an inscription on it. There is at least one known case of Harley Davidson actually buying one of Elvis' bikes, but the selling price was not anywhere near the $4 million dollars of the story.

4:    When Elvis died on August 16, 1977, the world was shocked. Elvis was only 42 at the time and still very active, playing concerts on a frequent basis throughout the U.S. Sure, there were the common critical reviews that Elvis had gotten fat, had more "off" nights than "on," and was frequently forgetting or slurring the words to his popular songs, but many either saw these stories as merely vicious gossip by the critics or just a phase Elvis was going through. Excuses were made and everyone assumed that Elvis would be around for a long time to come.

Then he died. The shock of his death due to "heart failure" had not even completely sunk in when it was discovered that Elvis' death had been accelerated by his dependency on prescription medication for a number of physical problems that he felt he was suffering from. No fan wanted to hear about these things, even if they did confirm thoughts made by some of Elvis' former bodyguards in the book released just before his death, ELVIS, WHAT HAPPENED? Elvis was the "King of Rock and Roll." He was the boy who struggled to make good and succeed by becoming a sex god but still the boy next door. Now it was turning out that Elvis was addicted to pills, had weird sex fetishes and lived his final years in somewhat of a daze. It was very hard for the fans or even the general public to take in so quickly.

Then, with the tenth anniversary of his death right around the corner, the word hit that maybe Elvis wasn't dead after all. Instead, he had faked his death in 1977 and with the tenth anniversary of his "passing" he would come back into the public eye to explain why he did it and what he planned to do next. The tenth anniversary came and went without his appearance and many people ignored the stories told altogether. May 1988 saw the first burst of major media attention about Elvis being seen alive when the WEEKLY WORLD NEWS reported a story about a women named Louise Willing who had seen Elvis standing in line at her local supermarket in Vicksburg, Michigan. Both the ASSOCIATED PRESS and the DETROIT NEWS picked up the story, which also included a mention that Elvis had been sighted at a Kalamazoo, Michigan Burger King, eating a Whopper and drinking a milkshake.

The news exploded with the release of a book in 1988 by Gail Brewer-Giorgio called THE MOST INCREDIBLE ELVIS PRESLEY STORY EVER TOLD. The book, sold only through a television advertisement, came with a sixty-minute cassette that contained taped telephone conversations supposedly by Elvis four years after his death. Brewer-Giorgio relates in her book that she had planned to write a novel about a singer named Orion that would be based somewhat on Elvis, with the exception that at the end of the novel Orion would fake his own death and disappear to Hawaii. According to Brewer-Giorgio, the book was all set to go to press and there was even talk of a movie being made from it when all negotiations collapsed. In digging into the cause of the failure of the book, Brewer-Giorgio unearthed information that led her to believe that Elvis was still alive and that he and those still running his business had put a stop to the novel because it was too close to reality.

Brewer-Giorgio's book sold well and was reprinted in 1988 as IS ELVIS ALIVE? A documentary based on the book was broadcast in syndication on August 14, 1991 called THE ELVIS FILES, and featuring Bill Bixby, a former co-star to Elvis in two of his films, as the narrator. The television special suggested that Elvis had been recruited by the FBI at one point in the 1970s to help convict a Mafia leader and that he had to fake his death and go into the government witness protection program to ensure that the Mafia would not come after him.

By that time the stories were everywhere about Elvis being alive and evidently frequenting every known convenience store and fast food joint in the entire United States. For many people, the whole thing was a joke to snicker at as being something only "dumb hicks" and "white trash" would believe. For conspiracy theorists, it was just another government-related cover-up, as so many before it.

Of course, there were "clues" that proved Elvis was still alive: that Elvis' name was spelled wrong on his grave, that it was a wax body in the coffin, that his autopsy report listed a wrong weight. Ultimately, no information faces up to the many facts that could refute them: eye witnesses that were at Graceland at the time of his death, the autopsy that gave details as to the cause of Elvis' death, the vicious legal ramifications that faced Elvis' estate after his death (something that surely would have brought Elvis back into the open), plus much more. Finally, it would impossible for Elvis to have simply left his family, especially his daughter, behind in order to "disappear" into Middle America as so many people would have the public believe.

As stated in an earlier essay in this book (see Death (and the Conspiracy of Life)), people wanted to give this urban legend a glimmer of hope because they wanted Elvis' life to end in some satisfactory and "happy" manner. His sudden death in such a dismal, traumatic way only helped to spring forth the ongoing legends of his hanging out at the 7-11 and ordering another Big Gulp. While some people merely see it as a joke being pulled on the gullible (and no doubt there are those that have certainly cashed in on this way of thinking), others see it as perhaps the best way to end the chronicles of Elvis Presley. With the constant urban legends of his faked death, Elvis will never ever die.

Sources: Brewer-Giorgio, Gail. IS ELVIS ALIVE? Tudor, New York. 1988
Gregory, Neal & Janice. WHEN ELVIS DIED. Pharos Books, New York. 1980. Pages 222-225.

Prince

> 1. Prince appeared in the movie FARGO as the passerby who is running through the snow and killed by the kidnappers early in the film.
> 2. Prince changed his name to a symbol of his own design because he had "advanced beyond using a name like other people."
> 3. Prince's notorious THE BLACK ALBUM was not released because the record label was afraid of the controversial nature of the lyrics.

1: Prince does not appear in FARGO, although a variation of the symbol he was using for a time as his name does appear in the ending credits. The film's storyboard artist played the part of a passerby wearing a red parka and when it came time for the credits to be selected for the end of the film, the artist asked that his credit be listed with a symbol instead of his name.

2: On June 7, 1993, Prince made a public announcement that he was changing his name to a symbol that he had used as the title of his previous album (the symbol was similar to a unisex symbol, reworked in Prince's own "paisley" style). The reasons for doing this were never adequately explained by Prince at the time, which was natural for the man who never had shown much interest in the media and their questions.

Rumors abound as to why he had done so, many of them are very unflattering towards the "Artist formerly known as Prince" (as the musician was commonly referred to in articles and books where either the capability to print the symbol was impossible, or where it was felt unnecessary to waste the time and hassle to obtain the symbol). However, things became a bit more obvious over time. 1992 had seen Prince sign a new contract with Warner Brothers, for which, within a year, he had regrets. By 1996 the artist had begun penciling the word "slave" on his face for some public appearances due (some assume) to his problems with Warner Brothers. After the contract with Warner was settled in 1996, there were still lingering problems which led to Warner being able to release more material from Prince up to the year 1999. On May 16, 2000, with his lingering publishing contract with Warner-Chappel completed, Prince announced to the world that he was going back to his original name.

With the dates falling into place, it takes little to see that Prince had no happiness with the idea that Warner would be selling his music and had switched to the symbol as a way to deal with the situation. Whether that meant that Prince wanted to make sure the label would not be able to sell the albums under his name, and thus not profit as much from them; or if he simply felt that he needed a different persona for the period he was tied up with Warner, the answer lies with Prince himself.

3: THE BLACK ALBUM was a Prince album set to be released in 1987. The heavy funk-oriented album did have explicit lyrics, and it was called THE BLACK ALBUM because of the completely black cover, which featured no information about the artist or track listings (please, no Spinal Tap jokes). The album was scrapped after supposedly hundreds of thousands of copies had been pressed (with a small number leaking out to the public before being destroyed by the record company). It later would become a collector's item among fans and turned up as a bootleg within a year.

When the album was pulled, the rumor circulated that the record label had canceled the album because of the explicit nature of the lyrics (one has to remember that this was at a time when there had been Senate hearings pertaining to obscene lyrics in modern music, so many record labels were a bit skittish about releasing material that would be deemed "obscene"). Another rumor circulated that Prince had canceled the project after having a religious experience, deciding that the nature of the lyrics was too strong for his new religious feelings.

Many agree that the real reason was because of Prince, but not due to a religious experience, but rather to a bad experience with the drug MDMA (also known as Ecstasy). Either way, the point made by Prince at the time and when the album was finally released by Warner Brothers in 1994 (through the protests of Prince, who was contractually obligated to allow the release of the album) was that the music represented a darker tone that he was no longer happy with.

Pulp

> Front man Jarvis Cocker of the group Pulp is the son or nephew of singer Joe Cocker.

Jarvis Cocker is not related to Joe Cocker. The rumor is just an assumption that because people share the same last name they have to be related in some fashion. Both being from Sheffield, England certainly helps to create the confusion, however.

Queen

> Due to a rare physical problem, Freddie Mercury's teeth continued to grow even after reaching adulthood. He would continuously have to go to a dental hygienist to have the teeth "clipped," which explains why in photos Mercury's teeth seem to fluctuate in size.

Mercury, a man who had exotic, dark looks that made him naturally attractive to many people, really did have an overbite that was very noticeable. From various photos and interviews it can be seen that Mercury was never completely happy with how his teeth looked, and tended to give a closed mouth smile if posing for promotional photos. Because of this, it is only in candid shots that his teeth can be judged accurately.

Mercury never did anything to correct the overbite, unlike other artists who had dental surgery once they achieved some level of success, so he must not have been too terribly upset about it. However, for such a flamboyant man, he did have a tendency to shy away from having his teeth seen. Because of this, it wasn't common to see how large his teeth really were, and thus an urban legend was started.

REM

> *A series of numbers on the covers of REM's albums make up a "countdown," and only the band knows for sure what it means.*

When the album GREEN was released, many fans noticed that a number "4" had been superimposed over the "r" in the album title, and they wondered what it meant. Fans then noticed that several of the albums had a single number on them: the number "5" on DOCUMENT, the number "10" on CHRONIC TOWN, a "9" on MURMUR, "8" on FABLES and "7" on RECKONING. All kinds of rumors flew around, but Michael Stipe eventually told fans on AOL back in August 1994 that it was nothing more than a coincidence after they decided to throw in numbers on the album covers just for the look of them.

It does not stand for some type of countdown.

Source: Henry, Ron. The R.E.M. – Usenet rec.music.rem Frequently Asked Questions List. http://people2.clarityconnect.com/webpages6/ronhenry/remfaq.htm. October 16, 2001.

The Rolling Stones

> 1. Mick Jagger was caught having sex with David Bowie by Bowie's wife.
> 2. Jagger performed with Bob Dylan, John Lennon, Paul McCartney and George Harrison on a "supergroup" album called THE MASKED MARAUDERS.
> 3. A drug bust during a Rolling Stones party found Jagger's then-girlfriend, Marianne Faithful with a Mars bar stuck up her vagina.
> 4. Keith Richards had (or still has) a complete blood transfusion in order to purify his body and kick his various drug habits.
> 5. Brian Jones was murdered.
> 6. Keith Richards has an abnormal fear of cheese.

1: Stories of the rich and famous and their supposed sexual escapades is nothing new, and this rumor is certainly not the only one of its type in this book. In particular, stories dealing with questions of one's orientation (Is he gay? Is she queer? Are they Bi? Is he a she? What did they do to that poor fish?) seem to pop up as soon as people make a name for themselves in the entertainment industry. In doing so, more than one celebrity has found the old cliché to be true – you're never famous until someone starts a rumor that you're gay.

In the case of Jagger and Bowie, however, such a story didn't seem so farfetched, even if the originator of the rumor backed down almost immediately from the story.

But first, some more details about the story itself: The time was the early 1970s and the rock scene was one that found performers displaying the new freedoms available to the young of the day. For some, this allowed them to state plainly their sexual orientation for the first time; for others, it allowed them to confuse the issue and leave people wondering, "Is he / is she?" Both Jagger and Bowie were masters of the game in this sense. Jagger first, with his overtly sexual nature on stage and stories (whether all were true or not) of all types of sexual conquests; not to mention an appearance in drag (with the rest of the Rolling Stones) for the cover of a 45 single. Jagger was also the seen during the 1973 Rolling Stones tour stroking a huge inflatable penis on stage as well. Bowie, meanwhile, spent the early 1970s turning the media on its ear with his androgynous look (mainly during his "Ziggy Stardust" period) and his up front "open" marriage with Angela Bowie that permitted not only outside heterosexual relationships, but homosexual ones as well. As time went on, however, David Bowie began to shy away from this image.

Many magazines printed articles and photos in the early 1970s showing a relationship building between Jagger and Bowie, but seldom anything beyond that of heading to the bars together or meeting backstage at shows. Still, there was an underlying question of where such a relationship would lead, especially during the sexual experimentation days of the 1970s.

Still, many people forgot about it and it never would have been more than a lingering, unanswerable question until May 4, 1990 when Angela Bowie spilled her guts on the relationship during an appearance on the American television talk show THE JOAN RIVERS SHOW. Angela had divorced Bowie in 1980 and found herself at that time under a ten-year gag order that restricted her from talking about several aspects of their ten-year marriage (although that did little to stop her from writing a book back in 1980 called FREE SPIRIT that dealt with some aspects of the marriage). By May 1990, the order had run its course and Angela could now talk, which was just perfect for a show like Joan Rivers' – a comedian that had based a career on snippy, insulting "jokes" about other celebrities.

At first, Angela was camera-shy in discussing aspects of their marriage, but it was apparent from the responses of Joan Rivers and her guest, radio personality Howard Stern, during and after her brief initial appearance that she was holding back on information promised before the show aired. Finally, Angela Bowie returned before the cameras and admitted that she had caught Bowie in bed with other men several times. The topper was when she stated that the "best time" she caught him was when she walked into the bedroom after returning from a trip only to find Mick Jagger naked in bed with Bowie.

For many fans of both artists, it was less than earth-shattering news. Many dismissed the story by Angela as just a bit of ugliness on her part to draw attention to herself; and just as many thought it was just a story from the past that had little to do with anybody's present nature. In fact, the story has rarely been approached in latter biographies of either man. The media, however, took off with the story and, while Angela never at any point stated that she caught the two having sex in bed, it was clear what the implications were. Within days, Angela state publicly that she only found them in bed together and nothing more – a statement completely opposite in tone from that of her Joan Rivers appearance, which suggested that David was routinely taking men to bed for sex and one being Jagger.

Both David Bowie and Jagger were quick to deny the story. For her part, Angela dismissed the story herself in her 1993 autobiography, BACKSTAGE PASSES, by bewilderingly suggesting that Americans were to blame for reading into the story what wasn't there, and in the next paragraph stating that she was "dead certain" they did have sex. Thus, conclusively stating that people could believe whatever they wanted to believe.

Which is exactly how such stories get started in the first place.

Sources: Bowie, Angela and Carr, Patrick. BACKSTAGE PASSES. G. P. Putnams, New York. 1993.
Bowie, Angela. FREE SPIRIT. Mushroom Books, London. 1981

2: See the entry for Bob Dylan for more details.

3: See the entry for Marianne Faithful for more details.

4: Anyone who grew up during the 1970s or knew anything about the Rolling Stones had heard the rumors about Keith Richards and his various blood transfusions. The stories that Richards was so rich that when he wanted to kick any one of his various drug habits, he would just fly off to Switzerland and have a complete blood transfusion done. This would reportedly stop his physical hunger for more heroin or whatnot, and then he could start the addiction all over again as soon as he returned.

It was nearly impossible not to hear about Keith's various run-ins with the law pertaining to his heroin addiction in the 1970s. His 1977 bust in Toronto, Canada on cocaine and heroin charges made international news and led to the belief that Keith was going to be able to kick the habit for good while rotting away in a prison cell for a few years. It didn't happen, but it did make it clear to Richards that he needed to start seriously cleaning up his act. Richards knew that he had become the poster boy for drug addicts, leading a charmed life that saw him surviving massive amounts of drugs, but physically resembling someone slowly burning away from the inside out.

It was also evident to those who knew Richards that he had tried half-heartedly at times to kick his habits in the past. Switzerland in the early 1970s was probably the worst place to go if that was the plan, however. For a time in the 1970s, Richards lived in Switzerland off and on, going back after tours and recording sessions to be with Anita Pallenberg and several hangers-on. People began spreading rumors that Richards was going to Switzerland not to just spend time there, but because it was the land of advances in medical surgery (it was infamous in the 1970s as the place to go to get plastic surgery and other body-changing operations done). It was only a short step to suggest that Richards was going to have something done about his drug addiction, and while it was true that he did seek out new ways of stopping his addiction, there was never any "complete" blood transfusion done in order to cleanse his body. Nor could a drug addiction be removed in such a manner, even if Richards had done such a thing.

It is known that Richards had extensive dental surgery done while in Switzerland, but that would hardly constitute a complete blood transfusion. Nevertheless, the story stuck in people's heads, and is still being used as the punch line to many jokes even today.

5: Brian Jones died July 3, 1969, drowning in his swimming pool at Cotchford Farm in Hartfield, Sussex, the former home of A. A. Milne who created Winnie the Pooh. It was the last step in a life that had progressively gone downhill since his glory days as the one the girls went nuts over in the Rolling Stones. He was also considered a musical genius, having the ability to pick up any musical instrument and learn to play it well within just a few hours. Many people in the band's early days saw Jones as the creative force behind the Stones, pushing them to experiment when the others just wanted to play Rhythm and Blues.

Yet Jones was never in the best of health. He had asthma, keeping an inhaler nearby most of the time in order to help with his breathing. He was known for spells where he would just topple over unconscious and then just as suddenly be perfectly fine again. He also quickly became dependent on drugs to the point where the band eventually got used to pushing Jones on to the stage and letting him essentially stand there and strum away while the rest of the band performed the actual concert. His career in music was also suffering from the drugs, making it mandatory for Keith Richards and Mick Jagger pick up the slack, contribute more material, and direct the band's progression whereas Jones had in the past.

The deterioration of his place in the band left Jones depressed, leading to more drug use. He had also suffered the humiliating action of losing his lover, Anita Pallenberg, to his fellow band member, Keith Richards. Jones was also running into legal problems, constantly being brought up on charges of drug possession, weakening his mental resources even further. By the spring of 1969, he was obviously close to a physical and mental breakdown, spending his time with the band in the studio – if he bothered to show up at all – passed out in a corner and contributing little to the recording sessions. If awake and given an instrument, he would not bother plugging it into the sound system or would go through the recording not even touching the instrument. It was a frustration to the band members who loved Jones as a friend, but could not simply keep Brian happy in the studio when work had to be done. As reported in several places, when Jones finally did ask Jagger what he could play on a recording, Jagger shot back, "I don't know, Brian; what can you play?"

The personal relationship between Jones and the others in the band had fallen apart, and even the two mildest members of the band, Bill Wyman and Charlie Watts, began keeping their distance from Jones. As Wyman stated after Jones' death, "I hung around with him as much as I could, to try and keep him going, and Charlie was pretty good as well. But there came a point when you couldn't, because he was so out of it, and it didn't matter who was there."

Everyone was fed up, and after the suggestion was made to Jones that he should leave the band, he quit on June 8, 1969 stating in a press release, "I no longer see eye to eye with the discs we are cutting." There was talk of Jones moving on to become a solo artist, but all he really did was coast towards his death less than a month later.

The events of the night he died are known but still deemed a bit sketchy, especially by those who insist that he was murdered. On July 2, 1969, Jones was staying at Cotchford Farm, which he loved passionately, even though it played havoc with his health because of the high concentration of pollen that amplified his asthma and frequent fits of hay fever. Work was being done on the home by builder Frank Thoroughgood, and although Jones did not get along well with Thoroughgood, Brian had invited him and a nurse who was staying with him, Janet Lawson, to stay for dinner and perhaps a swim in the pool. Jones' girlfriend, Anna Wohlin, was present for dinner as well.

Dinner went well, although both Frank and Janet would later comment that Jones' speech was slurred and garbled from taking sleeping pills (or so they thought; it turned out to be amphetamines) and alcohol together that night. After dinner, the party watched some television; at about 10:30 that night, Jones decided to go for a swim and asked the others to join him.

Janet declined, feeling that Thoroughgood and Jones were both unsteady on their feet and advised them not to go swimming. When they decided to go for a swim along with Anna, Janet reluctantly joined them in order "to keep an eye on them." Wohlin reported later that Jones made a big show of teasing Frank mercilessly while they were in the pool and at one point Frank even dunked Jones underwater and held him there in anger. Jones laughed it off and the two continued to swim when, after about twenty minutes, Anna and Janet decided to go back into the house.

It's at this point that the urban legends start, all of them ending with Jones being murdered. The first implication upon word of his drowning in a pool was a vicious rumor that Keith Richards and Mick Jagger had been at the get-together as well and held Jones under because of his "pretty boy looks" or even as a sacrifice to Satan (of whom the Stones were suspected of being worshippers). Of course, it soon became clear that neither Richards nor Jagger was at the party; still, that particular rumor goes around even today.

The second rumor was that Jones had been killed by drug dealers who had laid in wait in the bushes near the pool, awaiting the chance to kill Jones for stiffing them of payments recently. This would mean that one or more assailants would have jumped out of the bushes, pulled Jones out of the water and stick his head in a bucket of water (as per the legend typically told) and then throw him back into the water without making any noise to alert the others and in the time span of only a few brief minutes. An urban legend highly suspect, indeed.

The third possibility is one often claimed by the conspiracy theorists – that Jones was murdered by government assassins who saw him as a threat due to his leadership in the youth movement. His death, once again, supposedly occurred from being held head first in a bucket of water and then slipped back into the pool without the assailants being heard or seen – a feat, again, highly improbable. The only factor that made this urban legend better is that, with the government involved, cover-ups are a breeze and the threat of death to the remaining witnesses would keep it covered up for good. The problem with this is that the witnesses who were there have never suggested (even in Wohlin's book, THE MURDER OF BRIAN JONES) that it was a conspiracy. All other evidence is from people who either were not there, could not prove they were there, or wanted to make some money off the idea that such a thing was possible.

The fourth urban legend, and the one that has been mentioned the most, was that Frank Thoroughgood killed Brian in retaliation for Jones' constant taunting of him. In essence, Thoroughgood, in a drunken rage, supposedly held Jones under after the two women left the pool. Some people had suggested this for years, but in 1994, a book came out detailing an interview with a man named Tom Keylock. Keylock stated that he had seen Thoroughgood on his deathbed and that Thoroughgood had admitted to killing Jones that night in 1969.

This sent a flurry of press around and a bemused smirk on the face of conspiracy theorists everywhere; at least, it did, until Keylock was asked by the police about this story and Keylock readily admitted that he had made the whole thing up as a goof to play on the book's author. Seeing no story, the police went away. The newspapers and theorists, not wanting to admit to falling for a prank, couldn't let Thoroughgood's deathbed confession go, just ignored Keylock's confession to making it up completely. Anna Wohlin certainly fell for it in her book dealing with Jones' death, repeatedly implicating Thoroughgood as the killer. After all this renewed talk in the papers and in books during the 1990s, it's no wonder that people still believe that Jones was murdered.

We must consider the fact that Jones did have physical problems – known fainting spells, problems with asthma in an area of the country known for it's concentration of pollen, and known for taking pills mixed with alcohol earlier in the evening. The coroner's report showed that his liver was twice the normal size and degenerating into a mass of fatty tissue. He also had large quantities of alcohol and amphetamines in his system. With his asthma and known fainting spells, all evidence pointed to his death as being accidental in nature and nothing more than that.

When friends of Jones heard about his death, the other feeling that was generally expressed besides grief was inevitability. No one who knew him was surprised that he had died, as most felt he was on his way to doing so at the rate he was going anyway. The voice of his fellow bandmate and friend, Bill Wyman, really came through a few years back with the conclusive reason for Jones death:

"... Whatever happened, it was just an unfortunate accident. I don't believe there was anybody else involved. I don't see the reason. Why would they? He was a pathetic guy, there was no good motive; he'd left the band, he wasn't interfering with anyone else's life, there was nothing there. He was just a pathetic, wasted guy who had a huge problem with drugs, who had psychological problems, who had health problems. He really was quite unwell."

Sources: Herman, Gary. ROCK 'N' ROLL BABYLON. Plexus, London. 2002 Pages 44-45.

Thompson, Dave. BETTER TO BURN OUT. Thunder's Mouth Press, New York. 1999. Pages 38-44.

Wohlin, Anna. THE MURDER OF BRIAN JONES. Blake Publishing, London. 1999.

Wyman, Bill and Coleman, Ray. STONE ALONE: THE STORY OF A ROCK 'N' ROLL BAND. Viking, New York. 1990. pages 527/529.

6: Probably the silliest of all the Rolling Stones rumors. In an interview in 1994, Ron Wood jokingly stated that Keith Richards was afraid of cheese. Some people took this to heart and now believe that Richards will run screaming from a room if cheese is present. No, really.

Source: "Out for Blood," Rolling Stones. No. 689, August 25, 1994.

Satanic Rock

> *It comes down to this – every musician, writer, producer and anybody else that is involved with music made after 1954 is in league with Satan. This includes Rock, Rap, Soul, Country, and Pop, and any people who think there's such a thing as "Christian" Rock, Rap, or Country, are just fooling themselves. They will all burn in Hell, and so will you if you listen to it.*

Well, that urban legend listed above pretty much covers it. For years people had assumed that Rock and Roll music was sinful. In the 1950s this came about because of how Rock and Roll was introduced into suburban, white middle class America. Some people saw no harm in the music, but many were unsure what to make of it. It had their kids jumping around and singing nonsense words like a bunch of crazed animals – totally forgetting that many of them did the same back in the 1930s and 1940s when it came to Jazz. Why, there was that young guy Elvis, swinging his hips on the Dorsey Brothers show and singing about gosh knows what. Later on it became those four Brits on the Sullivan show with all that long hair, driving the young girls into hysterics. After that were the even longer haired people, obviously on drugs and burning their draft cards. Then came the freaks with the glitter and multi-sexual practices in the 1970s, not to mention those Punks from Britain who beat up on people and cut themselves up. Once you got rid of them, it was more Brits with their hypnotic organ grinders and weird hair, not to mention those heavy metal people who were going out of their way to sing about Satanic things. Finally people started dressing normally again in the 1990s, but then came the "cop killing" rappers and the "no future" punk-like, flannel-wearing musicians from Seattle. No wonder the older generations were panicking.

It should be pointed out that historically most people took music in stride, remembering their own days of wanting to rebel a little against the norm, trying to find their own voices as they became teenagers. Music was just a method to help the kids get through the difficult teenage years and people accepted the music as being an extension of that frustration and aimlessness. For others, however, because it couldn't be understood, it became something to fear.

With this fear grew the sub-culture in religious circles (particular the Christian bible belt of the 1980s) that Rock music was the work of the devil. Several people helped to perpetuate the legend by focusing on "facts" that they used to show how evil rock music was. The facts usually fell into the following categories:

Satanic Groups – bands and musicians who were already in league with Satan and were trying to drag children down to Hell with their music. Some of the bands would even go so far as to flaunt their relationship with Satan through their names or albums covers: KISS was "Knights In Satan's Service" and AC/DC was "Anti-Christ / Devil Children," for example. Album covers would have mystical symbols or bizarre images that could have only been done to show "some type of Satanic image."

Lyrics – songs about drugs, sex, violence, were written by bands to try and influence children to join in the Satanic rituals of the rock bands.

Subliminal Messages – including backward messages. Hidden ways to brainwash the children, while attempting to make the songs appear "innocent." (See the Backward and Subliminal Messages entry for more details.)

The Personal Lives of the Performers – the arrests, outrageous behavior, and thoughts of the performers as told in the news and interviews were research to prove that – surprisingly enough – young people were unsure of what they wanted to do and tended to go wild when given freedom and money.

Books were written about the evils of Rock music. Lectures were held. Record burnings took place, all in the name of trying to "save the children" from the evils of rock music. As can be seen throughout this book, urban legends propagated like mad thanks to the insistent tales of the religious leaders who wanted to find something evil about anything related to performers in rock music. Soon it became a good cash business for some of the less-than-honest people involved, with their marketing of videos, audio cassettes and lectures (usually using copyrighted material without authorization).

Rock wasn't the only form of music to be deemed Satanic by the religious leaders. Country was seen that because of its preoccupations with alcohol, wife-beatings, and suicide; while Rap was anti-authority, sexual, and drug-oriented. Even "Christian Rock," such as Petra and Stryper were looked upon as being Satanic simply because a rock beat was used in the music.

Eventually, in the 1980s, some bands got it into their heads that by being "Satanic" they may be have a better cash cow on their hands. This led to bands that displayed anti-Christian symbols and lyrics on their albums simply for shock value, in hopes of making some money. Oh, some were no doubt sincere about it, but many more were just in it for the money, hoping that the religious leaders would attack them so they could gain some publicity.

All of this eventually led to the PMRC Senate hearings of the late 1980s backed by Tipper Gore, wife of then-Senator Al Gore and later Vice-President under Bill Clinton. The PMRC hearings turned into a mockery for both sides, with little being done aside from record companies voluntarily putting stickers on albums stating that the music contained therein may contain material not suitable for young children. In the end, these stickers probably did more to increase sales than dissuade people from listening to the albums.

As the 1980s wound down, so did the hysteria about "Satanic Music." Every so often a blip can be seen on the radar, and a religious leader somewhere will pick up on the old urban legends of lore (that KISS legend still circulates even today) and start passing them around again. Music, however, has not gone through any major drastic changes in the past ten years so things have been fairly quiet on that front.

At least for now.

The Sex Pistols

> *Bassist Sid Vicious was the unknowing victim of a police conspiracy that pinned the murder of Vicious' girlfriend by a known drug informant.*

Sid Vicious, whose real name was John Simon Ritchie, had been known in Punk circles since 1976 when he played drums at the first appearance of what would become Siouxsie and the Banshees. He was 18 at the time and not very good. It was a start though and he continued to be seen here and there around the various bands in the Punk scene and was asked to be the bassist for the Sex Pistols. The Sex Pistols had commonly been regarded as one of the most popular bands in the movement – some would argue that they were actually the best of the bands around, but they were beyond argument well known.

Sid was brought into the band without ever having learned the bass, and only began learning how to play a few weeks before they were set to tour in 1978. He was very young (as were all in the band for the most part), easily impressionable and prone to violent mood swings that became more evident when he had a chance to be in the spotlight in front of an audience that readily accepting the violence in the clubs they played.

Nancy Spungen was a topless dancer from America who had made her way to England in order to latch onto a popular musician. She was generally seen as a violent, drug-addicted groupie, and for these reasons was avoided by nearly anyone who encountered her. After Johnny Rotten (a.k.a. Johnny Lyndon) managed to avoid her, she set her sights on Vicious, who was happy with the attention.

The two became inseparable, which was not looked upon favorably by any of Sid's friends or fellow band members. Both had violent episodes and Spungen was visibly disliked by those around Vicious. Many also believed that it was Nancy who got Sid hooked on heroin, which the band and their manager, Malcolm McLaren, attempted to help Vicious overcome. This even led to McLaren considering having Spungen kidnapped and forcibly returned to America in order to get her away from Vicious, but Spungen stuck it out.

When the Sex Pistols went on their ill-fated American tour of 1978, another attempt was made to get Vicious off heroin, and there were signs of progress until Vicious returned to England where Spungen got him hooked again.

Two things did come out of the disaster that was the 1978 American Tour – one was the break-up of the Sex Pistols over issues dealing with manipulations of the band by McLaren. The other was Vicious' spontaneous stardom in the public eye. Yes, he was still seen as being crazy and evil, but after seeing continuous images of Vicious' face in the papers and on television, people at least knew who he was. It was fame, even if it was of a dark variety, and Vicious was thrown into the middle of it without any way to focus. Spungen hung on for the ride.

With the collapse of the band, Vicious returned to Spungen and the two fell deeply in love. They also continued on their spiraling heroin habit. By October 1978, they were staying in Room 100 at the Chelsea Hotel in New York City, both junkies and both clinically depressed. Spungen had even talked steadily about suicide, or how she wished Vicious would kill her to put her out of her misery. On October 12, 1978, it appears that Sid did exactly that.

On October 11, the two went to visit an acquaintance. During the visit, Vicious had shown off a knife he had with a five-inch blade. Later in the evening, they arrived back at their room at the Chelsea hotel and went to bed about 1 a.m., after having an argument. Vicious' statement to the police the next day mentioned that he drifted off to sleep watching Nancy playing with the knife. He also mentioned that they had both taken something that night.

When he woke up the next morning at around 10:30, Vicious continued in his statement, he felt that the bed sheet was wet with blood. Going to the bathroom, he found Spungen propped up under the sink with a large knife wound in her stomach. According to Vicious, Spungen was still alive at the time and he then left to get himself methadone. When he returned, she was dead. Dazed, Vicious tried to clean off the knife and tried to clean up Spungen's body, but could not do it. He then called for help and the Police arrived soon after.

Vicious' statement to the police was rambling and incoherent. At one point early on, he stated that he had "stabbed her" but "didn't mean to kill her"; after that, however, he professed repeatedly that he did not stab her, insisting that she had somehow fallen on the knife and dragged herself into the bathroom. He would then later state that Spungen had not fallen on the knife, but had killed herself. In other words, he incriminated himself and then tried to back away from his statement.

The police didn't believe Vicious' innocence, and his having left the hotel to get himself methadone while she was, according to Vicious, still alive, did nothing to help. Vicious himself didn't even seem convinced, exclaiming that he "was a dog" for leaving her. He was arrested and taken to jail.

On October 17, he was released on $50,000 bail, paid by McLaren, but was arrested again on December 8, 1978 after attacking Todd Smith, the brother of musician Patti Smith, with a broken beer mug at a club. When he was released at the beginning of February, it was in the custody of his mother, Anne Beverly. Within just a few hours he was dead of a heroin overdose, heroin that his mother had gotten for him earlier in the day. He was only 21 years old.

So, where does the conspiracy come into play? Mainly thanks to the incoherent nature of Vicious' statement at the crime scene. Because he at first confessed and then denied that he had killed, some conspiracy theorists believe that Vicious had confessed in a stupor and didn't really know what he was saying. While some would believe that Nancy actually had killed herself and inadvertently made it appear to be of Sid's doing – she was known for suicidal tendencies before – many conspiracy theorist believed that it was an outside party who actually killed her that night.

The legend goes that a drug dealer known to the couple arrived that morning looking for money. Vicious was already passed at out that moment and Nancy told the drug dealer to leave. A fight ensued and when it was over Nancy had been stabbed with her own knife and left bleeding in the bathroom. It was then that Vicious woke up and found her dying. In the gray fog of panic and drugs, Vicious confessed to the crime, thinking it had to be him because it was possible that something like it could happen.

The police, according to the legend, had eye witnesses claiming that a man left the room that morning, but the police buried these reports because they knew the man who had killed Spungen – an informant. Not wishing to lose their informant, they planted evidence and changed Vicious' statement to read that he confessed, and then tried to cover.

Another variation of this conspiracy theory was that government agents attacked Spungen during the night and planted the evidence in order to implicate Vicious in her death. Of course the question with this scenario is, simply, why? Even if Vicious was considered some type of threat to the U.S. Government (or even the New York Police Department), there would be no reason to implicate Vicious in a murder when the couple's drug addictions were progressing to the point where they could barely leave their room, much less start some type of revolution.

One common thread of evidence given by the conspiracy theorists was the size of the wound on Nancy's body. Some have suggested that the five-inch knife did not do the damage and instead another weapon had been used. Yet there was no evidence to show that the knife was not the murder weapon.

With what is known about the case, it's clear that Nancy Spungen did die due to a knife wound to the abdomen. It was also clear that it was their knife and that the two had been fighting the night before. What remains unclear is if Spungen had killed herself or if Vicious had done it. Most friends and even the Nancy's mother went on record saying that they were sure that Vicious had done it, although possibly only in answer to Nancy's constant requests that she be put out of her misery. In the drug filled haze the two lived in, it would not be surprising to find out that he had done so with no malice aforethought and had no retentive memory of even doing it. The effect was still the same, however – Nancy had bled to death, and Vicious allowed her to die. After months of guilt over her death, Vicious would finally join Nancy in a violent type of peace.

Sources: "Sid Vicious' Biggest Hit," The Smoking Gun.
http://www.thesmokinggun.com/vicious/
Stallings, Penny. ROCK 'N' ROLL CONFIDENTIAL. Little, Brown and Company, Boston. 1984. Page 215.

Tupac Shakur

> *The death of Tupac Shakur involved a cover-up. He is actually alive and still recording and his death was only a way for him to get away from people who wanted him dead. On the other side of the fence, Shakur's death, as with that of Christopher Wallace (a.k.a. The Notorious B.I.G.), was supposedly covered up by the Police in order to avoid connecting police officers with the shooting.*

It's no surprise that controversial and contradictory urban legends grew up around the death of Tupac Shakur, for he was certainly one of the most controversial of performers in the 1990s. A rapper with strong political and poetic streaks in his work, he found himself on the wrong end of the law and the wrong end of a gun. In November 1994, he was robbed and shot five times – an incident that Tupac believed was staged by Biggie Small (The Notorious B.I.G), Sean "Puffy" Combs and others connected with Bad Boy Entertainment. The incident set into motion what some say was a "staged" rivalry between Bad Boy Entertainment on the East Coast and Marion "Suge" Knight and his Death Row Records on the West Coast, with Tupac in the middle. Tupac continuously made remarks about Small and the people connected with him, while signing with Knight and Death Row Records after Knight helped arrange parole for Tupac, who was serving time after being found guilty of sexual assault.

When Tupac was shot to death after a boxing match in Las Vegas, Nevada on September 8, 1996, and died five days later, the rumors started flying. Some assumed that Biggie Small was involved with the shooting, hiring people to take care of Tupac after Tupac repeatedly "bragged" about sleeping with Small's wife, singer Faith Evans. When the Las Vegas police couldn't find witnesses forthcoming, it only heightened the rumor that a cover-up was occurring and that the police were in on Tupac's murder. From the many stories told by those who believed in the cover-up – helped especially by articles and even books written about the topic, including Randall Sullivan's recent book, LABYRINTH – the off-duty police officers were hired to help kill Tupac. Thus, when the police found that they would be implicating their fellow officers, they covered up the story. Ironically enough, this same conspiracy by the police would be claimed after the shooting death of Biggie Small in Los Angeles just a few months later in March 1997, with many believing that, in this case, the Los Angeles Police Department ignored witnesses and the evidence because, as the rumor goes, Knight had hired off-duty police officers to kill Small.

While stories of police corruption do occur, there has never been enough evidence to support the story of a massive multi-state cover-up to both murders. Obviously, both were killed by someone wanting to gun them down and make some type of point (some have even suggested that Small's death was attributed to unknown gang members who wanted to pay him back for the death of their hero, Tupac), but the lack of evidence on the part of the police, the press and the public at large, compounded by latter cases of police corruption that would have readily exposed such a cover-up, makes the hopes and wishes of the theorists rather dicey. As it stands, it is quite possible that until someone comes forward with more information, Tupac's and Small's deaths will remain unsolved crimes.

The other rumor that arose from Tupac's death was that he had actually not died in September 1996, but had rather arranged the whole thing in order to go into hiding. The urban legend goes that after the shooting in 1994 Tupac became increasingly paranoid that people were after him. With the rivalry heating up, along with other controversies, Tupac knew that he had to do something or else he would be killed by someone soon. To avoid this, he staged the shooting at the MGM Grand the night of the boxing match. Slipping out of sight, everyone involved acted like he was actually dead, and he went into hiding. He is still in hiding today, waiting for the air to clear before he makes a public return.

This rumor started most probably because of the proliferation of musical material released after his death. All of it was recorded before his death, but so much of it appeared that it was hard not to wonder how he managed to record so much "ahead of time." Meanwhile, many of his lyrics dealt with death and dying, lending rather ominous meanings behind his songs after his death, leading to more theories that he could have only written about such things after he had "died." These theories have even led to web sites dedicated to listing all of the clues in his music, videos, and life to support the claim that he was still alive. In essence, it became the exact opposite of the many "Paul Is Dead" sites that exist (see the Beatles entry for more details), with the Shakur sites trying to prove he was alive although he was actually dead.

While wishing to have your favorite artist still alive is understandable, it doesn't stack up well against later lawsuits from many people who have fought not only with the police over the possibility of a cover-up, but also with each other over the rights to Tupac's estate. And the outrage felt by Tupac's family over the supposed cover-up wouldn't have existed if Tupac was simply hiding out.

Source: Herman, Gary. ROCK 'N' ROLL BABYLON. Plexus, London. 2002. Pages 253-256.

Carly Simon

Simon's popular hit You're So Vain *was written about Mick Jagger, Warren Beatty, or James Taylor.*

Whenever a song is written as a story told from a personal standpoint, many listeners wish to believe that the song tells a true story about the singer's past. The thinking boils down to the listeners thinking, "no one could have written about this experience unless they lived it."

The song *You're So Vain* deals with a woman spotting a former lover at a party. The man knows he is good looking and enters the party only to stop and stare at his reflection. While other women at the party jockey to get near him, the narrator obviously knows the man too well, pointing out his vanity.

When the song became a hit and people realized that Simon had written it, there was a natural tendency to try to figure out just who she was singing about who was "so vain."

Carly Simon was known as an artist who did fashion her songs around events in her life and the men she had known, so the assumption by listeners was really not that much of a stretch There were charges directed at many different individuals in Simon's past, but three men in particular were usually cited as the vain man in the song:

James Taylor. Simon had a long relationship with singer James Taylor (who has an urban legend dealing with autobiographical songs himself, see the entry for James Taylor for more detail), and they were married for a number of years. Taylor had been known for his charmingly "boy next door" looks and demeanor at time, while also considered a bit standoffish and "full of himself." The relationship between Simon and Taylor was also known to have been a constant struggle, leading to their eventual breakup.

Mick Jagger. At some point Simon and Jagger had dated for a brief time. Jagger has always come across in interviews and on stage as "sure of himself." Some would go so far as to suggest that he was more "full of himself" than "sure of himself," but the point is still made either way. He would have definitely been someone at a party that the women would have clamored towards and he was true that he would make sure he looked his best at all times, thus leading naturally to the presumption that he probably would be gazing at his reflection in a mirror when walking in to a room. Jagger actually sang some background vocals on this song (no, not the high female parts, as some people have joked over the years), leading people to deem it "ironic" that Jagger would be singing background on a song that painted him as "vain," like he didn't realize the song was about him. The problem with such irony is that the song repeatedly states that the man "probably thinks the song is about him," and so Jagger knew the song was about him. The logic loop doesn't make any sense (the song was about him, but he's so vain he didn't know the song was about him), although the other side of the argument in favor of Jagger being the man in the song is that Jagger did know it was about him and just didn't care.

Warren Beatty. Another man Simon dated for a brief time. Beatty was known as a notorious lady-killer. He was also a dramatically handsome young man who at times seemed more fixated on himself than about any of the beautiful women who practically threw themselves at his feet. He would be a natural for the song.

Many times the question has been raised to Carly Simon: who was the man in the song? Simon has gone so far as to admit that the song was written about a man she did have a relationship with, but has never gone on record as saying who the man was. There were reports at one time that Simon stated in an interview that the man was Warren Beatty, but there has been little record of where this interview took place. Simon has gone so far as to admit that the man was not James Taylor, although many assumed that he would have fit the song just as well as the others listed. As it stands, it is still unknown who exactly Simon was talking about, and she isn't offering any information to clear the air.

Skinny Puppy

The band brought out a puppy during an early 1990s concert in Chicago and kicked it about the stage until it died.

Ogre of Skinny Puppy

This industrial / metal / alternative band was known for the goth-oriented music that they created between 1982 through 1995. Because of this background, Skinny Puppy earned a variation of an urban legend that had been a staple rumor for such artists as Marilyn Manson, Alice Cooper and Ozzy Osbourne. This particular "puppy killing" event supposedly happened at a show in Chicago during the early 1990s. As mentioned in previous entries, such an event would have surely been noted by the audience and the public if it had actually occurred.

In the case of Skinny Puppy, however, the band actually did get involved in a situation where they were arrested under the assumption that they had actually killed a dog on stage. On the VIVIsectVI tour in 1988, the band's stage presentation consisted of a stuffed dog, named CHUD, being destroyed on stage in order to demonstrate the horrors of vivisection. While performing the show in Cincinnati, Ohio, an audience member thought the stuffed dog was alive and complained to the police about the supposed animal cruelty. As it happened, when the police arrived, they quickly found that no animal cruelty had occurred. The police did arrest two members of the band and the tour manager for disorderly conduct and they spent the night in jail.

Source: Goldberg, Corey M. "The Skinny Puppy (and Related Projects) FAQ."
http://www.monmouth.com/~sgoldberg/faqraw.txt. May 25, 2001.

Grace Slick

In April 1970, Grace Slick of the Jefferson Airplane (later, Jefferson Starship and then Starship) was invited to Richard Nixon's daughter Tricia's wedding.   At the wedding she put LSD into the water, causing everyone to hallucinate.

This was an urban legend from the early 1970s that has been mostly forgotten over time simply because the characters involved have been relegated to a time period nearly thirty years in the past. Nixon, of course, will forever be remembered as the first U.S. President to resign from office, because of the whole Watergate scandal. Grace Slick, as mentioned above, was at the time lead singer in the San Francisco-based, psychedelic rock band, the Jefferson Airplane. The band was well known for such hits as *White Rabbit* and *Somebody To Love*, both of which featured Slick's incredibly sonic vocals. She was also known for being an "uppity" liberated woman who was friends with several political activists who were against the politicians in office at the time; So, the older, conservative generations saw Slick as a danger to society.

So, if Slick was so anti-establishment that she was looked upon with suspicion, what is all this about her being at Tricia Nixon's wedding? Answer, it never happened, although there are elements of the story that actually have a basis in fact.

Finch College, referred to as a "bow and curtsey academy" by Slick, was a college that both Slick and Tricia Nixon (although not at the same time – Slick attended nearly ten years before Tricia). In April 1970, it was decided to have a tea party for some of the graduates of the college at the White House, with Tricia hosting. Even though a screening program was in place, an invitation was sent to Grace Slick. The opportunity for mischief of one type or another was too much for Slick to pass up, and her first stab at trouble was letting the organizers know that her "escort" for the party would be a "Mr. Leonard Haufman" – commonly known as left-wing activist Abbie Hoffman.

In her book SOMEBODY TO LOVE? Slick goes into great detail about what they wanted to accomplish upon arriving at the party – namely dropping pure "acid" into Richard Nixon's coffee cup. However, from her description of the event itself, it was clear that neither she nor Hoffman expected to get into the event in the first place considering the way they decided to disguise themselves. Slick states in the book that Hoffman, with slicked-back hair and a suit and tie, "looked like a hit man for the Mafia." Meanwhile, Slick wore a fishnet top, short black miniskirt and long back boots, making the pair look like a "pimp and a go-go-girl."

Upon arriving at security, the jig was up. Security recognized both of them, telling Slick that she was considered a security risk since she was on an FBI list. Although security finally relented and allowed Slick into the party, they refused to let Hoffman enter,

whereupon the two left – LSD still in their clothing, since they weren't searched. Slick went on to state in her book that evidently both Mrs. Nixon and Tricia wanted to meet Grace when word reached them that she was there, but Slick and Hoffman had already left by the time they found out about the incident.

As one can guess, Slick was not invited to Tricia's wedding, which happened several months later. Slick admits now that although the idea seemed prankish at the time, it probably was a dangerous thing to attempt. Perhaps both Slick and Hoffman realized that subconsciously that day, as the opportunity for their subversion was still available (Slick was, after all, invited into the party, but refused to enter without Hoffman).

Sources: Morgan, Hal and Tucker, Kerry. RUMOR!. Penguin Books, New York. 1984, page 88.
Slick, Grace. SOMEBODY TO LOVE?. Warner Books, New York. 1998. Pages 189-194.

Smashing Pumpkins

> *Billy Corgan of the Smashing Pumpkins played Jamie on the situation-comedy series, SMALL WONDER.*

Does anyone even remember the short-lived television series, SMALL WONDER? If not, the main point of this legend is to take a child actor and suggest that he or she grew up to become a famous musician. Similar rumors have also been attributed to Alice Cooper, Madonna, Marilyn Manson, and others over the years.

The part of Jamie on SMALL WONDER was played by Jerry Supiran. Corgan was not on the series.

Phil Spector

> *Phil Spector produced a single for the Crystals called* Let's Dance the Screw, *knowing that it would never be released commercially and his Philles Records partner, Lester Sill, would never get any royalties from the song.*

Here's the legend: Phil Spector, the genius producer behind the famous "Wall of Sound" of the 1960s, wanted out of his business relationship with his label partner, Lester Sill. Neither was happy with the other by 1963, and the break-up of their partnership eventually led to a lawsuit over royalties by Sill. Besides a cash buy-out (which later caused legal problems between the two), the settlement reached gave Sill a piece of the royalties from the next single released through Philles. Spector had just finished work on the Crystals' next single, *Da Doo Ron Ron*, and, knowing that it would be a smash hit and earn mega-royalties, he wasn't thrilled with the idea of letting Sill have a piece of the pie. Instead, Spector went into the studio and recorded a song called *Let's Dance the Screw Part 1 and Part 2*. "Part 1" consisted of an instrumental with backing vocals and Spector himself flatly telling the listener to "Dance the Screw." "Part 2" consisted of more of the same. The single, of course, never received any air play because of the nature of the song – it flopped and Sill received no royalties.

For anyone who has ever wanted to get back at a business partner, Spector's legend is a brilliant story. Of course, Spector was not really "sticking it to the boss" in this case, as Spector and Sill were partners in the Philles (a combination of both men's first names). Still, the legend makes Spector out to be the mastermind behind a flamboyant practical joke that allowed him to "screw" over his former partner, while saving a subsequent hit from making money for that same ex-partner.

Yet the details about this situation have never been completely uncovered. The first widespread, documented discussion of this story came in Mark Ribowsky's biography on Spector, HE'S A REBEL, although rumors circulated for quite some time in fan circles. Ribowsky tells a different variation of the story from that of what most fans had heard, however.

In Ribowsky's book, Lester Sill discusses the single briefly, describing it as a personal "fuck you, buddy" statement to Sill from Spector over their previous business relationship. In the space of one two-sentence paragraph, Ribowsky goes on to suggest that only one copy of the single was pressed, and that copy only went to Sill. This would seem to verify that Sill's memory of the recording is validated. After all, with only one single, there was certainly no point in assuming that Spector intended for the song to be anything more than a personal message to Sill. Others have suggested that this seems the logical reason for the single, especially in light of the fact that Philles would later reuse the catalog number of Philles 111 for Darlene Love. This would imply that Philles never intended to release the *Let's Dance the Screw* single commercially.

However, this statement neglects other aspects of the story. First, while it is not common, it is possible for record labels to reuse the catalog number of a pulled single. Commonly, such occurrences are rare and typical only in cases when a single was pulled before it was even released, but that still works within the confines of this particular legend. After all, any version of this story is built upon the foundation that Spector knew this single would never become a hit due to its nature. So, why throw out the use of a catalog number when it could be used for the next "real" single?

Keep in mind that Philles Records, as with other labels, was not always the best of record keepers when it came to catalog numbers. As pointed out by Mark Landwehr on his internet web site, The Phil Spector Label Gallery, the Righteous Brothers' single for *Unchained Melody* was reissued with the same catalog number, even though changes occurred to the single to make it different (*Unchained Melody* moved from the B-side to A-side, and listing Spector as the producer suddenly appeared as well). Another example was the Crystals' single for *He's Sure the Boy I Love*, which was released as both Philles 109 and Philles 109X for reasons unknown. If that isn't proof enough, Spector created a single called *Thanks for Giving Me the Right Time!* as a Christmas present in 1965 that didn't have any catalog number – which makes sense considering that Spector meant the disc to be a private gift to others and not meant for public consumption. If this was true, why would Philles bother with a catalog number for the one-copy joke *Let's Dance the Screw*?

Secondly, on his excellent web site, Mark Landwehr proves that Ribowsky was incorrect in suggesting that the only copy pressed was the one given to Sill. There are at least three known copies besides Sill's copy in existence, and rumors of three or four more on top of that. (It should be noted that bootleg copies of the single also exist.) Landwehr also made the excellent argument that no pressing plant would press only one copy of a single, no matter who was in charge. Fifty to one hundred copies would be an absolute minimum for a pressing plant; meaning that even as a vicious joke, Spector would have been aware that a lot of money was going into the presentation just to send off one single.

Moreover, why would Sill – a man who had been in the record business for some time at that point – willingly settle for just a cash buyout for a company that he helped create? Yes, Ribowsky reported correctly that Sill was so fed up with working with Spector that he wanted out any way possible, but it would seem highly unlikely that Sill would sign a settlement that cut him off completely from all activities of the company still being worked on while he was involved. A settlement that allowed him some future royalties would make sense, and this is why the original version of the legend seems more logical than the one so quickly glossed over in Ribowsky's book.

Either way the story is told, there is one portion of the legend that everyone agrees is true – Phil Spector masterminded an elaborate (and some say spiteful) practical joke on his former partner with this single. And, you can dance to it, as well.

Sources: Ribowsky, Mark. HE'S A REBEL. E. P. Dutton, New York. 1989, page 131.
Neely, Tim. "25 of the Most Collectible Phil Spector Records," Goldmine. February 22, 2002, Vol. 28, No. 4, page 19.
Landwehr, Mark. "Withdrawn & Unreleased Philles Records," The Phil Spector Label Gallery,
http://home.tbbs.net~msland/Specto/PS0004.htm

Rod Stewart

> *Stewart once had to be rushed to the hospital to have his stomach pumped of semen after a party with a group of football players.*

See the Stomach Pump Entry.

Stomach Pump

> *A popular rock star is forced to go to the hospital after passing out on stage. Complaining about severe stomach cramps, the doctors have to pump nearly a gallon of human semen out the rock star's stomach.*

One of the top ten rock music urban legends of all time, the "stomach pump" story has been told and retold for decades, usually with the newest, most popular performer being the unfortunate hospital patient. The only other major changes in the story over the years have been either the amount of semen that had to be pumped out of the stomach, the location, and perhaps the species involved. Otherwise, the story stays basically the same, with only the name changed.

As seen throughout the many entries here, there have been several performers that have had their names entered into the Stomach Pump sweepstakes over the years. The classic version deals with either Rod Stewart or Elton John (thanks to their obvious love for European Football, as will be discussed briefly), but many others have also suffered the same fate, including David Bowie, Mick Jagger, Jeff Beck, Jon Bon Jovi, Alanis Morrisette, Madonna, Lil'l Kim, Britney Spears, Fiona Apple, Marilyn Manson and even random members of groups like New Kids on the Block and the Bay City Rollers.

The build-up and resolution of the urban legend typically go as follows (Stewart will be used here as the example most commonly referred to during the 1970s): Stewart, a long-time fan of European Football (a.k.a. soccer), was happy to see his favorite team win a major game. In honor of their win, he invited the team to come to a pre-concert party to celebrate. Once there, Stewart and the football players got so drunk that Stewart decided to give them a special gift by performing oral sex on each member of the team. It was after accomplishing this feat that Stewart began to suffer from severe stomach cramps and had to be taken away to the hospital to have his stomach pumped.

The Elton John version of the story is the same, as is that of Jeff Beck. Other male performers have had the story changed to that of a large group of male prostitutes or male groupies. A more recent revision to the story has transferred the sex of the performer to female – quite a change since the story was told about male performers only in the past. This new variation goes one better – the female performer is supposedly involved with a number of dogs instead of men in many such retellings.

Of course, the story is nothing more than a shock-value tactic to make a performer look like a sexual pervert. Of course, in the case of the men, it was commonly told to present the performer as not only a homosexual, but a sexually-insatiable freak who would have indiscriminate sex with a large group of men at once. Typically, the story was told about performers that were either already known for their bisexuality or homosexuality; in other cases, it was attributed to male performers that the storyteller merely wished to put down by making them sound as if they were secretly homosexual. As for the women, the story evidently wasn't bad enough when it was a large group of men all at once, it had to be changed to an even stronger perversion by having the story include dogs. Again, a story simply told to make the performer look as unnatural and disgusting as possible, while also foolish and embarrassing with the outcome of their follies.

Source: "I've Got Love in My Tummy," Urban Legend Reference Pages. http://www.snopes.com/music/artists/rockstar.htm. February 4, 2001

James Taylor

The song Fire and Rain *is about a girl friend of James who died in a plane crash.*

The legend goes like this: During the early period of his music career, Taylor had a girlfriend named Suzanne, who he rarely got to see with his constant traveling. One day Taylor's friends decided to pay for Suzanne's airplane ticket so she could surprise Taylor after a show. Unfortunately, the plane crashed in a bad storm, killing Suzanne instantly. Because of the nature of her death, Taylor's friends waited several days before telling him about the tragic accident. The song is a direct retelling of the incident and his mind-set after being told.

A review of the song's lyrics would certainly support this story. The song, obviously about not being able to see someone again, begins with a verse explaining that the protagonist had just been told about Suzanne "being gone." Moreso, "the plans they made for you put an end to you." Thus, the plans made by Taylor's friends ended up with his girl friend being killed in a plane crash. So far, so good; yet the remainder of the song doesn't provide any further mention of Suzanne or her death until the very last line before the final chorus, where "Sweet dreams and flying machines [are] in pieces on the ground." This, therefore, talks about the plane crash itself. This is a bit of a jump from one context to another within the song. In fact, when reviewing the song, only about a quarter of it actually has anything to do with this version of the legend, making the rest of the song a bit non-sensical. That is, unless a listener believes a variation of the story, that the plane crashed in a rain storm and so, "I've seen fire and I've seen rain," is a reference to the plane crash itself.

In reality, while the lyrics are autobiographical, they are not about a girlfriend dying in a plane crash. In fact, the focus is not really on that of a friend's death at all, but rather how that friend's death was just one component of many that Taylor went through while recovering from physical and mental problems.

As fans know, James Taylor had a series of hospital stays over the years for clinical depression, substance abuse, and physical injuries. While recuperating from depression in the 1960s, he met a woman who was the Suzanne mentioned in the song. They became friendly and kept in touch, yet months after Taylor left the mental hospital he found out that the woman had committed suicide. The "they" of the song lyrics is actually a friend of Taylor's who withheld the information about her death until after he had finished recording an album for fear that the news would send him into another state of depression or into a spiral of drugs. This explains in more details exactly what is happening in the beginning of the song – the friends are not trying to hide their mistake (as the legend would lead one to believe), but rather to help Taylor until he was more mentally prepared for the news. This event in Taylor's life also jibes with the chorus, especially the line about always expecting to see the person again.

In full, the song deals with Taylor's mental well-being more than anything else. As Taylor himself stated in an interview with ROLLING STONE back in 1973, the song effectively dealt with three events in his life via the three verses in the song. The first verse dealt with the death of his friend that he missed out in knowing because of the concerns of his friends for his well-being; the second with the hardship of trying to get through his pain and suffering; and the third with his recuperation. As for "sweet dreams and flying machines," this pertains to his band, the Flying Machine, which had to break up in 1967 after he left the band due to drug problems.

Sources: "Fire   and   Rain,"   Urban   Legends   Reference   Pages,
http://www.snopes.com/music/songs/firerain.htm
Halperin, Ian. FIRE AND RAIN: THE JAMES TAYLOR STORY. Citadel Press, New York. 2000, pages 93-97.
Werbin, Stuart. "The Rolling Stone Interview: James Taylor and Carly Simon." Rolling Stone. January 4, 1973.

Van Halen

1. *After Gary Cherone left Van Halen, the band recorded with David Coverdale.*
2. *Van Halen had a stipulation in their contract that no brown M&M candies were to be found in bowls of M&Ms backstage at their concerts or else the show would be canceled. When brown M&Ms were found at a show at the University of Colorado, the band caused nearly $100,000 in damage to the arena in retaliation.*

1: In late 1999, after the third vocalist for Van Halen, Gary Cherone, had left the band, a rumor went around that David Coverdale was recording with them. Coverdale, a vocalist with Whitesnake and Deep Purple, was supposedly recording several tracks with Eddie and Alex Van Halen and bassist Billy Sheehan. The rumor was debunked eventually, but not before the story had spread throughout the Internet.

2: The band actually did have a clause in their contract stating that M&M candies were to be waiting in bowls backstage at their concerts, and that no brown M&Ms were to be found in the bowls "upon pain of forfeiture of the show, with full compensation." At the time, it was laughed at, assuming that the band had done it just as a joke. When a show at the University of Colorado included brown M&M candies in the bowl, and a dressing room was subsequently wrecked, the public began seeing Van Halen as a bunch of prissy prima-donnas. When it came out that over $80,000 worth of damage was done to the university's arena, the public then viewed them as a bunch of *crazy*, prissy prima-donnas.

David Lee Roth in his book CRAZY FROM THE HEAT offered up a logical reason for such a bizarre clause in their contract. The tours at the time were huge operations, consisting of several tractor-trailers and literally tons of equipment that had to be properly put together at a new location nearly every single day of the tour. If one thing went wrong, a problem would multiply and eventually either the show would not go properly or a dangerous accident would be waiting to happen due to careless work done by the people assisting at each new location.

David Lee Roth

The M&M clause was one to show whether the arenas that had signed to do a certain number of things to get the stage and lighting up and running had followed everything to the letter. Some arena managers were known for their simply glancing at a contract and/or finding cheaper ways of doing things than requested in order to save a buck here and there. The M&M clause was so minor and – some felt – ridiculous that it was readily ignored. If such a thing was ignored, the band and their management felt, then probably a dozen or more other things were also ignored in the contract. It would therefore be a sure sign that everything had to be checked out thoroughly before the show began or else something probably would go wrong.

When the brown M&Ms turned up backstage at the show in Colorado, Roth took it as a sign to go nuts and subsequently did wreck a dressing room to show his disapproval. As Roth points out in his autobiography, however, the damage he did to the room was about $12,000. The rest of the damage was not done by the band, but rather by the weight of all the equipment being too heavy for the floor of the arena, therefore causing about $70,000 worth of damage – just as the band had anticipated if the details of the contract were not followed.

When the word went out to the press about the dollar amount of the damage, little was said about the majority of the damage being done by non-adherence to the contract. Instead, it was usually addressed as being due to the "Van Halen concert," and with word of Roth's wrecking of the dressing room, it was just naturally assumed that the damage done backstage by Roth was the sole cause of all the damage caused in the area.

As Roth said in his book: "Well, who am I to get in the way of a good rumor?"

Source: Roth, David Lee. CRAZY FROM THE HEAT. Hyperion, New York. 1997. Pages 97-98.

The Who

1. *Keith Moon was a young kid who happened to go to a pub to see the Who playing on stage. He thought the drummer was terrible, and during a break between sets, told Pete Townshend and Roger Daltrey that he could play rings around the drummer they had. Pete and Roger, humored by the brass attitude of the kid, decided to let him try it, whereupon Keith amazed everyone with his abilities on the drums. After the gig, Pete and Roger fired their drummer and asked Keith to join the band.*

2. *In a drunken rage, Keith killed his chauffeur by backing his car over the man.*

3. *Keith Moon did not die from an overdose of Heminevrin (a prescription drug taken to help with his alcoholism); instead, he choked to death on his own vomit. Or, maybe died from a cocaine overdose. Either way, he died in Paul McCartney's house and had to be moved back to his own place before calling for an ambulance.*

4. *Pete Townshend's song Rough Boys, from his solo album EMPTY GLASS, was an attack directed at a group of punk rockers who had insulted the Who in an interview.*

5. *Pete Townshend is bisexual.*

6. *The stuttering done by Roger Daltrey in My Generation was an accident in the recording studio that sounded so good that the band decided to keep it in the song. It was supposed to represent a nervous, angry young man, trying to speak while hooked on amphetamines.*

7. *Keith Moon celebrated his twentieth birthday while on tour by destroying a Holiday Inn, climaxing the carnage by driving a brand new Lincoln Continental automobile into the motel pool.*

1: As the story goes, it was the middle of May, on a Thursday night, when the Who was taking it easy between sets at a pub called the Oldfield. They had lost their drummer in April and had been going through an unsuccessful series of try-outs for a new drummer since then. They were finally down to paying a studio musician named Dave to play with them when doing shows, but the expense was high and no one saw it as a permanent position. With the word on the street being that a band called the Who had a rich manager, a series of gigs awaiting them, and a possibility of a record deal, many drummers were eyeing the band. On that Thursday night, Keith Moon, a drummer struggling to make a go of it, sneaked into the pub and between sets offered his services to the band.

As stated in the well-known story told about Moon joining the band, Townshend, Daltrey and John Entwistle were amused by the brashness of the kid, and decided to let him have a go at the drums in the next set. The story then goes on to say that Moon not only impressed the others, but literally destroyed Dave's drum kit because of the way he pounded on the kit during the set. When Moon left the stage and Dave returned to finish the set, he found that the kit was in horrible shape and even the drum pedal for the bass drum had been broken in two. Because of all the damage, Dave finished the set sounding terrible, making Moon look even better when the set was completed. After the gig, Dave supposedly charged the band for the damage done and left. Meanwhile, Roger and Pete hurried out to find Moon and immediately asked him to join the band. The rest was history, so to speak.

It's a great story and one that has been told time and time again. It is also possibly the genesis of an urban legend commonly told about Eric Clapton (see the entry for Eric Clapton for more details). The only problem is that there are no eye witnesses to this story as claimed, and the only witness that has gone on record about Moon joining the band at the Oldfield claims that it never happened. In Tony Fletcher's excellent biography on Keith Moon, MOON, the manager of the Oldfield at the time, Louis Hunt, remembers what had happened quite differently. The Who did play at Oldfield, Hunt states in the book, but the bands that played there had a specific night of the week that was theirs to use, and Thursdays were not a normal night for the Who to have played. He did remember Moon being told about the Who looking for a drummer and distinctly remembered Moon coming into the Oldfield on that particular Thursday looking for the band. When told that they were practicing in a drill hall in Acton, Moon departed anxiously, leaving Hunt obviously assuming that Moon was going down to try out for the band that very instant.

As Fletcher points out in his book, while Hunt's story conflicts with the standard story told about Moon joining the band, there is some logic to what he said. First, Hunt had no reason to change the story since Keith and the band had always mentioned that it was Hunt who told Moon about the Who needing a drummer; therefore, Hunt's version of the story certainly doesn't favor his involvement in any way (unlike some stories by people who supposedly "introduced the famous people to each other" as presented in some bands' biographies). Furthermore, the incident as always told seems to lean towards "collective amnesia," since none of the regulars who knew of the Who (and the band was fairly popular in the area at the time, even before Keith joined) have ever have gone on record as seeing this event occur at the Oldfield.

Fletcher speculated that what may have occurred is that Moon did go to the hall where the band was practicing that night and did audition for them as has always been part of the story. Fletcher also deduces that it may have even been a case where he went home and had his parents drive him to Acton with his personal drum kit, as a latter retelling of the event by Keith's mother places her at the audition as well.

Fletcher concluded that perhaps the main thrust of the story is close to being true, only the names and places be changed to make the story more exciting – after all, what would be more exciting than having Moon be established in the band during the middle of a show and astonishing everyone there at the club? For Fletcher, the changes in the story from the facts were not surprising, since the band was known for going for the "legend" even though the "facts" were almost as interesting.

Source: Fletcher, Tony. MOON. Avon Books, New York. 1999. Pages 78-81.

2: By the late 1960s, rock stars were becoming so famous that they were beginning to invest in businesses outside of the music field. In some cases, these activities were pursued because the artists had a creative or personal stake in the new business; for others, it was a tax dodge or simply a glorified ego trip. In Keith Moon's case, he had become involved in a disco, not only for the ego stroke, but also because it meant establishing a type of place he felt most at home in: a party atmosphere with a lot of drinking and the chance for him to be the life of the party.

The disco was the Cranbourne Rooms and was located in Hatfield, very close to his home at the time. The plan that night in January 1970 was to go with his wife, Kim Moon, and a few other friends to the club to celebrate its opening and have a few laughs along the way. Driving them to the disco that night was Neil Boland, Keith's chauffeur.

The problem was that the atmosphere at the club was not the most inviting, with several skinheads in the crowd that night who didn't look pleasantly at the long haired "freaks" in attendance. With the drinking going on during the night, the feelings of anger and hate only grew, and with Moon as the center of attention, the hatred was directed at him.

Moon tried to keep the crowd happy, but things only worsened and by the time the club closed that night, ugliness was prevalent in the crowd. Moon and his party made their way out to their Bentley, but not before Moon made a parting insult to one of the skinheads in the crowd. With a large number of people leaving at the same time, Moon's party found themselves surrounded in the parking lot by well-wishers, drunks, and, unfortunately, skinheads who decided that they wanted a chance to have a go at the celebrity in the Bentley.

With people starting to beat on the car with their fists and with rocks, Boland took it upon himself to try to clear a path in front of the car so they could leave. Doing so only led to Boland being pounced upon by the skinheads and he was swallowed up in the crowd. Moon, taking matters into his own hands, slipped behind the wheel and gunned the car forward through the crowd.

Moon, in a panic, drove through the crowd, little realizing that Boland had made a dash for the car. In the confusion, Boland somehow fell under the car; exactly how it happened was something which no witnesses could agree on. People tried alerting

Moon and his party to what had happened, only to appear to the frightened people in the car to be attacking, leading to a further acceleration of the Bentley by Moon. By the time they were finally made to understand that someone was under the car, still being dragged down the street, it was too late. Boland was dead.

When the newspapers got hold of the story, it was very easy to embellish the incident (especially in the early days of the police investigation into the event) to make it appear that Moon had murdered his chauffeur. Within days, stories were going around that Moon had gotten into a fight at the club with Boland and had intentionally run over him when Boland stepped out of the car in the middle of the fight. There was also a rumor that Moon knowingly ran over Boland just to get away from the crowd after they started attacking the car.

When the investigation was completed, however, it was clear from the witnesses' stories (including one of the skinheads involved in beating on Boland after he got out of the Bentley) that Boland had run after the car and somehow slipped underneath it as it was moving. The court found in Moon's favor, seeing it as an accident and nothing more. Even so, Moon would be left with the stigma that he had murdered a man, thanks to the rumors that surrounded the incident. Moon would also be left with the feeling that for some reason the rumors were perhaps true and he was eaten up by guilt and haunted by the death for the rest of his life.

Source: Fletcher, Tony. MOON. Avon Books, New York. 1999. Pages 272-278.

3: As discussed earlier in the book (see the entry for Death (and the Conspiracy of Life)), when people we knew as "bigger than life" die, we expect to die in some "bigger than life" manner. Keith Moon, who was considered by many to be superhuman in his wild and crazed behavior, both on the stage and certainly off, did not strike fans and friends as the type who would just die from something like an overdose – that is to say rather, die from an overdose of a prescription drug that he was taking for a legitimate reason. If he was to go at all, it was expected to be in a blaze of glory, or at least in an act so amazingly bizarre that it would be talked about for years; or at least from an overdose of something a bit more Keith-like in nature. No doubt, this is why many of the rumors came about after this death.

Yet there was no way to avoid the issue, Keith Moon died in his sleep on September 7, 1978 from an overdose of Heminevrin. Not from a mad conspiracy plan; nor from a large, deadly cocaine or alcohol binge; nor from a dramatic attempt to purge the deadly toxins from his body and choking to death, just in a very non-Moon manner. The coroner's report stated that 25 undisolved and seven partially-dissolved Heminevrin tablets were in Keith's stomach at the time of his death – an amount close to 18 times the normal dosage of the drug used as a type of sedative. In fact, the drug was considered addictive and dangerous and normally only prescribed for hospitalized patients and for short periods. If we compound that with the knowledge that, although Keith was taking it to help with his alcoholism, he was still drinking a small amount of alcohol on top of the drug (and was known for taking cocaine above all that), it's no wonder that Moon overdosed, no matter how superhuman his strength appeared to others.

As for the cocaine overdose rumor, the coroner's report stated that no trace of such the drug was found in his system. Nor were there signs of his death occurring due to choking on his own vomit, since the coroner's report showed no signs of it and Annette Walter-Lax (Moon's girlfriend) stated that she performed mouth-to-mouth resuscitation on Moon and found no obstructions in his breathing passages. This would discount the long-held legend that Moon had choked to death on his own vomit in a similar manner to Jon Bonham (who died after a massive drinking-binge — a death that some considered more in-line with Moon's behavior). It would also dismiss comments from some of Keith's associates that he choked to death on a combination — taking so many the Heminevrin resulting in his body did not having the strength to cough up the food lodged in his throat during the course of throwing up the recently-eaten steak that Keith had on the morning of his death. Nevertheless, the legend that Moon choked to death was the most persistent of all rumors about his death, with even members of the band believing that his death was for this reason. As it was denied by the coroner's report and the person who tried to administer resuscitation, such a notion must have come to people as a way to make his death more dramatic than the silent one that had occurred.

Suicide is always a consideration when we hear about any type of overdose and such a thought certainly was on some people's minds when Moon's death was reported. With his alcoholism being presumed or known by many by that time, and depression playing a common factor in such addictions, some assumed that Moon might have killed himself intentionally. His struggle with his addiction was also less than promising, and the band was considering the possibility that he not tour with them if he could not straighten himself out, further leading to suggestions of depression. However, many that knew Moon knew him to be active and happy most of the time and certainly not the type to consider suicide. He also felt that the Heminevrin might be helping him and was even suggesting to some that he would be marrying his girl friend sometime in the near future, and so hardly in a state where he would be pushed over the edge. Moon was also known for his overabundance when it came to drugs just as when it came to alcohol and, with little background knowledge of the drug that was supposed to be helping him (it was, after all, prescribed by a doctor who he had faith in to help him) Moon probably thought nothing of taking another tablet when he felt it was fine for him to do so.

All indications point to an accidental overdose of a prescription drug that killed Keith Moon in his sleep. There was also no evidence as to the wildest and most sinister of all the rumors pertaining to his death — that of Moon dying of a drug overdose in Paul McCartney's house and McCartney having Moon's body moved back to his own place in order to avoid any suspicion. This story clearly conflicts directly with the testimony of Moon's girl friend and with the coroner's report, but it was just another remarkable story that many believed because it was about an over-the-top man who had to have an otherworldly death to match is otherworldly life.

Source: Fletcher, Tony. MOON. Avon Books, New York. 1999. Pages 551-562.

4: *Rough Boys* was a hit from Pete Townshend's 1980 solo album EMPTY GLASS and it was rumored that the song written in direct response to a group (or one, depending how the story is told) of punk rockers who tore up the Who claiming that they were old and washed-up in an interview. The lyrics were supposedly an indictment against the meaningless, anarchy-driven nature of the Punk movement, with Townshend essentially asking the "rough boys" what their point was supposed to be. Thus, *Rough Boys* was Townshend's musical revenge on the insulters.

Townshend, however, in an interview with Timothy White in 1989 stated that the song actually dealt with homosexuality, along with a comparison of the gay and punk cultures. similar in dress and style, yet obviously not associated with each other beyond both trying to obtain a "rough" visual look. In a way, the song did speak to the meaningless nature of the style and attitude of the groups discussed, but it was not written specifically in response to some insult hurled at the Who at some point.

While Townshend's response to White cleared up the issue of the song's intentions somewhat, it created another urban legend right on top of it (see next entry for more details).

5: The legend that Pete Townshend was bisexual or gay came from an interview Townshend did in 1989 for his IRON MAN album. The interview was by Timothy White as part of his syndicated radio program, Timothy White's Rock Stars and later transcribed in his book, ROCK STARS in 1999. During the course of the interview, White touched upon the rumor that Townshend's song *Rough Boys* was viewed as a song about homosexuality. Townshend discussed the song and further stated that he was surprised when the solo album that contained the song, EMPTY GLASS, appealed to both a gay and a female audiences that he felt he'd never had before.

In discussing this, Townshend said the following:

> "... One of the things that stunned me when EMPTY GLASS came out was that I realized I'd found a female audience, just by being honest. Not necessarily by saying, 'I am gay, I am gay, I am gay.' But just by being honest about the fact that I understand how gay people feel, and I identify. And I know how it feels to be a woman. I know how it feels to be a woman because I am a woman. And I won't be classified as just a man. To an extent the gay lobby infuriates me sometimes. With EMPTY GLASS I got lots of letters from gays who said, 'Good on you, Pete, for coming out.' And I would write back and say, 'No, I haven't come out.' And then I realized maybe that was just pride. That in a way it was a coming-out. That it was a real acknowledgment of the fact that I'd been surrounded by people that I really adored – and was actually sexually attracted to – who were men. And that the side of me that responded to those people was a passive side, a subordinate side."

The newspapers and magazines, especially those in Britain, had a field day with this statement when it was published. Headlines screaming that Townshend had come out of the closet began appearing, reading more into Townshend's statement than he had meant. His silence for years after the interview just fanned the flames even further and critics wishing to take a quick jab at him could be depended upon to dig up the comment whenever necessarily.

In 1999, Townshend finally did discuss the Timothy White quote in an interview with PLAYBOY magazine, clarifying his thoughts:

"It was [to do with] that song, which is ironic because the song is actually taunting both the homosexuals in America – who were, at the time, dressing themselves up as Nazi generals – and the punks in Britain dressing the same way. I thought it was great that these tough punks were dressing as homosexuals without realizing it. I did an interview about it, saying that *Rough Boys* was about being gay, and in the interview I also talked about my "gay life," which – I meant – was actually about the friends I've had who are gay. So the interviewer kind of dotted the t's and crossed the i's and assumed that this was a coming out, which it wasn't at all. But I became an object of ridicule when it was picked up in England. It was a big scandal, which is silly. If I were bisexual, it would be no big deal in the music industry. If I ran down a list of the men who have tried to get me into bed, I could bring down quite a few big names in the music business. And no, I won't do it."

Sources: Sheff, David. "Pete Townshend," Playboy. Issue #468, February 1994.
White, Timothy. ROCK LIVES. Henry Holt, New York. 1999.

6: The story about the stuttering in *My Generation* being an accident appears to be true from interviews with and biographies about the band over the years. With both Pete Townshend and Roger Daltrey as known stutterers, it was inevitable that some would occur while working in the studio. After a time, it was realized that using the stutter in the song make it sound like the person speaking was having trouble forming the words – a situation all of the band members had run into with people they knew in the "Mod" scene who stuttered while popping amphetamines (a favorite drug of the Mods). The stuttering stayed and formed the basis of the seething anger lying underneath the lyrics, helping to make it a huge hit when it was released.

7: Keith Moon was well known for his destructive behavior while on tour (and even when not on tour). Destruction seemed to amuse Moon greatly and the stories told over time about his demolitions of hotel rooms remain legendary today. While many other artists have been known for the occasional trashing of a dressing room or hotel room, Moon had turned it into a fine art. He could even make a room appear to be destroyed when nothing had actually been touched (disassembling furniture and arranging the pieces or putting black masking tape on the television set to make everything appear to be broken were just some of his eventual tricks of the trade). So when the story went around that Keith Moon celebrated his twentieth birthday by not only trashing a Holiday Inn he was staying at, but driving a Lincoln Continental into the motel's pool, people just shook their heads, smiled and believed every word of it.

The problem is, it never happened. At least the automobile in the pool part. Furthermore, what did occur that night at the Holiday Inn wasn't even Keith's fault, as he was miles away getting a broken front tooth fixed. He wasn't even turning 20 at the time of the birthday party.

The story began on August 23, 1967 in Flint, Michigan while the band was touring the U.S. as the opening band for Herman's Hermits (the band best known for such hits as *I'm Henry the Eighth (I Am)* and *Mrs. Brown, You've Got A Lovely Daughter.* Moon, being born in 1946 was celebrating his 21st birthday while on tour and a party had been arranged after the show at the Holiday Inn that the bands were staying at. The rumor went around for years that Keith was actually celebrating his twentieth birthday and that he told everyone it was his 21st so that he could get into the bar and have a drink; however, it just a rumor to make Keith appear even "naughtier" than he was. There was certainly enough drinking by everyone before even hitting the bar to make such a story unnecessary on Keith's part.

As mentioned, because of the amount of drinking on everyone's part (not just Keith's), when the party got started everyone was in a drunken mood and the party turned into a good-natured food fight, with gobs of cake flying everywhere. Still, no damage beyond some carpet cleaning being required was apparent at the time and everyone at the hotel (including the police who were there as part of security for the tour) took the matter lightly.

The problems began when a group of the musicians decided to "de-bag" the birthday boy. For those who do not know the term, to "de-bag" means to hold someone down and rip their pants off. It's a joke and usually taken with a certain amount of humor. Unknown to anyone, however, was that Keith was not wearing any underwear, so when he was "de-bagged" (and his pants torn to shreds), he stood naked from the waist down in the middle of a party with band members, girl friends, fans and the police.

Suddenly feeling a bit out of place and embarrassed, Moon ran out of the room. In doing, so he tripped over something and landed face first on the floor, breaking a tooth in half. Even with the drinks inside of him, Keith was in a lot of pain and ended up spending the night finding a dentist to put fit him with a cap for the tooth and missed the party.

With the mishap of the birthday boy over, the police and the hotel staff decided it was time for the party to end. So it was for the band members in the Who, with Daltrey and Townshend retiring, and Entwistle helping Moon find a dentist in the middle of the night. Members of Herman's Hermits, however, didn't like have the party ending and decided to take out their frustrations by tearing apart the hotel. This included destroying a piano, throwing people into the motel's pool, smashing vending machines, and spraying cars in the parking lot with fire extinguishers. The police finally calmed everyone down and the carnage ended. By the time Moon and Entwistle came back, everything had returned to normal and Moon was in no mood to do anything more than head for bed.

So the irony of the urban legend is that not only was Moon not involved with a destructive episode at a hotel he was staying at, but instead members of a band that most considered to be completely harmless – Herman's Hermits – were the real culprits in the damage.

As to the Lincoln Continental, Moon obviously did not drive it into the pool that night, nor were there ever any documented cases of Moon actually driving a car into

URBAN LEGENDS of Rock & Roll

a swimming pool anywhere. Yet, the perpetuator of the legend about driving an automobile into a pool was none other than Keith himself. As he discussed the party in grander and grander terms as the years went by, he would eventually bring to life the fable that he had somehow dashed out of the room half naked, found a Lincoln Continental with the keys in the ignition in the parking lot, and drunkenly drove it straight into the pool. While it sounded like a hilarious caper added to the evening's events, it never happened.

Source: Fletcher, Tony. MOON. Avon Books, New York. 1999. Pages 209-212.

"Weird Al" Yankovic

1. *"Weird Al" Yankovic is the son (or nephew) of famous accordionist, Frankie "Polka King" Yankovic.*
2. *The number 27 has a deep, personal significance to Al, which is why the number repeatedly appears in most of his music, videos and other projects.*
3. *Rapper Coolio turned down Yankovic's request to use his song* Gangsta's Paradise *for a parody called* Amish Paradise *Al then went ahead and did the parody anyway.*
4. *Weird Al committed suicide back in the 1980s, depressed over the lack of sales of his albums.*

1: The rumor that Weird Al Yankovic is related to Frankie Yankovic is understandable. It hardly even seems worth pointing out the reasons for such a connection in people's minds, as they are self-evident: first, that they both share the same name; second, that Weird Al is a comedic musician known for playing the accordion in his musical parodies, while Frankie "Polka King" Yankovic was world famous as an accordionist.

Al Yankovic was born October 23, 1959 to Nick and Mary Yankovic in Lynwood, California. His parents can be seen in a few of Al's projects, including the "mockumentary," The Compleat Al. He is not related to Frankie Yankovic at all.

2: In 1994, fans writing for a Weird Al fanzine called MIDNIGHT STAR, noticed that Al had used the number 27 many times in his projects. A list was put together of the many coincidences of the number popping up (such as a counter advancing to 27 in the video for *Like a Surgeon*, Al wearing a shirt with the number 27 on the cover of his album RUNNING WITH SCISSORS, and lyrics that include the number, amongst others). Because of this reappearing number, many fans wondered what the significance of the number was to Al, believing that there had to be more to it than just a coincidence. Of course, being fans of Weird Al, many of them didn't take it seriously, even when resorting to a "Paul Is Dead" fixation (see the entry for Beatles) with the number and the clues supposedly found on Al's work. Even so, it was thought that there was a personal reason for the number.

As Al himself mentioned to Chuck Miller in an interview for GOLDMINE:

> "I suppose I used the number 27 originally because I just thought it was a funny number or maybe it was the right number of syllables . . . But some fans brought that up to me, and some fans started to think maybe there was some kinds of deeper significance to the number . . . And I was aware this was going on, so I would kind of feed the flames a little bit and from that point on started putting the number in more consciously."

Therefore, this urban legend was unintentionally started by the artist involved, and then built upon once he knew people were looking for it.

Source: Miller, Chuck. "Weird Al" Yankovic: the Clown Prince of Parody," Goldmine. Issue 514. Page 18.

3: The rapper Coolio complaining about Weird Al using his popular song *Gangsta's Paradise* for a parody is really a case of "He said / She said." Coolio, in 1996, told a reporter backstage at the Grammy Awards that he never agreed to the usage of his song for the parody and that Al's record company ignored him. In his statement, Coolio made it clear that he saw it as the record company's fault and not that of Al himself (although he also made it clear that he did not want Yankovic anywhere near him). With the backhanded slap, Yankovic felt terrible about the situation. As he told Chuck Miller in an interview with GOLDMINE, he was assured by his record company that Coolio had okayed the parody.

Al had a history of getting acceptance on his parodies to back up his statement. Al had experienced the pain of working on material that had to be abandoned when the original artists refused to cooperate, and had gone out of his way in the past to make sure everything was in good order before creating such material. (One of the reasons why Yankovic has never parodied a song by the artist Prince is due to the artist never okaying such a parody.)

The situation with Coolio did convince Al to change one aspect of his parody work: from that point on he would not rely on a third party to get permission for material use and would instead get the permission directly from the artists themselves.

Source: Miller, Chuck. "Weird Al" Yankovic: the Clown Prince of Parody," Goldmine. Issue 514. Pages 18-19.

4: The rumor that Weird Al Yankovic had committed suicide goes back to, oddly enough, a joke made on a television series in 1997. The show was the animated comedy series, KING OF THE HILL, which revolves around a man named Hank Hill, who lives in Texas with his wife and son. The episode that aired on November 23, 1997 on the Fox Network, *The Son That Got Away*, had a couple of jokes made at Yankovic's expense.

In the series, Hank's son Bobby wants to grow up to be a comedian and mentions in this particular episode that he wants to be like Weird Al. Hank replies: "Don't be stupid son! Weird Al Yankovic blew his brains out in the late 80's when people stopped buying his albums."

Later in the show, Bobby runs away and gets lost. In fear he cries out: "Oh No! I'm going to die friendless and alone like Weird Al Yankovic!"

Although rude and upsetting to some fans of Yankovic, the obvious point of the jokes is that they are not true. Nothing would be funny about them if Yankovic really had committed suicide, and they would have not only have been in bad taste, but poor jokes on top of that. Still, some people assumed that there was truth behind the jokes and assumed that perhaps Weird Al really was dead. Or perhaps even that he had died and the point of the jokes was that his death wasn't from suicide, but something else and it had been twisted to be a suicide in connection with what the characters in the show believed.

It probably didn't help that Yankovic had taken some time off after the release of his 1996 album BAD HAIR DAY, returning in 1999 with his album, RUNNING WITH SCISSORS. Because of his absence, people stopped to wonder if there was any truth behind the jokes, which probably help cement the urban legend even more.

Although some fans were upset over the jokes, Weird Al himself thought they were funny. As Yankovic's drummer stated on the Weird Al newsgroup back in June 2001, Yankovic used clips from the episode during his 2000 tour.

Frank Zappa

1. Zappa took part in a "gross-out" contest with Alice Cooper back in the early 1970s.
2. Zappa was the son of the actor who played Mr. Greenjeans on the CAPTAIN KANGAROO television series.
3. Zappa once urinated on audience members during a show.

1: See the entry for Cooper, Alice for more details.

2: CAPTAIN KANGAROO was a popular television series for children throughout the 1960s and up into the middle 1980s. The live action show (a curiosity today in children's programming) feature Bob Keeshan as Captain Kangaroo, the host of the series. The Captain would have some whimsical adventures on the show, but for the most part (especially as the show got into the 1970s) the Captain spent his

Frank Zappa

time talking with other characters on the show. One such character was Mr. Greenjeans, played by Hugh Brannum. The character was a popular supporting role on the program and kids watching certainly knew who he was.

Meanwhile, Frank Zappa had recorded a song on his 1969 album, HOT RATS, called *Son of Mr. Green Genes*. The song was a sequel of a sort to a track from the 1968 Zappa album UNCLE MEAT. Although the name in the title does not match at all the name of the character from the television series, some listeners got it into their heads that Zappa was actually saying he was the son of the actor.

Rumors also spread in the Boston area at one time that Zappa was the son of children's show host, Bob Emery. Zappa's father was Francis Vincent Zappa, Sr., as reported in many sources.

3: As stated by Zappa when presented with the rumor that he urinated on audience members during a show: "I never had my dick out on stage and neither did anybody else in the band."

Source: Sheff, David. "Frank Zappa," Playboy. April 1993.

I've Heard a Rumor:
How to Decipher Facts from Urban Legends

As any book about Urban Legends can attest, there is never an end to the growing number of fictional stories told about people, events, and things. It's certainly true about rock music, with new artists coming along all the time and new urban legends passing on from one listener to another as their careers grow.

Some newer legends are even just rehashed, brought-up-to-date older legends, with one artist's name replaced by another. Stories about the stomach pumps or about killing puppies on stage have been around for decades now and probably will continue into the future with each new generation. You simply remove "Artist A" and insert "New Artist B" into the handy slot for protagonist(s) in the story and the fans are all set to go.

Musicians themselves sometimes happily add to the confusion, letting publicists and managers create stories about them in hope of getting some press coverage. In some cases, it was deemed easier to ignore slanderous stories in order to avoid giving the legends even more press than it already had, only to have people become convinced that the legends were true because the artist refused to refute them (such as what happened with Mariah Carey's "starving children" quote). In other cases, artists decide to let stories ride as they feel any publicity is better than no publicity at all. There are even cases where artists have created stories themselves, just to see if anyone would believe them, or have told the "true" version of a story so many times that they invent information just to liven the story up for themselves when telling it again for the umpteenth time.

The Internet has been of little help in dispensing of these legends as false. In fact, it has spread urban legends about artists that would normally have taken months to cross the country back in the 1970s and 1980s with instantaneous, worldwide distribution. The Internet has also proven the old saying that people believe what they read. Anyone can get on the Internet, post on a newsgroup, message board, or mailing list the worst rumor they can possibly think of about a musician, and even if 99% of the readers disregard it, there will always be a few who put total faith into what the storyteller had written. From there it grows and is reported in other areas; by the end of the day it could end up being reported in several different places, and once people see it being reported on several web sites, they naturally assume that there must be some truth to the story, and thus another legend is born.

Some fans are perfectly happy with these stories, totally convinced that Mama Cass choked on a ham sandwich. They know for sure that Mariah Carey actually said that she wanted to be thin like the starving children. They truly believe that the "gross-out" story really occurred between Alice Cooper and Frank Zappa . . . or was that Zappa and Captain Beefheart? Or maybe it was Ozzy Osbourne and Alice Cooper? Or maybe even Ozzy Osbourne and Marilyn Manson? No matter who it was, the fans are convinced it happened to someone, and that is the point.

Many people are not as easily spoon fed stories about their favorite musicians. Even when a story at first sounds plausible, there is still an element that tells people that something doesn't quite fit – why weren't the people involved reported to the police or the SPCA? Why is the event never discussed in biographies or articles about the individual? Where are the sources? After all, when it's a story heard "from a friend of a friend of a friend" alarm bells should be going off inside people's heads as to the accuracy of the story being told.

While people may be able to deduce that a story doesn't quite ring true, they are sometimes unsure how they can go about checking into the story to find out the facts. Books such as the one you're reading and those of others are a start, yet new stories spring up almost daily. The purpose of this section is to help the reader do his or her own detective work in tracking down information.

Check out the books: In 1981, one of the first books dealing with modern myths, these "urban legends" was writing by the foremost authority on the topic, Jan Harold Brunvand. The book, THE VANISHING HITCHHIKER, has been reprinted numerous times since then and Brunvand has since written a number of other books that are essential (and entertaining reading) for anyone that wants to settle the score on rumors they have heard since they were kids. Some of his books have gone out of print, but can be found in used bookstores in the Folklore section. Here's a few of the titles he has done:

THE VANISHING HITCHHIKER. W.W. Norton & Company, New York. 1981. ISBN 0-393-95169-3.
THE CHOKING DOBERMAN. W.W. Norton & Company, New York. 1984. ISBN 0-393-30321-7.
THE MEXICAN PET. W.W. Norton & Company, New York. 1988. ISBN 0-393-30542-2.
CURSES! BROILED AGAIN! W.W. Norton & Company, New York. 1989. ISBN 0-393-02710-4.
THE BABY TRAIN & OTHER LUSTY URBAN LEGENDS. W.W. Norton & Company, New York. 1993. ISBN 0-393-31208-9
TOO GOOD TO BE TRUE: THE COLOSSAL BOOK OF URBAN LEGENDS. W.W. Norton & Company, New York. 2000. ISBN 0-393-04734-2.

Jan Harold Brunvand was also involved in the 1994 book, THE BIG BOOK OF URBAN LEGENDS, a book from Paradox Press, New York, ISBN 1–56389-165-4. This book, and many of the above deal with non-celebrity oriented urban legends, but any of them are a good place to start in order to get a good understanding about urban legends of the past.

Other books have been written about urban legends in the past few years, many which just rehash Brunvand's work. THE STRAIGHT DOPE by Cecil Adams (Ballantine Books, New York, 1984) and its many sequels, along with a web site, http://www.straightdope.com, is one of the few that can be depended upon to display questions about stories heard over the years. In addition, an "Ask Cecil" section on the site will help people with questions about new legends, although answers can come with a smirk by the writer at times.

Biographies and autobiographies are also a great place to start in separating fact from fiction when dealing with rumors. Although not all biographies are written on a level that can be construed to be "factual": some are slapdashed to cash in on a celebrity's popularity and merely rehash the same urban legends with no fact finding involving; others are written as a mouthpiece for the celebrity to carry forth their own vendettas against others. There are also too many books that are written at a tabloid level in order to reprint old gossip and scandals, rarely with any interest in determining fact from fiction. Oh, and Jackie Collins novels are never to be considered "factual." They are called novels for a reason, after all.

Still, there are writers who want to dig up the truth about the people they are writing about, and as more time goes by more biographies about a variety of artists have appeared, making for easier fact finding for readers who want to investigate the tales told about their favorite musicians.

Check out the Internet: While the Internet does have too many writers who like simply to stir the pot with new added urban legends, there are a few defenders of reality out in cyberspace. The already-mentioned Straight Dope site is a good place to start, and there are other sites that deal solely with urban legends – the new and the old.

The Urban Legends Reference Pages at http://www.snopes2.com, by Barbara and David P. Mikkelson is the best web resource for anyone looking up new legends. It's highly recommended, and has new additions posted nearly every day.

The AFU & Urban Legends Archive at http://www.urbanlegends.com is another highly-recommended site, which is linked directly to the newsgroup dealing with folklore of this type alt.folklore.urban (and the reason for the initials "AFU"). The newsgroup is a good source for discussing new urban legends as well.

While you're on the Internet checking out those sites, you may want to see if there is a newsgroup or web site about the artist you are trying to research. This is not always the safest way to go, since newsgroups are notorious for having fans that like to puncture what they see as the pomposity of other fans, and do so by making up legends in the newsgroup just to cause problems. Some newsgroups also suffer from occasional meltdowns, where running feuds between individuals on the newsgroup lead to little or no information being passed around for fans to read.

FAQs available on the internet about some artists are a good resource, and usually can be found on web sites pertaining to those artists. FAQs are "Frequently Answered Questions," and are commonly put together by a group of fans to answer the routine, everyday questions that come from new fans and/or those not in the know about a particular artist. This is why, if you ask a general question about someone on a newsgroup, you sometimes get the curt reply of "check the FAQ!" These FAQs sometimes go into detail about rumors and urban legends told about the artists, giving documented information to explain the legend and how the artist themselves view the stories told about them.

Check out current news sources: Main sources of information are newspapers and magazines. News sources such as the national news are a good resource as well for immediate details pertaining to the more dramatic stories being passed around at times about musicians. Entertainment oriented news programs can be a bit "iffy" at times.

Many are done to promote celebrities and their projects, so it's common to see news stories reported unchecked or with a knowing "wink to the camera."

Here's an example of how this would work: it is not uncommon for someone to think it humorous to go to a newsgroup or message board about an artist and exclaim that the person had died that morning in some type of "horrible gerbil accident" (okay, the stories made up are usually a little more serious than that, but you get the idea as to the level of the poster in most cases). The thing is, even marginally known musicians will get a mention in the press about their deaths if they actually occur; on-line national news services, such as CNN or AP, will post information about these stories within minutes of the initial reports if they turn out to be true. Official web sites for an artist (and in many cases the fan-owned web sites as well) commonly will make mention of such rumors as well if when they're deemed vast enough or had circulated enough to be discouraging.

Think before you react: When one hears a new story about a favorite artist, it's easy to react without thinking. Before reacting, try to step back and look at the story to determine how much information is true. Asking the following questions will help:

Who was the source? (If it was Cousin Ernie's mechanic's brother, then they probably are not the most reliable source for news.)

How, when, and why did the event happen? (For example, Charles Manson's try-out for The Monkees supposedly occurred at a time when he was actually in prison, automatically voiding the urban legend without further research needed.)

Where is it being reported and who reported it? (If a story about Britney Spears needing the stomach pump appears on a web site called "Ihate$&(@#*$#*Britney.com," then the story is probably to be questioned.)

Where can additional information be found about the story? (If the answer is, "Nowhere! They've covered it up!" as in the "Elvis Presley is alive" urban legend, then be ready to suspect the story.)

Are there any inconsistencies in the story? (Madonna may have been just a child in the 1960s, but she still would have been too old to play Tabitha on the old Bewitched television series, in addition to the fact that she was not a child actor.)

Is the story even feasible? (Gene Simmons getting a cow's tongue surgical grafted onto his own tongue is implausible after even a split-second of thought. Still people believe it.)

When asked for further information, does the person who supplied the story elaborate in order to cover up the inconsistencies? (Just ask a question. You'll be surprised how often people will try to cover up their errors in the story when put on the spot.)

If there are any problems in getting answers to these questions, then it is best to research further and not take the story on face value. Most urban legends are readily discountable once one thinks about the possibilities of such a story being true. Others can be discredited when facts are gathered.

Of course, the one argument that fans of made-up stories use is that disputing urban legends is like shooting fish in a barrel – not only is it easy, but it's being a spoilsport about the age-old custom. The answer to that argument is that, yes, urban legends can be fun, if people understand that the stories are being told in jest and are not true. The problem is that too often the stories are taken as fact by people who do not want to bother finding out the truth. Other times, the stories are used as ammunition against artists by those who wish to tear down their work because it is not liked or considered evil (look no further than the many books discussing backmasking or the Satanic imagery in all rock music for signs of this). Some are maliciously done to purposefully wreck a person's career. There is a potential danger in these stories, and because people do believe in them, it's necessary from time to time to remind people that rumors sometimes do not have any truth to them whatsoever.

There's nothing wrong in having some fun and taking a look back at the stories we remembered hearing as we grew up listening to our favorite musicians. Nevertheless, there are times when it is good to remind ourselves that all the stories were never more than just fables made up along the way.

The Top Ten
Rock and Roll Lessons of All Time
(and they just have to be true!):

10. Stomping baby chicks and puppies on stage during a concert is a common and age-old tradition in rock and roll.

9. Phil Keaggy is the best guitarist of all time, according to Hendrix . . . or was it Clapton?

8. If you can't become a Monkee, there's always Helter Skelter. Your family will love you anyway.

7. An audience will pay good money to see two popular musicians stage a "Gross-out Contest." Better yet, no one will complain to the press or the authorities about it.

6. Never eat a ham sandwich unless you have a friend nearby who knows the Heimlich Maneuver.

5. As Jim Morrison, Elvis, and Tupac Shakur have taught us, faking your own death is easy and is the best way to avoid a government, Mafia and/or drug-oriented conspiracy.

4. Every rock musician uses backward masking in order to communicate with Satan – and it really works!

3. A complete blood transfusion will help you kick your drug habits automatically. Just ask Keith.

2. Paul Is Dead. Really. In fact, he's the only rock star who has ever died. Everyone else is just hiding out. Right, Elvis?

And the Number One Rock and Roll (Urban Legend) Lesson of All Time . . .

1. Always keep a stomach-pump handy.